Abortion Counseling

Rachel B. Needle, PsyD, received her Master of Science (MS) and Doctor of psychology (PsyD) from Nova Southeastern University in Fort Lauderdale, Florida. She received her BA in psychology from Barnard College, Columbia University. Dr. Needle completed an internship in clinical psychology at the University of Medicine and Dentistry of New Jersey (UMDNJ): Robert Wood Medical School in Piscataway, New Jersey. She is a Florida Certified Sex Therapist. Dr. Needle is currently a postdoctoral fellow at the Center for Marital and Sexual Health of South Florida.

Dr. Needle is an adjunct professor of psychology in the Department of Behavioral Sciences at Nova Southeastern University in Fort Lauderdale, Florida. She is also the director of Health Information Services at Positive Friends, an Internet dating Web site for individuals with viral sexually transmitted infections (STIs).

Dr. Needle cofounded Florida Friends for Choice (FFC), a nonprofit organization whose mission is to provide legal aid to women and health care providers to guarantee access to safe, quality reproductive health care for all women.

Dr. Needle's clinical and research interests include sexual function and dysfunction, relationship concerns, sexual compulsivity, battered women, and trauma. She has a particular interest in working with individuals both during and following cancer treatment. Dr. Needle has presented her research and clinical work at national and international conferences.

Lenore E. A. Walker, EdD, is a professor at Nova Southeastern University Center for Psychological Studies and Coordinator of the Clinical Forensic Psychology Concentration for doctoral students training to be clinical psychologists. She currently has an independent practice of forensic psychology and is executive director of the Domestic Violence Institute with affiliate centers around the world. Dr. Walker specializes in work with victims of interpersonal violence, particularly battered women and abused children. Her expert witness testimony opposed to the numerous challenges to *Roe v. Wade* dealing with notification or consent laws helped established judicial by-pass procedures, especially needed when teens come from homes where there is domestic violence. Dr. Walker earned her undergraduate degree in 1962 from The City University of New York (CUNY) Hunter College, her Master of Science in 1967 from CUNY City College. and her Doctor of Education in psychology from Rutgers University in New Jersey. In 2004, she received a postdoctoral Master's Degree in Clinical Psychopharmacology at Nova Southeastern University (NSU). She has worked on high-publicity cases, such as with battered women who kill their abusive partners in self-defense, and testifies on behalf of protective mothers who are being challenged for custody by abusive fathers. She lectures and does training workshops all over the world about prevention, psychotherapy, legal cases, and public policy initiatives for abused women and children. Dr. Walker has authored numerous professional articles and 15 books, including *The Battered Woman* (1979), *The Battered Woman Syndrome* (1984/2000), *Terrifying Love: Why Battered Women Kill & How Society Responds* (1989), and *Abused Women & Survivor Therapy* (1994). In addition, she wrote *Introduction to Forensic Psychology* (2004) with coauthor David Shapiro and *A First Responders Guide to Abnormal Psychology* (2007) with coauthor William Dorfman.

Abortion Counseling

*A Clinician's Guide to Psychology,
Legislation, Politics, and Competency*

Rachel B. Needle, PsyD
Lenore E. A. Walker, EdD

SPRINGER PUBLISHING COMPANY

New York

Springer Publishing Company, LLC
11 West 42nd Street
New York, NY 10036
www.springerpub.com

Acquisitions Editor: Sheri W. Sussman
Project Manager: Carol Cain
Cover design: Mimi Flow
Composition: Apex Publishing, LLC

08   09   10/   5   4   3   2   1

Library of Congress Cataloging-in-Publication Data

Needle, Rachel.
   Abortion counseling : a clinician's guide to psychology, legislation, politics, and competency / Rachel Needle, Lenore Walker.
      p. cm.
   Includes bibliographical references and index.
   ISBN-13: 978-0-8261-0257-7 (alk. paper)
   ISBN-10: 0-8261-0257-3 (alk. paper)
1. Abortion counseling—United States.   2. Pregnancy, Unwanted—United States.   3. Pregnant women—Mental health services—United States.   I. Walker, Lenore E.   II. Title.
   HQ767.4.N44 2007
   363.46—dc22   2007022455

Printed in the United States of America by Bang Printing.

We dedicate this book to all of the abortion providers who work against a backdrop of violence and legislative restrictions that attempts to limit access to abortion services.
You are the true unsung heroes of this movement.

Contents

Foreword

Good health is essential to leading a productive and fulfilling life, and the right of all women to control all aspects of their health, in particular their own fertility, is basic to their empowerment. . . .

The human rights of women include their right to have control over and decide freely and responsibly on matters related to their sexuality, including sexual and reproductive health, free of coercion, discrimination and violence. . . . (United Nations, 1996, sections C.93, C.96)

These words from the national platform for action of the United Nation's Fourth World Conference on Women reflect an international consensus on a fundamental point: The ability to time, space, and limit childbearing is a necessary condition for women to live healthy, productive, and fulfilling lives. As Needle and Walker underscore in their book, *Abortion Counseling: A Clinician's Guide to Psychology, Legislation, Politics, and Competency,* reproductive rights are crucial for women's physical and psychological health, and political attempts to restrict these rights constitute a basic threat to women's health and empowerment.

UNINTENDED CHILDBEARING IS DESTRUCTIVE TO THE MENTAL HEALTH OF WOMEN AND THEIR FAMILIES

Unintended (mistimed or unwanted) childbearing has negative health, social, and psychological consequences to women, their families, and society (Brown & Eisenberg, 1995). Health problems include a higher probability of mortality and morbidity for both mothers and children. In addition, such childbearing has been linked with a variety of social problems, including child abuse, divorce, poverty, juvenile delinquency, and criminality (Berk, Sorenson, Wiebe, & Upchurch, 2003; Denious & Russo, 2000; Russo, 1992).

Mistimed childbearing (e.g., teenage pregnancies, closely spaced births) has negative physical, psychological, and social effects on mothers and their children. Spacing births more than 2 years apart would reduce the risk of low birth weight and neonatal death in the United States by an estimated 5 to 10% below current levels (Miller, 1991). Longitudinal research has also found close childspacing intervals to be *predictive* of child abuse (Altemeier, O'Connor, Vietze, Sandler, & Sherrod, 1984).

The deleterious effects of unwanted childbearing are well documented. In one longitudinal study, unwanted children were found less likely to have had a secure family life. As adults they were more likely to engage in criminal behavior, be on welfare, and receive psychiatric services (David, Dytrych, & Matejcek, 2003). As the Committee on Unintended Pregnancy of the Institute of Medicine has observed:

> The child of an *unwanted* conception especially (as distinct from a *mistimed* one) is at greater risk of being born at low birthweight, of dying in its first year of life, of being abused, and of not receiving sufficient resources for healthy development. The mother may be at greater risk of depression and of physical abuse herself, and her relationship with her partner is at greater risk of dissolution. Both mother and father may suffer economic hardship and may fail to achieve their educational and career goals. Such consequences undoubtedly impede the formation and maintenance of strong families (Brown & Eisenberg, 1995, p. 1).

Although unintended pregnancies are experienced by women of all reproductive ages, including married and unmarried women, and women in all income levels, women at highest risk for unintended pregnancy are women who are already under substantial stress and who have less access to coping resources—adolescents, unmarried (single, divorced, and separated) women, and women over 40 years of age (Boonstra, Gold, Richards, & Finer, 2006). In this book, Needle and Walker articulate the cognitive processes that diverse women and girls experience when they find they are carrying an unintended pregnancy.

ABORTION PLAYS A SUBSTANTIAL ROLE IN ENABLING WOMEN TO TIME, SPACE, AND LIMIT THEIR CHILDBEARING

It is a sad fact of life that despite the development of modern methods of contraception in the 20th century, 1 in every 10 women of reproductive age in the United States each year becomes pregnant; about half of these pregnancies are unintentional. This means approximately 3 million U.S.

women a year are confronted with an unplanned pregnancy, with all the stress such a situation entails. Approximately half of these pregnancies are terminated by abortion. It is estimated that 20% of American women of childbearing age have already had an abortion, and one out of three American women will have had one by age 45 (Boonstra et al., 2006).

Women have abortions in order to time and space, as well as limit, their number of children. In the United States, for example, nearly one-half of abortion patients in 1987 were mothers, and nearly one in four of those mothers had a child under two years of age (Russo, Horn, & Schwartz, 1992). Given the widespread and negative effects of unwanted childbearing and the critical role that access to abortion plays in avoiding unwanted births, attempts to restrict women's access to abortion have profound implications for the public health in general and for women's health in particular.

WOMEN'S MENTAL HEALTH HAS BECOME A POLITICAL WEAPON IN EFFORTS TO RESTRICT LEGAL ACCESS TO ABORTION

In the United States, avoiding the destructive effects of unwanted child-bearing was a key element in the complex rationale underlying the United States Supreme Court decision in *Roe v. Wade,* which legalized abortion in 1973. Needle and Walker review the legislative history and subsequent policies that have affected women's rights and access to a safe abortion. In their book, they detail how, in keeping with the goal of overturning *Roe,* political forces opposing abortion have developed a new emphasis on the psychological well-being of the mother to construct new arguments for restricting access to abortion. The claim is that the Court failed to balance its concern for the negative effects of unwanted childbearing with the detrimental effects of abortion on women's mental health. This argument, based on anecdotal reports and uncontrolled or misrepresented studies, has been increasingly raised in other areas of the world as well, and has been found in areas as diverse as New Zealand and Central and Eastern Europe (David, 1999).

There is now an organized attempt to pass restrictive abortion legislation with the aim to stimulate legal challenges that will work their way up the court system to ultimately be used as an opportunity to revisit and overturn *Roe v. Wade* (Russo & Denious, 2005). For example, the claim that abortion damages mental health was a prominent feature in testimony in support of legislation to ban abortion in South Dakota (SD), (SD Task Force to Study Abortion, 2005).

The idea to use abortion's damage to women's mental health as a strategy to restrict access to abortion originated as a strategy called the Jericho Plan, which had the stated goal of making abortion inaccessible despite its legal status by making physicians "fully liable for all the physical, psychological, and spiritual injuries they inflict on women" (Reardon, 1996). Related actions include seeking out women who are depressed or feeling sad and guilty after having an abortion and under the guise of "healing" convincing them that they did not receive full, informed consent about the procedure. Women are encouraged to translate their sadness into anger at their abortion providers and to consider themselves "victims of abortion." They are then referred to pro-life attorneys who will sue for damages on their behalf. For example, a Web site sponsored by Priests for Life has asked supporters to "encourage mothers who have been harmed by abortion to bring suits against the abortion industry," and provided a list of telephone numbers of organizations to help women sue their doctors. Life Dynamics, one of the organizations listed, is described as developing a nationwide network of 600 lawyers ready to file such suits (Farley, 1995).

These activities represent the views of extreme elements of a pro-life political movement that have taken it on as their mission to force their religious view of abortion, which confers personhood at the beginning of conception, on the country as a whole. From this extreme point of view, abortion is immoral, no matter what the cost: Death or disability for the women, a sick infant that will suffer horribly and die, a child born into a violent home to experience battering and abuse, adding an additional mouth to feed that will mean the women's other children will go hungry—the reason that a women seeks to avoid having a child doesn't matter in this context of religious righteousness.

There is little basis for this view of personhood in history or in biology. Nonetheless, by glossing over the complexities of unwanted pregnancy and encouraging simplistic and judgmental thinking, ignoring the fact that the label "abortion" encompasses a range of procedures and experiences, misrepresenting the facts of prenatal development, and using positions of religious authority to warrant myths and misinformation, these extremist elements have embarked on a campaign to manipulate and misinform well-intentioned individuals with pro-life views who have concerns about abortion and want to help women in this stressful time.

Needle and Walker, as psychologists, provide the antidote to this strategy by critiquing the research and demonstrating how these groups may lead women to misattributing their mental health issues to abortion when the roots of the women's problems lie in other life experiences. The analysis benefits from Walker's long background in the psychology of battered women, as she applies her knowledge to the results of unintended pregnancies of abused women and children. Successful counseling techniques used for women and children who have been victims of domestic violence have been modified here for those women with abuse in their background who decide to terminate their pregnancy. Needle, who has worked in abortion centers counseling women before and after abortions, has used her expertise in the psychology of reproductive health to help mental health counselors develop skills in working with their patients.

THE POLITICS OF ABORTION POSE A DIRECT THREAT TO WOMEN'S MENTAL HEALTH

Increasing women's confidence in their ability to cope with an abortion has been found to lower their depressive symptoms after having an abortion (Major et al., 1990). Conversely, constructions of abortion that increase its social stigma can affect women's psychological well-being by encouraging them to feel shame and guilt at their decision to terminate pregnancy. This can then be used as further evidence of abortion's "harmful" mental health effects. It is important to remember that the meaning of abortion is socially constructed and can be made to seem wrong and shameful, despite the fact that it may represent a courageous act of a women acting out of a desire to meet her responsibilities to others and do the best she can under stressful conditions (Russo & Denious, 2005). Indeed, 74% of women cite concern for or responsibility to other individuals as the reason for their abortion (Boonstra, et al., 2006).

Anti-abortion demonstrations and harassment at abortion clinics are also designed to create guilt and shame in women obtaining abortions. In a study of women's psychological responses to anti-abortion activities, Cozzarelli and Major (1998) found that women experiencing shame and guilt in response to anti-abortion activities such as picketing and blocked entrances to clinics reported greater levels of post-abortion distress. Women who possessed more negative pre-pregnancy attitudes were more depressed overall and were more strongly affected by anti-abortion activities. In other words, these strategies are most effective when used on women who already had negative mental health indicators. Needle and Walker present poignant comments from abortion providers that illustrate both the negative effects that the protesters have had on health care professionals as well as the courage that these health care providers have shown as they put themselves on the line to provide reproductive health care for women they serve.

Undeniably, abortion occurs in a stressful context; it can be difficult to disentangle psychological effects of pregnancy—wanted and unwanted—from an abortion experience. However, the controversy surrounding abortion rights also threatens women's health by clouding and dismissing the effects that negative life events correlated with unwanted pregnancy may have on women's mental health status. Negative mental health indicators in women with abortion histories are deliberately mislabeled as psychological sequelae and are attributed to the woman's experience of abortion. Experiences of childhood abuse, partner violence, and other predictive risk factors for unwanted pregnancy are integral to women's health. Yet they are ignored in the attempts to link abortion to psychological health. When a large proportion of women experiencing unwanted pregnancy are victims of childhood abuse and have partners who are abusive, violent, or uncooperative in using contraception, misattribution of the mental health effects of such experiences to having an abortion can distract women from working on the sources of their problems. Confidence in their ability to cope with the stress of their unwanted pregnancy can also become undermined.

In this context, well-informed abortion counselors have an important role to play in helping women sort out their feelings and understand the complexities of the roots of their distress. Accurate information about the relationship of unwanted pregnancy to mental health and recognition of the diversity of women's responses to unwanted pregnancy are essential if counselors are to cut through extremists' political agendas and focus on the therapeutic goal of enhancing women's mental health and well-being (Rubin & Russo, 2004).

WOMEN'S RESPONSES TO UNWANTED PREGNANCY

Responses of women who discover they are pregnant are as variable and unique as the women themselves and typically reflect a combination of positive and negative emotions. When abortion is legal, a woman is given the opportunity to decide whether she is willing and able to assume the responsibility for having a(nother) child. This is a complex and personal commitment that will have profound consequences for the lives of women and their families, and women do not make the decision lightly.

The mental health of women who have had abortions reflects their mental health at the time they seek and obtain abortions. Given that abortion most often occurs in the context of unwanted pregnancy, it is not surprising that women who report having an abortion also report higher levels of anxiety and depression, suicidal ideation, and lower life satisfaction. These are risk factors for unwanted pregnancy, and are common outcomes of partner violence, and of childhood physical and sexual abuse, which are more likely to be experienced by women who have unwanted pregnancies (Russo & Denious, 2001). This is not to say that no individual woman is ever troubled or distressed by having an abortion—indeed, ambivalent feelings are the norm and most women feel very relieved and happy but also somewhat sad and guilty.

But being upset and feeling guilty is not the same has having a mental disorder. Although a minority of women report feeling distressed after having an abortion, there is no scientific evidence that having a voluntary, legal abortion increases risk for actual mental disorder. Some women may feel distressed and feel the need for support and counseling, but this is not the same thing as having a "post-abortion syndrome" or "post-abortion psychosis" (Adler, et al., 1990, 1992; Denious & Russo, 2000; Posavac & Miller, 1990; Russo, 1992, in press).

ABORTION COUNSELING FROM A PRO-CHOICE PERSPECTIVE HAS A CRITICAL ROLE TO PLAY IN ENSURING THAT NEGATIVE MENTAL HEALTH OUTCOMES ASSOCIATED WITH ABORTION ARE AVOIDED OR AMELIORATED

Give the poisonous political context created by pro-life efforts to construct a "post-abortion syndrome," it is critical that everyone involved—women, their friends and family members, mental health professionals, and policy makers—understand what is known about women's responses to unwanted pregnancy and its outcomes, the relationship of pregnancy outcome (abortion vs. delivery) to mental health, and how potential negative mental health effects can be avoided or ameliorated.

Abortion counseling has a critical role to play in ensuring that women's mental health is the priority and not the goals of a political agenda, whether that agenda be driven by pro-life or pro-choice advocates. Thus, Needle and Walker, in *Abortion Counseling: A Clinician's Guide to Psychology, Legislation, Politics and Competency,* have taken on a complex, profound and essential task—equipping therapists and abortion counselors with the knowledge and skills needed to help their clients—and they have done it well.

Their work can inform mental health professionals who seek to advocate for public policies and programs that will improve mental health. Readers of this book should have an increased understanding of how women's diverse life circumstances affect their ability to cope with the difficult decisions and circumstances surrounding abortion. They will also be better able to build women's resilience and coping skills by having considered them both in the context of women's lives (e.g., coping resources, social support, partner violence and early experiences of abuse, incidence of depression) and in the context of socio-political agendas that seek to manipulate women's mental health in order to undermine women's reproductive rights.

In the final analysis, it is important to remember that abortion counseling is not about abortion—it is about women confronting the decision to bear a child, with all of the profound and life changing commitments and responsibilities that entails. Some women need help and support to sort out what is the right thing for them to do in their personal situation and to deal with their feelings about the process afterwards. Such women deserve our trust, support, assistance, and respect for their decision.

Nancy Felipe Russo, Ph.D

Regents Professor of Psychology

Arizona State University

June 2007

REFERENCES

Adler, N. E., David, H. P., Major, B., Roth, S., Russo, N. F., & Wyatt, G. (1990). Psychological responses after abortion. *Science, 248,* 41–44.

Adler, N. E., David, H. P., Major, B., Roth, S. H., Russo, N. F., & Wyatt, G. E. (1992). Psychological factors in abortion: A review. *American Psychologist, 47,* 1194–1204.

Altemeier, W. A., O'Connor, S., Vietze, P., Sandler, H., & Sherrod, K. (1984). Prediction of child abuse: A prospective study of feasibility. *Child Abuse and Neglect, 8,* 393–400.

Berk, R. A.; Sorenson, S. B.; Wiebe, D. J., & Upchurch, D. M. (2003). The legalization of abortion and subsequent youth homicide: A time series analysis. *Analyses of Social Issues & Public Policy, 1,* 45–64.

Boonstra, H., Gold, R. B., Richards, C. L., & Finer, L. B. (2006). *Abortion in women's lives.* New York: Alan Guttmacher Institute.

Brown, S. S., & Eisenberg, L. (Eds.) (1995). *The best intentions: Unintended pregnancy and the well-being of children and families.* Washington, DC: National Academies Press.

Cozzarelli, C., & Major, B. (1998). The impact of antiabortion activities on women seeking abortions. In L. J. Beckman & S. M. Harvey (Eds.), *The new civil war: The psychology, culture, and politics of abortion* (pp. 81–114). Washington, DC: American Psychological Association.

David, H. P. (1999). Overview. In H. P. David (Ed.). *From abortion and contraception: Europe from 1917 to the present* (p. 322). Westport, CT: Greenwood Press.

David, H. P., Dytrych, Z., & Matejcek, Z. (2003). Born unwanted: Observations from the Prague Study. *American Psychologist, 58,* 224–229.

Denious, J., & Russo, N. F. (2000). The socio-political context of abortion and its relationship to women's mental health. In J. Ussher (Ed.), *Women's health: Contemporary international perspectives* (pp. 431–439). London: British Psychological Society.

Farley, C. (1995). Malpractice as a weapon. *Time, 145*(10), 65.

Major, B., Cozzarelli, C., Sciacchitano, A. M., Cooper, M. L., Testa, M., & Mueller, P. M. (1990). Perceived social support, self-efficacy, and adjustment to abortion. *Journal of Personality and Social Psychology, 59,* 452–463.

Miller, J. E. (1991). Birth intervals and perinatal health: An investigation of three hypotheses. *Family Planning Perspectives, 23*(2), 62–70.

Posavac, E., & Miller, T. (1990). Some problems caused by not having a conceptual foundation for health research: An illustration from studies of the psychological effects of abortion. *Psychology & Health, 5,* 13–23.

Reardon, D. C. (1996). *The Jericho Plan: Breaking Down the Walls Which Prevent Post-Abortion Healing.* Springfield, IL: Acorn Books.

Rubin, L., & Russo, N. F. (2004). Abortion and mental health: What therapists need to know. *Women & Therapy, 27*(3/4), 69–90.

Russo, N. F. (1992). Psychological aspects of unwanted pregnancy and its resolution. In J. D. Butler & D. F. Walbert (Eds.), *Abortion, medicine, and the law—4th edition* (pp. 593–626). NY: Facts on File.

Russo, N. F. (in press). Understanding emotional responses after abortion. In J. C. Chrisler, C. Golden, & P. Rozee (Eds.), *Lectures on the psychology of women, 3rd edition.* NY: McGraw-Hill

Russo, N. F., & Denious, J. E. (2001). Violence in the lives of women having abortions: Implications for public policy and practice. *Professional Psychology: Research and Practice, 32,* 142–150.

Russo, N. F., & Denious, J. E. (2005). Controlling birth: Science, politics, and public policy. *Journal of Social Issues, 61,* 181–191.

Russo, N. F., Horn, J., & Schwartz, R. (1992). Abortion in context: Characteristics and motivations of women who seek abortion. *Journal of Social Issues, 48,* 182–201.

South Dakota Task Force to Study Abortion (2005). *Report of the Task Force submitted to the Governor and Legislature of South Dakota.* Pierre, South Dakota: Author.

United Nations (1996). *The Beijing declaration and the platform for action: Fourth World Conference on Women: Beijing, China: 4–15 September 1995.* New York: UN/DPI/1766/Wom.

Preface: On a Personal Note

RACHEL

MURDERER

This was the word that was spray painted across the street from my house on October 31, 1986. I was 8 years old and I was leaving to go trick-or-treating with some other kids from the neighborhood. I was shocked and frightened when I saw this. Growing up as the daughter of an abortion clinic owner, I have been exposed to many things that a typical child doesn't see. I have had to deal personally with the violence that has been associated with this contentious issue. It has been like living in a war zone with bomb threats, tasteless messages spray painted on my driveway, and notes left on my front door and in my mailbox. As I grew older and began to understand more about the abortion controversy that caused these things to happen, I became even more fearful than I had been as a small child.

For my mother, being involved with the abortion issue was and is a choice, but for me, it was just something that I was born into. Let me be clear; I have nothing but the utmost love and respect for my mother and her dedication to this issue. My mother never flinches. She displays enormous commitment to her business and the issues surrounding it, even when the matters involved are frightening and dangerous. This, to me, is very admirable. And very scary. I have had to live with inconsistent and confusing feelings all of my life.

After watching a terribly disturbing television show in the fall of 2000 about a group called The Army of G-d, an infamous and extraordinarily zealous antiabortion group, I called my mother and spent an hour begging her to find a new line of work. The show included graphic scenes of buildings being blown up, shots being fired, and people running for cover. I was weeping as I begged my mother, those horrible war scenes flashing in my mind. My mother, in her calm, even-keeled, and inimitable way, reminded me of the importance of the work she does and the reasons why it is the only job for her. Her calm demeanor helped me become more rational and less emotional. She believes in the importance of her center, she loves her work, and she has devoted too much of her life to women's rights to give up now under the threats of a zealot organization. Though this was quite obviously not the response that I was hoping for, I do understand and greatly respect my mother for her decision. Unfortunately, it puts our entire family into the same war zone as she is in.

Though I have had feelings like these before, I never really allowed myself to get as emotionally disturbed as I did after watching that TV program. I decided then that it would be a good thing for me to speak to other children of clinic owners, directors, or doctors in order to learn how they cope with the constant threat to the lives of their parents. Although there have been a number of books written on the abortion issue and the impact on the doctors and clinic directors and staff, as far as I know, I have never read anything from the perspective of their children.

When I began graduate school at Nova Southeastern University I was privileged to be introduced to Dr. Lenore Walker by a good friend of mine, Kate. I knew of Dr. Walker, of course, because of her research with battered women, but I had no idea, at that time, what an outspoken, dedicated, and inspirational woman she was, and how passionately she too felt about women's reproductive rights. Since the moment I was introduced to her, Dr. Walker and I have gotten along well and agreed upon issues. Even when I have not seen or spoken to her in a week or so, I will receive e-mail forwards from her relating to the abortion issue.

When I told Lenore about my idea of writing a book from the stance of a clinic owner's daughter, she supported the idea. We then continued talking and ideas began to fly. When I left her office that day, we had a working outline for our book with more ideas than could fit in one volume. I am fortunate to have Lenore as a mentor. She goes out of her way to get students motivated and more involved in whatever ways that she can and works with them in doing so.

Despite my fears, I have always supported the battle for abortion rights. I have attended political rallies since I was a child, and I even did some outreach and fundraising for the issue when I was in college. In November 2002 a friend and I began a not-for-profit organization entitled Florida Friends for Choice. Our organization provides education and funding to fight legislation being passed to restrict abortion services. I guess at this point you can say that I am "out" as an activist myself and am more involved in the issue than ever.

However, it is still scary for me. While at a Florida Friends for Choice event in May 2004, I did a phone interview with a reporter from a local newspaper. Of course I could not tell my own story truthfully without answering questions about my background including who my mother is and what she does. I spoke to this journalist for a little less than an hour.

When I got off the phone, I felt myself becoming more and more anxious with each passing second. I called back asking questions such as, "Is there any way we can leave the information about my mother's work out of the article?" Just then, I got another call. It was my mother. I told the journalist that I would call her right back. But, before I had a chance to call her back, she called me to say that she would not include my personal information in her article, but if at any time in the future I felt more comfortable with it to call her. I felt a great sense of relief that the pressure was off me to have to make the decision.

I got lucky. Most journalists would have printed the story as I told it because of its human interest. I said more to her than I had intended, perhaps because she was so engaging and interesting herself. It made me realize that other people, like this reporter, can be sensitive to the personal and political feelings that are such a part of this issue, which taught me that I can go forward with this project.

So even I, who have been immersed in this issue and the controversy surrounding it for my entire life, got nervous and then brave again. Why not speak up for something you believe in so strongly, as I do about a woman's right to choose what she does with her own body? Well, I can and now I will, in this book.

It is our hope that this book will educate others and appeal to politicians, civilians, psychologists, journalists, and many more people. Let the truth be told and let people make informed decisions about how they feel about the abortion issue with the correct understanding and education of the issue and the politics surrounding it.

I am so honored to be working with Lenore on this book. I want to thank her for believing in this issue as she does and for this wonderful opportunity.

LENORE

When I first met Rachel, 6 years ago, she was a first-year graduate student in psychology, and I was a psychology professor on the faculty. She was introduced to me by one of my other students, Kate, who was absorbing my feminist ideas like a sponge. Kate had pulled together my research program on battered women and culled through our graduate student body of more than 300 people for other women to work with us on learning more about the world of women who have been abused at some time in their lives. Rachel immediately joined this at-first small feminist group of women who appealed to her sense of social and political activism. There was something about Rachel that made me think of my own daughter, Karen, who also struggled with a socially and politically active mother while growing up, never knowing what the next day might bring.

I tried to expose both my daughter, Karen, and my son, Michael, to my political activism, understanding that it would take more than one generation to make the changes so women and men would be treated equally. There was a time during her teen years when Karen's favorite phrase was, "Mom. Please do not make a scene!" As she got older, like Rachel, she often expressed her ambivalence—both admiring my commitment to political activism but also frightened of it.

I often tell the story of Karen and my trip to Ireland, where I was presenting my work on battered women at the International Congress on Women's Studies. Karen was back at the hotel waiting for me to finish a workshop, as I had promised her we would then go shopping. When I got back I asked her if it would be all right if we stopped at a rally where the Irish women were going to protest their laws that made it illegal for psychologists and counselors to give women information about abortion as a safe alternative to pregnancy. Karen, who was only 16 at the time, agreed but set clear limits. We could go to support the Irish women but only for 1 hour. As soon as I got there, one of the women from my workshop recognized me and asked if I wouldn't mind holding one of the ends of the large sign they had made until the person who had agreed to do so arrived. I looked at Karen and she shrugged her shoulders as a typical 16-year-old might do. Of course, the person who was supposed to hold that part of the sign never showed up, and it was my picture that was splashed over the front page of the Irish newspapers and television the next day. Karen and I did get to go shopping afterward, but as she would say, life with her mother was always unpredictable.

When I was Karen and Rachel's age, I remember hearing the stories of the girls who got pregnant and had so-called back-alley abortions. The sweet daughter of the neighborhood shopkeeper was one. She was close to my age and had gotten pregnant. Like so many women of the day, she became infected from the unsterilized methods and died. I can't remember her name but I can still feel the fear that was meant to keep us girls from becoming sexually active. I never forgot that lesson: the issue of abortion and reproductive health was inexorably linked with politics. Others still use it to control women.

As I grew older and became a teacher, mother, and a psychologist, I watched many of my young students and clients become pregnant and have babies before they were even out of school. Those that came from poor homes stayed buried in the cycle of poverty and welfare. They could not develop job skills as they had no means of obtaining an education. Then, along came the new feminist movement, bringing with it a political activism that centered on women's issues—keeping children safe from abuse, helping battered women become violence-free, protecting women from rape and sexual harassment, and providing reproductive health choices including the right to choose an abortion. I found it interesting that the fight about the woman's right to make her own choices came after the so-called sexual revolution and birth control were established. *Roe v. Wade*, the monumental U.S. Supreme Court decision in 1973, changed everything, we thought.

But, it was not to be. Almost immediately, the backlash began and across the country people took sides. The religious and conservative political coalitions banded against the new law. As an elected delegate from the state of Colorado to the National Women's Conference held in Houston, Texas, in 1976, I worked with my state delegation as well as others when we arrived in Houston, petrified that there would be violence that antiabortionists threatened. I left a husband and two children back home concerned about my safety but I could not stay away. Men walked up and down the aisles of delegates with walkie-talkies, trying to tell the women delegates how to vote on every issue. But, we met in the streets, hallways, bathrooms, and food concession lines. We talked woman-talk, and in the end, all the issues voted on were passed despite the harassment. We sent our work on to the United Nations Conferences on Women. I attended the conference in Nairobi, Kenya, in 1986. The delegates worked hard but the real action was at the Non-Governmental Organization meetings and informally on the lawn and in the women's bathrooms on the University of Kenya's lovely campus. Each day we all eagerly read the newspaper distributed to conference attendees to learn what would be the day's offerings.

Although my research and clinical psychology work focused on battered women and child abuse, my political interests focused on the entire feminist agenda: giving women the right to make informed choices about their lives. When the women from the Center for Reproductive Law and Policy (then housed within the Americans for Civil Liberty [ACLU] but today a separate organization) and from Planned Parenthood came to me in the early 1980s and asked me to testify in the now-famous *Hodgson v. Minnesota* and *Casey v. Pennsylvania* cases requiring married women and teenage girls to get husbands and parents to sign their permission before they could get an abortion, I flashed back to the grocer's daughter lying dead in her own pool of blood from a botched-up abortion and the women at the Houston conference controlled by men with walkie-talkies, and then I flashed forward to my own daughter and granddaughters. Of course, I agreed then, and later accepted that the best we could do was win young women the right of a judicial by-pass if one parent didn't give consent or at least acknowledge notification. I continued to testify in the many cases that came afterward, working with many of the young and old, mostly women attorneys, in the pro bono centers of large commercial and small public law firms. I worked with Planned Parenthood attorneys in *Casey,* the Pennsylvania case described that wanted to require a husband's signature before a married woman could get an abortion while permitting a single woman to sign for herself. The undue burdens and inequality between men's and women's ability to obtain health care continues until today.

During the early 1990s, before the Racketeer Influenced and Corrupt Organizations Act (RICO) suits that we discuss in Chapter 2 made clinic violence too expensive for protestors to continue on a regular basis, I worked with Planned Parenthood's abortion clinic workers in Denver. We trained volunteers who shielded patients from the jeers and taunts of the mostly male protestors who littered the sidewalk outside the clinic. Police on horseback guarded those brave enough to make it through the gauntlet. Post-traumatic stress reactions were common in those who worked inside, putting up with the harassment and danger day after day.

Until I met Rachel, I thought the battle to keep women's rights to make their own health choices was being fought mainly by women of my generation who remembered the back-alley abortions that we were forced into. Although it seemed clear that the politics of choice were still inexorably linked to male domination of women 30 years after *Roe v. Wade,* my daughter's generation did not see the loss of these legal rights as possible. Those who were fighting the battles in court went about it in a quiet way. Rarely did books published on the topic become popular and scholarly work on the topic was not rewarded in the university. Rachel's generation, who have more experience with recent publicity around the partial-birth abortion ban and the revival of post-abortion as a mental health problem, are not very outspoken. Even I did not publicize my testimony in the abortion rights cases.

Perhaps that is changing. Ron Reagan, President Reagan's son's outspokenness to support stem cell research funding, chilled by the current political climate, gives me more hope. The personal really is political!

In January 2004 my cousin telephoned me and announced that 40 years earlier, before abortion rights, she became pregnant and at age 17 she gave birth to a baby boy. Alone and in secret from the rest of her family, she and her mother hid in another state until her baby was born and immediately placed him for adoption. Then, she went back home to finish high school. Her child was lucky. He had loving adoptive parents and grew up to be a fine person who was happy to find his biological mother. She told only one other person about her child, her husband when they were married. It was much more difficult for her. Every day of every year she says she went through heartbreak, wondering about that child's fate. With her husband's encouragement, she went looking for him at around the same time he was searching for her. They found each other and have become part of each other's families.

How did she live with that secret for 40 years? What did that do to her, her son, her other children, and their extended families? Would she make the same choice, today, knowing the statistics about risk of child abuse in foster and adoptive homes? She says, definitely no, and is active in the open-adoption movement today. For her, living with the terror of not knowing if he was in harm's way and guilt about placing him for adoption still overwhelms her and sometimes even overshadows the joy in having been reunited. There was no choice then. She was told by her mother that adoption was the only thing to do or their lives would be ruined. My daughter and grandchildren have choices today. I hope to help them keep them.

Introduction: Why We Wrote This Book

Abortion rights activists don't want to talk about the bad times—they need to stay upbeat to put up with the continued harassment. Psychotherapists rarely provide abortion counseling and do not really know what women face when they make this choice. Abortion protestors also have dwindled in number. We have only to look at the current U.S. policies to know that the real battles are being fought in the legislatures and executive branches of our government.

Who counsels the women who choose to get an abortion today? Before the choice is finally made, women usually turn to family, friends, and counselors who work at women's centers where abortions are performed. Rarely do they turn to their psychotherapists to help them make the decision, even if they have one with whom they have been working for a long time. And, if they do, it becomes clear that most psychotherapists, even those who do support a woman's choice to terminate a pregnancy, do not have the factual information about the procedure itself nor the theoretical framework for helping the woman to make a competent decision.

To whom do women turn when they want to talk about the abortion, afterward? Rarely do abortion centers provide counseling for women because when they did offer groups, few women came to them. What if a woman with mental health issues prior to becoming pregnant has an abortion and then needs to talk about how this action affects all her mental health issues? Many abortion counselors are not fully trained to work with women who have diagnoses such as bipolar disorder or even abuse victims with post-traumatic stress disorder (PTSD). These women usually turn to their own psychotherapists who are skilled in working with the client but again may not know a lot about the typical post-abortion effects. Thus, many people wonder whether or not there is a post-abortion syndrome and may blame a woman's emotions and behavior after the abortion on the procedure rather than understanding the interaction between the woman's biology and hormones, her previous mental health problems, the secrecy and shame under which the woman may be acting, the political climate and harassment she may have faced by protestors outside of the center, and the religious and moral values with which she may have grown up. When all the data are reviewed, it becomes clear that few women have negative reactions from an abortion today and even fewer women develop psychological symptoms that last longer than a few days or weeks. Those who do have a longer psychological reaction usually have had serious psychological problems before they became pregnant. Many of these women are also survivors of physical and sexual assaults, both as children and as adults. When appropriately treated for PTSD from the abuse, most are able to go on with their lives.

It is time for a book to educate all those who are engaged in both pre- and post-abortion counseling. In order to do so, it is important for therapists to understand the politics and legislative history affecting women's decision-making, which we describe in Chapters 1 and 2. Chapter 3 reviews the psychological theories that guide the way women and girls think about important decisions so that counselors and therapists can determine each person's competency to make an informed choice. In Chapter 4, we present accurate information about the abortion procedure itself along with descriptions of the global human rights movement for women's access to reproductive health care. In Chapter 5, we review the psychological theories about the development of stable emotions to assist counselors and therapists in determining the woman's emotional state both pre- and post-abortion. It is important to review the empirical studies about the effects of abortion, and in Chapter 6, we provide a summary of the studies of post-abortion syndrome, which shows that post-abortion syndrome does not exist, even though some women may have some temporary negative or ambivalent feelings afterward.

In Chapter 7, we describe the areas that may elicit negative emotions so that therapists may recognize them in the few clients that may demonstrate such feelings. Suggestions for counseling sessions with individuals or groups can be found here. Abortion counseling has had profound positive and negative effects on those who have been working in women's centers. In Chapter 8, we present interviews with some of these courageous women who share their experiences to assist counselors who may want to share some of that optimism in the face of political backlash and fears for their own safety. Finally, in Chapter 9, we attempt to summarize the major points that have been found helpful in clinical practice.

Stories of real people are interspersed together with the facts and scientific data. There are lists of the many legal cases and continuous legislative agendas together with those laws that have passed and, to get people stirred up, those that are still in danger of passing. We have traveled within the countries about which we write, where huge disparities exist and poor women cannot get health services to which rich women have access. But this discrepancy exists in the United States also. Personally, we have seen children who go hungry because there is no food and treated unwanted children who have suffered horrendous abuse. Real people have fallen prey to the U.S. policies that refuse money to the family planning clinics around the world. It is time to stand up and send out a clear message. We do not have any argument with people who oppose abortion due to moral or religious grounds. We want them to have the same choice not to have an abortion that people who do support choice have to obtain an abortion.

We have no shame in saying that we are political activists. Like many of the activists we write about in this book, our goal is for everyone to have the right to make their own choices. Activists in this movement support those who have different opinions, and it is important for everyone's opinions to be respected and honored. Our vision is a world where everyone has tolerance for the other points of view. Hopefully, the generations that follow us will live without the fear that the abortion controversy has brought.

Throughout the book, we present stories of various people who are directly and indirectly affected by the struggle for women's reproductive health freedom. We offer descriptions of those who work in abortion clinics and those who protest outside the clinic, lawyers who work on reproductive rights cases, women who have had abortions and those who have chosen not to, and those who have had no choice at all. Information is included that counselors and therapists will find important to include when they counsel women before they choose to have an abortion or afterward, whether their sad or guilty feelings have remained longer than most do or they just want to talk with someone who understands. We review the important literature and conclude that there is no post-abortion syndrome, though we agree that some women may want or even need some counseling afterward. Usually good pre-abortion counseling identifies women who may be at risk and helps avoid problems afterward. Counselors and therapists will be able to identify medically safe abortion centers and Web sites that give up-to-date information. We end this book with some ideas about the psychology of tolerance and suggestions on how to teach it to others.

Acknowledgments

I would like to dedicate this book to my beloved mother for her strength and dedication to women's reproductive rights. Thank you for fighting tirelessly to ensure that women have access to safe reproductive health care. You have taught me the importance of always standing up for what I believe in, and never giving up. You are my inspiration and my rock. I love you.

Thank you to my father, grandparents, and brother for believing in me and for your unconditional love and support. I also want to thank Paul, Dale, J.B., Lauren, Marci, and my beautiful nephews and niece for being part of my life and for all of your encouragement.

My thanks to my good friend Kate Richmond, whose passion for equality and women's rights has inspired me. She introduced me to Lenore knowing that we shared this same passion. My deep gratitude to Lenore, for whom I have the utmost respect and affection; I could not have asked for a more fabulous mentor, dear colleague, and friend.

Also, my appreciation to my incredible friends who have been a source of ongoing support. Many thanks to Stephanie, Melia, Elissa, Elise, Nicole, Jill, Randi, Sharon, Chrissy, Tamra, and Stacey. And to R.J., without whom I could not have done this.

I am grateful to the staff of the women's center for their candidness and honesty in sharing their experiences as providers. Your devotion to the women you care for has left an indelible impression on my heart.

I also want to acknowledge and thank my colleague Dr. Stanley Althof, who has provided me with a wonderful opportunity working with and learning from him.

Rachel Needle

I would like to thank my parents for giving me the strength of my convictions; my family, especially my children, grandchildren, nieces, and nephew for being there, along with my students, as a reminder of the future generations who must not lose their right to choose when and if to have children; all my friends and psychology colleagues for their support, especially when I tackle the tough, controversial issues; and my partner, David, for his unwavering love and companionship.

I would also like to thank Rachel for her enthusiasm and energy for this project. Her ability to work with me as a friend and a colleague on a project of this magnitude is a testimony to her incredible intelligence and maturity. She, Kate Richmond, and the other women in my feminist therapy class are an inspiration for all young women today. They represent the true meaning of how women can share friendship and collegiality with one another.

Lenore Walker

Both of us would like to thank Sheri W. Sussman, our wonderful editor at Springer who believed in us and gave us encouragement every step of the way. Her support and knowledge made this a much better book.

We also want to acknowledge the important work of all of the organizations that are out there supporting women and the right to choose—especially Planned Parenthood, the National Abortion Federation, the Guttmacher Institute, the Center for Reproductive Rights, and the American Civil Liberties Union. We admire your commitment to this issue, and value the help you have given us while writing this book.

We would like to thank Dr. Nancy Russo for all of her help in obtaining documents and for assisting us in understanding the past 30 years of the work she has been doing with health providers and the American Psychological Association. We admire her scholarship, her generosity of her time and knowledge, her friendship, and her courageous convictions.

RN

LW

May 2007

CHAPTER 1

Perspectives for the Mental Health Professional

Since the monumental U.S. Supreme Court decision of *Roe v. Wade* in 1973, which made it legal for a woman to obtain an abortion, an abundance of anti-choice legislation and regulations have restricted access to safe and legal reproductive health care services. Hundreds of potential laws are filed each year across the United States that threaten access to abortion services. This legislation includes (but is not limited to) broad bans on abortion, often without exceptions for a woman's health; imposed waiting periods on women seeking abortion in addition to requiring abortion providers to give their patients certain state-mandated materials; restricting a minor's access to abortion, generally in the form of parental notification or consent bills; and excessive, politically motivated restrictions and requirements on medical facilities providing abortions. It is important for therapists who are counseling women pre- or post-abortion to understand these legislative efforts and their possible impact on the women and abortion providers.

PERSPECTIVES FOR THE MENTAL HEALTH PROFESSIONAL

After years of struggle to make a woman's right to choose a reality, and almost immediately after *Roe v. Wade* created the new law, antiabortion

1

politicians began crafting legislation to limit access to abortion services. The Hyde Amendment was the first barrier for women to safe and competent medical care, and it is still is one of the most restrictive pieces of antiabortion legislation. In a sophisticated political move that stifled debate on the amendment, then U.S. Congressman Hyde added it to other important but nonrelated legislation. The Hyde Amendment, passed in 1976 and first enacted in August of 1977, prohibits the use of federal funds to pay for abortion services with the only exception being if continuing the pregnancy would endanger the woman's life. The Hyde Amendment, which includes U.S. aid to other countries and their birth control clinics, universally affects poor women around the world. The amendment creates an economic barrier to poor women in need of abortions and is discriminatory: a significant portion of those affected are women of color. These women, many of whom cannot afford to put three nourishing meals a day on the table for their children, will either have to forgo paying bills to scrape together upwards of four hundred dollars to pay for an abortion or are forced to continue their pregnancies. A report by Boonstra and Sonfield (2000) states the following: "An analysis by researchers at Princeton University's Office of Population Research and the Alan Guttmacher Institute of the number of abortions to Medicaid-eligible women in two states before and after the law was enforced in the late 1970s, concluded that about 20% of the women who would have obtained an abortion had funding been available were unable to do so in the post-Hyde period and carried their pregnancy to term."

In 1978 the limitations of the Hyde Amendment were expanded to include pregnancies that resulted from rape or incest. In reality, however, the ability of providers throughout the years to actually receive payment from Medicaid has been minimal. According to the Alan Guttmacher Institute, a minimum of 9,100 abortions annually result from pregnancies that occur due to forced sexual intercourse (Jones, Darroch, & Henshaw, 2002). In 2001, only 81 abortions to end pregnancies that resulted from rape or incest or that endangered the life of the mother were paid for by Medicaid (Sonfield & Benson Gold, 2005). One of the more frustrating aspects of the Hyde Amendment is that it must be renewed and voted on by Congress every year. In essence, every year for the last 30 years, poor women, and women who have been sexually assaulted, have been discriminated against and denied access to a life-changing, and more importantly, legal medical procedure. Thus, although more than half of the people of the United States believe women should have the right to choose abortion if they wish, their Congressional representatives continue to vote against poor and otherwise marginalized women to continue a pregnancy and then force the states to pay with inadequate funds for her to raise that child.

Abortion providers are charged with the challenge of providing quality care to women at an affordable cost, as well as maintaining accessibility for those women who have limited financial means. Many providers reduce their fees, their work, or both with local grassroots organizations that provide funding for women seeking abortions. On a national level, the National Network of Abortion Funds (NNAF) helps over 22,000 women annually with a total of over $2 million in financial assistance (National Network of Abortion Funds). Currently, there are approximately 125 funding sources throughout the United States. Most of the funds have eligibility requirements and an application process that women seeking financial assistance must go through before being approved. The funds' primary source of income is usually donations and many funds have limitations on how much they are able to donate per patient so they can help as many women as possible. These funding agencies often times run out of money and therefore there is no guarantee that a women applying for assistance will receive it. A majority of these funding agencies are staffed by volunteers and truly the unsung heroes are the abortion provider's staff who will spend countless hours on the phone networking to try and arrange funding for women who do not have the resources or ability to find it themselves. Certainly one of the most emotional aspects of any abortion counselor's job is to hear the desperate stories of the women needing help while knowing that there are limited resources available to help them.

One of the most difficult situations occurs when counseling women who became pregnant as a result of rape and are prosecuting their attackers. Abortion providers who cooperate with local law enforcement agencies to provide fetal tissue for DNA comparison with the suspect's are not compensated by any agency providing victim services for those women seeking abortions. Women who are dealing with the emotional trauma of a sexual assault, incest, or both, who then find themselves pregnant as a result of that violation, are forced to tell their story over and over again, this time in order to qualify for financial assistance. They are victimized all over again. Beyond the women who are cooperating with the prosecution of their offenders, there are women too numerous to count who have been raped or coerced into having intercourse who do not report the attack but still find themselves pregnant. These women must now tell their stories to strangers once again, this time in hopes of receiving funds to pay for their abortions.

FUNDING FOR ABORTION

The women who need help to find funding are primarily those of limited means financially, educationally, and emotionally. They are often single

---

Box 1.1   Highlights (Guttmacher Institute, 2007d)

- Thirty-two states and the District of Columbia follow the federal standard and provide abortions in cases of life endangerment, rape, and incest.
- Four of these states also provides state funds for abortions in cases of fetal abnormalities.
- Three of these states also provides state funds for abortions that are necessary to prevent grave, long-lasting damage to the woman's physical health.
- One state provides abortions only in cases of life endangerment, in apparent violation of the federal standard.
- Seventeen states use state funds to provide all or most medically necessary abortions.
- Four of these states provide such funds voluntarily.
- Thirteen of these states do so pursuant to court order.

---

parents and women who are struggling to make ends meet, living paycheck to paycheck. Regardless of why a woman is choosing to have an abortion, having to seek out financial assistance is a humbling experience. Many women wait to have an abortion because either they are not aware that funding exists or they are trying to raise the funds themselves. Yet every week a woman waits, she is aware the pregnancy is growing and developing, which adds to her emotional stress. Many women unwittingly wait too long to find help and either have higher fees or are no longer able to have abortions due to the longer gestation of the pregnancy. Box 1.1 gives an overview of the funding requirements for abortions in the various U.S. states that have their own laws.

PARENTAL NOTIFICATION AND CONSENT LAWS

One of the most time-consuming and burdensome legal restrictions on access to abortion is the requirement of mandatory parental notification or consent. In the United States, 34 states require parental involvement before a minor can receive abortion services (Guttmacher Institute, September 2006). These laws vary greatly state by state. Twenty-one states require that the abortion provider obtain proof of parental consent, and 11 states require that the provider notify a parent. Two states require both parental consent and notification (Guttmacher Institute, November 2006).

State-by-state, the difference in wording of these laws can be significant. On one end of the spectrum, laws can require the consent or notification of both parents. Minnesota requires that both parents be notified, and Mississippi and North Dakota require both parents' consent (Center for Reproductive Rights, 2005). The difficulty inherent in coordinating notification or consent of both parents, as well as the potential difficulty in locating both parents, makes these laws particularly burdensome. Many parental involvement laws also create an additional burden by delaying a client's medical care. These laws often amount to a waiting period for abortion, requiring that notification or consent take place 24–48 hours in advance.

On the other end of the spectrum are six states that recognize the diversity of families' structures and have, in turn, made these laws more flexible. In these states a grandparent or other adult relative may consent or be notified of the abortion in place of the minor's parents (Center for Reproductive Rights, 2005). Also, 13 states have the ability to waive the consent or notification requirement altogether in cases of neglect or abuse (Guttmacher Institute, November 2006).

Unfortunately, the implementation of a mandatory parental involvement law can be very burdensome. Depending on the wording of the law, notification or consent may have to take place in person, by mail, or by phone. In many cases it may require multiple office visits. In other cases, providers may have parents sign a form waiving the requirement of notification or consent and the associated waiting period, allowing notification or consent to take place on the day of the abortion procedure. Penalties if notification or consent is not properly executed vary state by state and may include criminal penalties, fines, or revocation of the doctor's medical license. Therefore it is important that the abortion provider insure that a legal definition of consent or notification has occurred.

In their practical application, notification laws often have the same result for the client as do consent laws. Both consent and notification require the client to discuss her situation with her legal guardian. If the client is unable to do so, it means little to her whether she must legally notify them or have their consent. Depending on the way the law is written, a parent may have to come to the doctor's office with the client or receive a phone call or accept a certified letter. If the parent refuses all attempts to contact him or her, notification may be impossible.

PARENTAL NOTIFICATION OR CONSENT: HIDDEN ASSUMPTIONS

Proponents of mandatory parental notification or consent laws claim that their purpose is to involve the parent in the client's decision and to foster communication, but the reality is that the majority of clients involve their parents in this decision even when the law does not require it. Those who do not discuss the abortion with their parents often have substantial reasons for not doing so. If a client does not involve her parent, she will often involve a close family member or trusted adult. If the client is not able to talk to her parent, this law does not transform that relationship. It only adds another burden on the patient.

Underlying these laws is an assumption that all clients have a certain type of family life where involving her parents would benefit her. This notion of family does not incorporate the many diverse family styles that occur in homes where culture, ethnicity, socioeconomic status, or other circumstances are predominant. The reality of the young woman's situation may prevent her from discussing her situation with her parent or legal guardian. There are many factors that may affect her decision. She may be facing a physically, emotionally, or sexually abusive parent. Her parent may in fact have his or her own agenda about whether or not the client continues the pregnancy. For instance, they may not believe in abortion or they may believe the client should have to carry an unwanted pregnancy as punishment for sexual activity. In fact, the parent may not be thinking about what is best for the client, and disclosure to this type of parent may worsen the girl's family relationships.

Another problem in these laws occurs when they involve the legal guardian of the client. But some teens' legal guardians may not be involved in their lives. A minor may be living with a grandmother, aunt or uncle, step-parent, sibling, or friend. In some cultures, it is common for the client's primary caregiver not to have gone through the proper legal channels to be considered a legal guardian. Thus, the teen may discuss the desire to have an abortion with the caregiver but he or she has no legal standing to sign the consent form. Many of these teens are actually emancipated but have not obtained legal documentation to prove their lifestyle.

Furthermore, many clients may not have the documentation to show that parental notification or consent has legally been given even when they have discussed the procedure with their caregivers. They may not have documents such as an identification cards, birth certificates, or adoption or custody papers to confirm who their legal guardians are. Clients may also be undocumented residents of this country. While politically it may be better for the United States for these young women not to give birth on U.S. soil, in fact this is not a good health practice. However, without paperwork it can be difficult to verify the mothers' ages and identify the parents or legal guardians to insure compliance with law. Because these documents may not be readily available, services may have to be delayed even longer, further endangering the mothers' health.

EXCEPTIONS: JUDICIAL BYPASS AND MEDICAL EMERGENCY

One of the most important components of the parental notification or consent laws is the option for judicial bypass. All 34 states that have laws include a judicial bypass procedure (Guttmacher Institute, 2007). Judicial bypass allows a minor to apply to a court to waive the parental consent or notification requirement. The ease or difficulty of the judicial bypass process often depends on local officials and may vary judge by judge. While it is of utmost importance to have a compassionate judicial bypass option, it certainly does not alleviate all of the problems of this law.

The process of seeking a judicial bypass can be very intimidating. It may seem to the client that the purpose of this law is punitive, since court may be seen as a place where criminals go. The client may find it difficult to speak about intimate details of her life with a judge. In smaller communities, the client may know the judge or court employees and confidentiality may therefore be compromised. Furthermore many courts are only open during business hours when the client is in school. Scheduling

---

Box 1.2   Highlights (Guttmacher Institute, 2007c)

- Twenty-four of the states that require counseling also require women to wait a specified period.
- Thirty-four states require some parental involvement in a minor's decision to have an abortion.
- Twenty-one states require parental consent only, two of which require both parents to consent.
- Eleven states require parental notification only, one of which requires that both parents be notified.
- Two states require both parental consent and notification.
- All of the 34 states that require parental involvement have an alternative process for minors seeking an abortion.
- Thirty-four states include a judicial bypass procedure, which allows a minor to obtain approval from a court.
- Six states also permit a minor to obtain an abortion if a grandparent or other adult relative is involved in the decision.
- Most states that require parental involvement make exceptions under certain circumstances.
- Twenty-eight states permit a minor to obtain an abortion in a medical emergency.
- Thirteen states permit a minor to obtain an abortion in cases of abuse, assault, incest, or neglect.

time for the doctor's visit as well as time for the judicial bypass may require several days out of school.

Only 28 of 34 states have a medical emergency exception (Guttmacher Institute, 2007). This leaves young women who reside in the other six states in a very dangerous situation. Should an emergency arise, a young woman's health and safety may very well be compromised. Without a medical emergency exception, she is at the mercy of the law and the delays associated with parental involvement laws.

The injustice of mandatory parental involvement laws is that they target one of the most vulnerable groups in our society—young women— by creating additional obstacles and delaying their access to abortion services. These laws most dramatically affect those who may not have a supportive relationship with their parents or legal guardians. Understanding these elements of the law will greatly improve your ability to counsel and prepare your clients who are seeking abortion services. Box 1.2 is an overview of the parental notification and consent laws for the different U.S. states.

FEDERAL PARENTAL NOTIFICATION LEGISLATION

During the 109th Congress (2005–2006) the U.S. House of Representatives heard and passed the first federal parental notification act, called the Child Interstate Abortion Notification Act (CIANA; GovTrack, 2006). Although the Senate had previously passed another version of the bill, the one passed by the House is more strict, and the Senate, therefore, voted against the act. If passed, the Child Interstate Abortion Notification Act (CIANA), also called the Teen Endangerment Act or the Child Custody Protection Act (CCPA; H.R. 748, S. 8, 396, 403), would create two main penalties. The first would make it a federal crime for a person to transport a minor across state lines to receive an abortion if she does not fulfill the parental consent or notification laws of her home state. The second part of the law states that the client would also have to meet new federal parental notification guidelines and face an associated delay if she leaves her state of residence to seek abortion services. This law would make a physician's noncompliance with the notification procedures a federal crime. The young woman would have to meet the legal requirements of her home state as well as provide federal notice to the legal guardian. If the young woman's home state does not have a judicial bypass option, this law does not provide an option for a federal bypass.

Many parts of the country have limited access to abortion providers, and crossing state lines to obtain abortion services is often a necessity. If passed, this law will significantly limit access for minors across the country. Although it does not appear that this so-called Teen Endangerment Bill will pass during the 2007 Congress, now that the political majority are not in favor of it, the fact that it has gotten this far is of great concern to those who believe that most young women and girls have the cognitive and emotional maturity to make the decision whether or not to tell their parents about their choice of an abortion. We discuss this issue further in the Chapters 2 and 3 in this book.

In Box 1.3 we reprint a story by Bill and Karen Bell to illustrate how dangerous these parental consent and notification laws can be. The Bells' 17-year-old daughter went forward with an illegal abortion without telling her parents and died from unforeseen complications. The Bells have become outspoken proponents of repealing the parental involvement laws, believing the research that young women who do not tell their parents about an abortion usually have their reasons and that these laws will not prevent young women from seeking and obtaining an abortion. Sometimes, however, as in Becky Bell's case, doing so may be unsafe and more dangerous than if they had obtained appropriate pre-abortion counseling from abortion centers with counselors who are trained to determine these young women's ability to make informed choices. We describe the research on the cognitive abilities of these teenagers in Chapter 3 and on the development of their emotional abilities in Chapter 5.

Box 1.3 Bill and Karen Bell

Sixteen years ago we would have supported legislation mandating parental involvement laws. Bills have been introduced by legislators to require minors under the age of 18 to notify their parents before obtaining an abortion, and to require minors to receive their parents' consent for an abortion. While these pieces of legislation seem reasonable on the surface, our experience has taught us that parental involvement laws seriously endanger the very families and teens they are intended to protect.

In 1988, our beautiful, vibrant, 17-year-old daughter Becky died suddenly, after a six-day illness. The pathologist who directed her autopsy concluded that the cause of her death was streptococcus pneumonia, brought about by an illegal abortion. Learning this, we finally understood our daughter's last words. In the hospital, she had taken off her oxygen mask and said, "Mom, Dad, I love you. Forgive me."

How could this have happened? Why would Becky have risked an illegal abortion? How could parents as close to their daughter as we had always been not have known that she was pregnant and desperate to deal with a situation that she believed she couldn't share with us?

(continued)

We learned the sad answers to these questions in the weeks following our daughter's death. Becky had told her girlfriends that she believed we would be terribly hurt and disappointed in her if she told us about her pregnancy. Like a lot of young people, she was not comfortable sharing intimate details of her developing sexuality with her parents.

Becky discovered that our state has a parental consent law, which requires girls under the age of 18 to get their parents' permission before they can get an abortion. A Planned Parenthood counselor told her that she could apply for a judicial bypass as an alternative to parental consent. The counselor remembered Becky's response: "If I can't talk to my parents, how can I tell a judge who doesn't even know me?" We now know that in over 10 years on the bench, the judge in our district has never issued a waiver to a teen for an abortion.

Desperate to avoid telling us about her pregnancy, and therefore unable to go to a reputable medical establishment, where abortions are provided compassionately and safely every day, Becky found someone operating outside the law who would help her. Becky had a back-alley abortion. Indiana's parental involvement law ultimately led our daughter to her death.

Studies have established that the majority of teenagers (60%–70%) do talk to their parents when they become pregnant. Of those who don't, about one-third are at risk of physical or emotional abuse. The rest, like Becky, believe for myriad reasons that this is a problem they must face without their parents.

Parental involvement laws further isolate girls in this last category, who feel it is impossible to turn to their parents, forcing them to instead make decisions and arrangements on their own.

All parents would want to know if their child was in a situation like Becky's. In fact, we would have supported the law in our state before we experienced the loss of our daughter. We have been forced to learn in the most painful way imaginable that laws cannot create family communication. We would rather have not known that our daughter had had an abortion, if it meant that she could have obtained the best of care, and come back home safely to us.

Many of you have daughters and granddaughters, and we are sure that you would want to be involved in any issues relating to their health and well-being—just as we did. Yet, the law in Indiana did not force Becky to involve us at her most desperate time.

As much as we would have wanted to help Becky through this crisis, the law did not succeed in forcing her to talk to us about issues she found too upsetting to share with us. For the sake of other parents' daughters, we urge legislators who are considering these very dangerous bills to remember Becky Bell, and to pass no laws that will increase the chances that even one desperate girl will feel that her only choice is an illegal abortion.

The law in Indiana did not make Becky come to us. Will other parental involvement laws be any different?

CRISIS PREGNANCY CENTERS

We first introduced the concept of Crisis Pregnancy Centers (CPCs) earlier when detailing the federal funding of these mostly faith-based groups that mislead women with erroneous advertisements and information designed to stop a woman from choosing to have an abortion. The mission of CPCs, first established in 1967 in Hawaii after the state legislature successfully repealed its laws criminalizing abortion, are to keep women from having abortions. Robert Pearson, the man who initiated these centers, stated, "Obviously, we're fighting Satan. A killer, who in this case is the girl who wants to kill her baby, has no right to information that will help her kill her baby" (National Abortion Federation [NAF], 2006b). In 1973 when *Roe v. Wade* became the law of the land, he then created the Pearson Institute in order to teach other antiabortion groups how to open CPCs throughout the country. An investigation conducted by the Democratic Staff of the U.S. House of Representatives Committee on government reform found that in the past 5 years, taxpayers have spent over $30 million underwriting these centers all over the United States (NAF, 2006b).

This Congressional study authorized female investigators to pose as teenagers trying to make a decision on whether or not to have an abortion. The investigations contacted 23 out of the 25 CPCs in 15 states that had received grants through the $150 million "Compassion Capital Fund," part of President Bush's faith-based initiatives. It was reported that 87% of the CPCs that were contacted provided false and misleading information linking abortion to breast cancer, infertility, and mental illness (Cramer, 2006).

Obviously these centers are giving biased information and ignoring the findings of an expert panel of the American Psychological Association (APA) and the Surgeon General by telling the women that there were serious psychological aftereffects from an abortion when none have been found in other studies. We discuss these studies further in Chapter 6.

By giving erroneous information that abortion is more likely to cause breast cancer, the CPCs also ignored the National Cancer Institute's conclusion that abortion does not increase the risk of breast cancer (National Cancer Institute, 2003). Box 1.4 contains the *New York Times* editorial that exposed the erroneous health information supported by those politically opposed to abortion ("Abortion," 2003). It is unknown how many women were frightened by this misinformation.

Across the country, many women seeking a place to obtain an abortion respond to the CPC advertising and visit these centers only to learn that they do not provide abortion services. These women report being misled and then harassed, bullied, and given blatantly false information

> **Box 1.4** *New York Times* **Editorial (January 6, 2003)**
>
> The National Cancer Institute has been bullied by Congressional conserva-tives into revising its best judgment on whether abortion increases the risk of breast cancer. Unless the institute can summon the courage to express its true views, it will be severely damaged.
>
> Researchers have long debated whether abortion increases the risk of breast cancer, possibly by altering hormones and tissue development in the breast. A fact sheet distributed by the institute last March noted that stud-ies conducted before the mid-1990s produced inconsistent results but that subsequent studies generally found no association between abortion and breast cancer. The American Cancer Society reached the same conclusion.
>
> Those judgments were anathema to antiabortion groups, which have been trying to scare women away from abortion by raising the specter of breast cancer. A group of 28 antiabortion members of Congress com-plained to Tommy Thompson, secretary of health and human services, that the institute's formulation was "scientifically inaccurate and mislead-ing." So in June, the institute removed the fact sheet from its Web site and later replaced it with a statement that some studies have found an increased risk of cancer while others have not. That statement, while tech-nically accurate, is such an egregious distortion of the evidence that one can only hope it is an interim statement, as some staff members suggest, not a final surrender.
>
> The institute plans to address the issue at a conference on pregnancy and breast cancer in February. If the experts at the meeting agree that there is no link between abortion and breast cancer, the institute will have no excuse to suppress the information. It will have to issue a new fact sheet or admit that it can no longer provide objective guidance on matters that inflame social conservatives.

by the CPC staff. Many assert that their confidentiality had been vio-lated and that mistreatment by CPCs had threatened their health (NAF, 2006a). As a result, NAF has published a Web site page to counter some of the misleading information that CPCs have been found to give women in an attempt to persuade them not to have an abortion.

As we have found through our interviews for this book, the tactics of the CPCs are geared toward preventing women from having an abortion by delaying, scaring, and intimidating them. Often the CPCs intention-ally make women wait longer than necessary for pregnancy test results or sonograms and deliberately use this waiting time to show the women vid-eos and pictures depicting gruesome and graphic images of bloody and dismembered fetuses that have allegedly been aborted (Women's Health Action and Mobilization, 2007).

The NAF Web site provides a fact sheet that describes and gives the most relevant information about CPCs available to assist women so that they understand the attempt of many CPCs to mislead women and persuade them against choosing an abortion. The NAF Web site reports that most CPCs historically have not been licensed as medical facilities and are staffed mostly by volunteers who must share a commitment to Christianity and anti-choice beliefs. The CPCs offer select services that are not always accurate and do not include any information on contraception for women or men. In addition, CPCs do not make referrals to abortion centers. Reports show that the number of CPCs is growing while the number of abortion providers is shrinking (Finer & Henshaw, 2003).

The NAF–Patient Partnership program (2006) collects information from women who have sought abortions after their experience with a CPC. This has been one of the ways that the misinformation being provided by these CPCs can be monitored. As we discuss in Chapter 5, this kind of scare tactic may well produce significant difficulties in healing rather than preventing the procedure itself. Some of their stories that have been published are as follows:

"I asked for the results of my pregnancy test and she told me it was negative anyway so I don't need to get so worked up. Luckily I knew that these places often try to confuse women by telling them they aren't really pregnant so they are tricked into carrying the fetus past the time for a safer abortion. I repeated a home pregnancy test which was positive, so she was lying to me."

NAF CPC Patient Partnership Participant

"All I heard about was how bad abortion was and that it was more dangerous than any other choice, that it would completely ruin my relationship with my boyfriend and it would make me depressed, and that I would regret it for the rest of my life."

NAF CPC Patient Partnership Participant

"Last thing was the video. She left the room and said it was required for me to watch this video. I could immediately tell what kind of video it would be when the host came on and said in a very concerned voice, 'Millions of women have chosen abortion but few know the medical risks that can be associated with this procedure.' It went on to say that abortion doctors are the lowest on the figurative 'totem pole' of doctors and are often not as skilled as other doctors. They don't have the correct knowledge or tools to perform this complex procedure and therefore are 'working blind'."

NAF CPC Patient Partnership Participant

"The woman at 'Caring' Pregnancy Center did not inform me about my legal rights to birth control, abortion. . . . She did not tell me how to protect myself against a deadly STD or a future pregnancy. She did not care whether I was raped, or if I had sex recently enough to use the emergency contraceptive. . . . 'Caring' Pregnancy Centers will only continue to hurt women like me and this makes me angry. And I agree that something must be done."

NAF CPC Patient Partnership Participant

"I went to this clinic thinking I was going to have an abortion. They did a pregnancy test, and ultrasound, showed me a video, showed me pictures and a development chart, and then I spoke with someone. She told me that they did not perform abortions. They offered to provide me with clothes and told me about a home that I could go stay in until I have the baby. They also told me that I should keep my baby or put it up for adoption. They told me the abortion was going to be very painful and that I might not be able to have a child later in life if I have an abortion."

Florida Abortion Center

"They told me that abortion centers use drills and knives to cut you open and that the Doctor hates women."

Florida Abortion Center

"They told me I could die from an abortion and that I would never have kids. They preached about religion and told me that I should have the baby or put it up for adoption. They told me I had a formed baby and how it was a sin."

Florida Abortion Center

TARGETED REGULATION OF ABORTION PROVIDERS (TRAP)

Another group of legislative attempts to prevent women from choosing to terminate a pregnancy include what are called the TRAP laws, which attempt to regulate the medical practices of doctors who provide abortions by imposing burdensome requirements that are different and more stringent than regulations applied to comparable medical practices. These excessive and unnecessary government regulations ultimately harm women's health and inhibit their reproductive choices (Center for Reproductive Rights, 2004).

Currently, 19 states and Puerto Rico enforce TRAP laws that apply to abortions performed in both the first and second trimesters of pregnancy. Fourteen states currently have laws that apply only to abortions performed after the first trimester (Center for Reproductive Rights, 2004).

The real purpose of the TRAP laws is to make accessing an abortion even more difficult than it is presently. States already require facilities that provide abortions to have a state license including yearly inspections and reviews on top of these additional laws. When these state laws are implemented they take abortion centers outside the existing regulatory licensing procedure applicable to other physicians and impose unfair requirements that have already reduced the number of places for women who need these services to go. The legislation treats abortion differently than all comparable medical procedures and creates a double standard for those physicians who provide abortions within their medical offices (these physicians' offices do not have to have a separate state license). As a medical service, abortion is not any different from other outpatient procedures that do not have state laws regulating them. Because in the year 2007 the provision of abortion care is already marginalized, these laws can only be interpreted as a direct form of harassment to physicians and add unnecessary and unwarranted barriers to women seeking a part of their legal rights to comprehensive reproductive health care. The important thing to remember is abortion, especially when performed early in the pregnancy, is one of the safest and most common medical procedures performed today. The American College of Obstetrics and Gynecology (ACOG) reports that the risk of death from an abortion is much lower than an appendectomy, childbirth, or even a tonsillectomy (ACOG, 1990).

Many requirements are stipulated in these laws. Although they might seem innocuous in theory, the implementation could successfully force the limited number of free-standing abortion facilities to have to close. As it is, 86% of cities do not have any providers (Center for Reproductive Rights, 2004). Mississippi, North Dakota, and South Dakota each only have one provider. Many women are forced to travel great distances for their care, often across state lines. In addition, physicians are deterred from becoming or remaining abortion providers because these TRAP laws carry criminal and civil penalties to include large fines, imprisonment, and suspension of one's medical license. These laws violate the constitutional laws, forcing them to comply with unreasonable searches and by violating their right to equal protection of the laws (Center for Reproductive Rights, 2004).

The TRAP regulations are seen as a stealth way of imposing Ambulatory Surgery Center status on facilities providing abortions. This makes it extremely difficult for providers to keep their doors open. In order to do so they must have physicians trained in abortion surgery and staff who have not left because of the threat of violence and harassment. They must also keep their fees affordable despite the necessary security needs and cost increases due to the limited availability of not only outrageous malpractice insurance costs, but also property insurance, and overall health care costs with limited reimbursement, if any, offered as a benefit. Requirement on the physical design and function of a regulated facility are often imposed by the TRAP laws (Center for Reproductive Rights, 2004).

Many of the TRAP laws clearly serve as a violation of abortion providers' rights by allowing unannounced search and seizures at times when surgery is being performed. Some of the mandated requirements include airflow and circulation requisites; square-footage minimums for hallways, recovery rooms, counseling rooms, and changing rooms; specific sink designs; and lawn care standards. Those who continue to provide abortion services would have difficulty seeking new space due to the reluctance of landlords to rent to them. The reality is that abortion providers remain targets of arson, clinic bombings, large demonstrations, and other forms of domestic terrorism.

Some TRAP schemes permit review and even copying of patient medical records during searches by the state health department. This is a serious concern of abortion providers because such provisions create a serious threat to patient confidentiality and are likely to deter some women from safely seeking abortion services (Center for Reproductive Rights, 2004). This threat to patient confidentiality could clearly deter a woman from seeking a safe abortion, especially if the patient lives in a small rural community where everyone knows one another. Patients might even withhold important medical information that could have a disastrous outcome during surgery. These laws are often purposefully written in vague language so that it becomes even more difficult for a provider to comply with them.

PARTIAL-BIRTH ABORTION

Perhaps the most misunderstood, divisive, politically strategic and motivated issue regarding abortion today is the so-called Partial-Birth Abortion Bill. One must be clear that this is a political battle cry, not a movement that will improve access to any medical technology. Those who want to end all abortion rights have been forthright that this manipulated and intentionally named procedure causes great discomfort among the American public. They have been successful in clearly chipping away at access to legal abortion by initiating these laws. There has never been medical terminology that is called partial-birth abortion. Major medical associations have come out strongly opposed to this legislation, going so far as to declare that "The courts were correct each time they struck down such ill-conceived and unconstitutional restrictions on physicians' ability to provide patients with the safest possible medical care . . . The term 'partial-birth abortion' was purposely contrived to be inflammatory" (ACOG, 2006). This is a very clear attempt from those who want to overturn *Roe v. Wade* to mislead the American public into thinking that abortions in the final months of pregnancy are easy to obtain. Also, the attention is turned from the woman to the fetus without understanding or taking into account the woman's physical or emotional health.

Until this legislation, which named the procedure partial-birth abortion, no such medical procedure by that name existed. However, once the government took a stand against abortion, despite it being the law of the country, the officials used their power to frame the debate using false information about a medical procedure. This is a dangerous precedent, because this will give the government the ability to attempt to set a medical standard of care separate from physicians who write the criteria for protocols and teaching.

The Guttmacher Institute (2007a) discusses the background of this legislation in the following paragraph:

> Since the mid-1990's, a majority of states have enacted laws prohibiting "partial-birth" abortions, although that term is not recognized by the medical community. Overwhelmingly, these laws permit the procedure only when necessary to preserve the woman's life but not to protect her health. In 2000, the U.S. Supreme Court, in *Stenberg v. Carhart,* struck down a Nebraska statute as unconstitutional because it did not include an exception for the woman's health and because it found the language used to define a "partial-birth abortion" to be so broad as to potentially outlaw a range of abortion procedures, including the most common form of second trimester pre-viability abortions. Nonetheless, President Bush in 2003 signed into law a federal ban that was virtually identical to the Nebraska law. In 2004, the ban was declared unconstitutional by three district court judges on the grounds that it shared the same constitutional flaws identified in *Stenberg;* appeals are currently underway.

A list of the current so-called partial-birth laws in the various U.S. states is provided in Box 1.5.

In the act, the definition of partial-birth abortion reads:

> "The person performing the abortion deliberately and intentionally vaginally delivers a living fetus until, in the case of a head-first

---

Box 1.5   Highlights (Guttmacher Institute, 2007a)

- Twenty-six states have bans on partial-birth abortions that apply throughout pregnancy.

  - Eighteen bans have been specifically blocked by a court.
  - Seven bans remain unchallenged but are presumably unenforceable under *Stenberg* because they lack health exceptions.
  - Ohio's ban has been challenged and upheld by a court.

- Five states have bans that apply after viability.

  - Utah's ban has been specifically blocked by a court because it lacks a health exception.
  - Montana's ban remains unchallenged but is presumably unenforceable under *Stenberg* because it lacks a health exception.
  - Three bans are currently in effect.

- Four states have bans that include a health exception.

  - Two states broadly allow the procedure to protect against physical or mental impairment.
  - Two states narrowly allow the procedure to protect only against bodily harm.

- Twenty-seven states have bans without a health exception.

  - Nineteen bans have been specifically blocked by a court.
  - Eight bans remain unchallenged.

---

presentation, the entire fetal head is outside the body of the mother, or, in the case of breech presentation, any part of the fetal trunk past the navel is outside the body of the mother for the purpose of performing an overt act that the person knows will kill the partially delivered living fetus." (Wright & Katz, 2006)

It is frightening to understand that any physician who violates the law could face up to 2 years of imprisonment, civil lawsuits, and other penalties including revocation or suspension of their medical licenses. The physician would also be held responsible for "all injuries, psychological and physical" (Wright & Katz, 2006). There is no health exception for the mother demonstrating little regard for women and the realities of their pregnancies. This doesn't withstand the fact that a woman might have other children at home who could possibly lose their mother if she is forced to continue pregnancy to term despite the danger to her health.

In fact, Wright and Katz (2006) describe a very rarely used procedure called intact D & X (dilation and extraction) that accounts for

0.17% of all abortions in this country. Originally this method became available to reduce complications in late second-trimester abortions. It is almost always performed over a protocol of 2–3 days. The procedure begins with inserting an osmotic dilator, called a laminaria, which dilates the cervix. Most providers use this with a combination of Cytotec on the actual day of the procedure. Cytotec is given vaginally or bucally (between the gums and cheek). This combination provides sufficient dilation so that the fetus can be removed intact. Intact D & X clearly minimizes the risk of uterine injury and cervical tears. Also, this procedure retains the products of conception without the barbaric dismemberment described by abortion opponents.

Intact D & X allows a woman to emotionally part with her pregnancy. It gives her and her family a dignified experience, allowing them to say goodbye to the fetus if requested and the time and ability to express their loss and sadness. It also allows further testing for the woman in case of fetal anomalies, so that important medical information can be assessed. This would help the woman to understand her risk factors and the possibility for a healthy pregnancy in the future.

Focusing on the woman is the most important part of this discussion. The heart of this should be about understanding the often life-threatening situations that place women in the position of making this difficult decision that for many women may be life saving but also emotionally devastating.

In a movie made in the mid-1990s, *Legislating a Tragedy*, four women were interviewed about this procedure that allowed them either to be there for their families despite an illness that combined with pregnancy could have killed them, or to prevent the fetus from further suffering due to a disease or abnormality that deemed them incompatible with life (Center for Reproductive Rights, 1996). These women's stories assisted then President Bill Clinton to understand what this issue was about and to veto the bill that was initially passed during his term as president.

GONZALES V. CARHART: A SHIFT IN ABORTION RIGHTS AT THE SUPREME COURT

On April 18, 2007, the U.S. Supreme Court issued its decision in *Gonzales v. Carhart*, upholding Congress's ban on so-called partial-birth abortion in a 5–4 opinion authored by Justice Anthony Kennedy. The ban, passed by Congress and signed by President Bush in 2003, criminalizes abortion procedures frequently used in the second trimester of pregnancy, procedures that doctors say are safe and are often the best ways to protect women's health. Violation of the ban can result in 2 years' imprisonment, fines, and civil suits. While the broadly worded ban (which seems to reach intact or relatively intact D & X procedures) contains an exception to save a woman's life, it lacks a health exception, which has long been required by the Supreme Court. In other words, it does not contain an exception to that ban for cases in which the health of the woman is at risk. In upholding the ban, the Supreme Court disregarded opinions of leading doctors and medical organizations that opposed the ban because of its threat to women's health, and undermined a long-standing core principle of *Roe v. Wade* that women's health is paramount.

In 2000, just 7 years prior, the Supreme Court struck down a similar Nebraska law in *Stenberg v. Carhart* by a vote of 5–4 because there was no exception allowing such abortions when necessary for the health of the woman. Congress then passed the Partial-Birth Abortion Ban Act of 2003, creating a nationwide ban. That law was struck down by three district courts and three appeals courts, but the retirement of Justice Sandra Day O'Connor and confirmation of President Bush's appointee Judge Samuel Alito in 2006 changed the composition of the Supreme Court. The decision upholding a ban on abortion in *Gonzales v. Carhart* represents a major shift by the Supreme Court.

One of the most disturbing aspects of the decision is the adoption of anti-choice language and rhetoric in Justice Kennedy's decision. Throughout his opinion, Justice Kennedy called physicians "abortion doctors" (Gonzales v. Carhart, 1614, 1618, 1625, 1632, 1636) described the fetus as an "unborn child" (1616, 1629, 1630, 1634, 1650) or "baby" (1620, 1622, 1623, 1650), and dismissed the expert medical opinions by physicians skilled in abortion care as preferences motivated by "mere convenience" (1638, 1650). Kennedy also wrote "respect for human life finds an ultimate expression in the bond of love the mother has for her child" (1617), and that "while we find no reliable data to measure the phenomenon, it seems unexceptionable to conclude some women come to regret their choice to abort the infant life they once created and sustained. Severe depression and loss of esteem can follow" (1634). Assertions such as these have long been debunked by the scientific community.

Justice Ruth Bader Ginsburg, writing in dissent, called the decision "alarming," stating that, "for the first time since *Roe*, the Court blesses a prohibition with no exception safeguarding a woman's health" (Gonzales v. Carhart, 1640). Further, she said, the federal ban "and the Court's defense of it cannot be understood as anything other than an effort to chip away at a right declared again and again by this Court. A decision so at odds with our jurisprudence should not have staying power" (1653). Justice Ginsburg also noted in her dissent that "the Court deprives women of the right to make an autonomous choice, even at the expense of their safety" (1649). Justice Ginsburg addressed Justice Kennedy's arguments about protecting women from abortion stating "this way of thinking reflects ancient notions about women's place in the family and under the Constitution—ideas that have long since been discredited" (1649).

The *Carhart v. Gonzales* decision has broad implications for medical practice and the doctor-patient relationship, both in abortion and in other contexts. Until this opinion, the Supreme Court recognized the importance of not interfering with medical judgments made by physicians to protect a patient's interest. For the first time, the Supreme Court has permitted politicians' judgment to supersede a clinician's medical judgment. Women, in consultation with their physicians, have always been able to make appropriate medical decisions and receive safe, quality care based on their individual circumstances. This is no longer the case. While other safe abortion procedures remain legal, many physicians may need to make changes in the care they provide to women. According to the American College of Obstetricians and Gynecologists, the decision will chill doctors from providing a wide range of procedures used to perform induced abortions or to treat cases of miscarriage, and will gravely endanger the health of women in this country (ACOG, 2007).

The ruling will also make it easier for states, as well as the federal government, to further limit a woman's ability to choose abortion. Justice Kennedy stated "when medical uncertainty persists. . . . The Court has given state and federal legislatures wide discretion to pass legislation in areas where there is medical and scientific uncertainty" (Gonzales v. Carhart, 1636). Despite the fact that safety advantages of the banned procedures were recognized in medical texts, peer-reviewed studies, clinical practice, and expert testimony, the Supreme Court still favored politicians' views rather than health care providers' medical opinions in the face of such "uncertainty." The impact of this decision is to invite politicians around the country to pass additional restrictions on abortion with arguable justification that could further jeopardize women's health.

Many states will now attempt to enact new laws restricting abortion access. As Louise Melling of the ACLU stated, "You have the Court issuing a decision that radically undermines the long-standing protection for women's health. The Court is saying that in the face of any uncertainty, the tie goes to the legislature, not to the doctors" (Hughes & Crary, 2007). Troy Newman, president of Operation Rescue, said, "The Court has now said it's okay to ban procedures. We can do more than just put hurdles in front of women seeking abortions—we can put roadblocks in front of them" (Crary, 2007). Anti-choice activists have already started planning new attacks. Pro-choice supporters expect even more anti-choice bills to be introduced in the states and additional direct assaults on *Roe* to be launched. Other states may try to strengthen their reproductive privacy laws or to codify *Roe*. Such legislation has already been introduced in Congress in the form of the Freedom of Choice Act. It is essential that health care providers closely monitor legislation in their states to prevent more erosion of *Roe*.

BIASED COUNSELING AND MANDATED WAITING PERIODS

The precounseling and postcounseling aspects of abortion care are very significant in obtaining positive outcomes of both the physical and emotional concerns of the provision of care. With the majority of abortions being performed in outpatient, nonhospital settings (it is important to know that because of religious organizations buying or merging with hospitals today, in-hospital abortions have decreased significantly), women and their families are given a great deal of attention from the staff.

This includes the ability to meet with a counselor and patient advocate, physician, or both, who is supportive, honest, educating, and kind. Each staff member is respectful of an individual's needs and particular life situations during this time of good and thorough decision making. This model was developed in the early 1970s by one of the first outpatient abortion centers called "Pre-Term." Their counseling approach and training centered around the woman and her ability to make good choices. The dignified environment allowed an opportunity to share feelings. Many women, for the first time, had the opportunity to have important thoughts, feelings, and questions expressed.

Each session is tailored to a woman's own individual needs, and the woman receives the necessary information based on her choice of pregnancy termination—surgical or nonsurgical. The information is given with respect, understanding, and sensitivity to what each woman requires for this experience. Many women are appreciative of this approach and the unique environment of women who make up the counseling staff. Despite the success of this approach and thousands of letters of thanks received from abortion providers throughout the country, state laws want to integrate the mandated so-called counseling information.

Biased counseling laws are a form of anti-choice legislation. Biased counseling bills are often misleadingly titled "Women's Right to Know Act" or "informed consent" bills (NAF, 2003). Most states have a law that requires this state-directed counseling for women seeking abortions. Although the requirements may vary state to state, the specified information is designed intentionally to dissuade women from having abortions. In many of these states, the legislation actually mandates that the information and literature be written by the states. This literature usually consists of pictures of a fetus during various stages of development. Often, there are inaccuracies in this information, and the brochure writers are generally not physicians or even experts in the field.

Biased counseling laws are often accompanied by waiting periods. Mandated waiting periods require women to wait 24 hours, 48 hours, or even longer between the state-mandated counseling and the actual abortion procedure. This usually requires a visit in person, which requires a woman to have to make at least two trips to her health care provider. Obviously, this is an undue burden for many women in finding childcare, transportation, and time off from work, and could even make a difference as to whether or not she would be within the time frame to have the abortion completed at all. For the battered woman who chooses to have an abortion without telling her husband in order to avoid being beaten, getting away from home twice in a short period of time is extremely dangerous. As we describe in Chapter 2, women are capable of making the decision to choose to terminate a pregnancy through abortion and do not need extra time to think about their choice any further than they themselves require. The message most women get from these forced counseling laws is that the state is saying to her that she needs more time to think about this—obviously hoping she will change her mind.

In addition, the waiting periods often imposed by such bills could, ironically, force women to seek abortions later in their pregnancies, exposing them to increased health risks and added expense. The delays caused by waiting period requirements disproportionately harm low-income women, young women, battered women, and those who do not live close to a clinic. A listing of the states with counseling and waiting period requirements is provided in Box 1.6.

In summary, antiabortion activists have used two distinct methods to attempt to change the ability of women to choose to terminate their pregnancies by a safe medical procedure. The first are the various types of legislation that have been introduced into state and federal legislative sessions and the resulting judicial challenges that create case law. In Box 1.7 we provide a summary of the major legislation that has been decided by the U.S. Supreme Court.

The second is the creation of counseling centers that concentrate on providing false and misleading information to women as they try to decide whether or not to abort the pregnancy. Then, these centers provide unnecessary and biased counseling and therapy for women who have made the decision to terminate their pregnancies but may be struggling emotionally with that decision and falsely name this emotional struggle Post-Abortion Syndrome. We discuss the accurate cognitive and emotional issues around abortion and provide evidence of the nonexistence of a Post-Abortion Syndrome in the next few chapters.

Box 1.6   Highlights (Guttmacher Institute, 2007b)

- Thirty-two states require that women receive counseling before an abortion is performed.

  - Twenty-three states direct the state department of health to develop the abortion-related materials that are provided to women seeking an abortion in the state.
  - Twenty-nine states also mandate that women seeking an abortion receive specific information about the procedure.

    - Three states include information on a purported link between having an abortion and an increased risk of developing breast cancer.
    - Five states require that women be told that the fetus may be able to feel pain and be offered the option of having anesthesia provided directly to the fetus.
    - Twenty-one states require that women be told there may be assistance available for prenatal care, childbirth, and infant care.
    - Three states require that women be given information on the possible psychological impacts of abortion.
    - Seventeen states require that women be given a detailed list of agencies that provide educational, referral, or counseling services designed to help women carry their pregnancies to term.

  - Eighteen states specify how information is to be delivered, with six requiring that counseling always be provided to women in person.

- Twenty-four of the states that require counseling also require women to wait a specified amount of time—most often 24 hours—between the counseling and the abortion procedure.

  - All six of the states that require that all counseling be provided in-person also require that the counseling take place at least 18 hours prior to the procedure, thereby necessitating two separate trips to the facility.

Box 1.7   Timeline of Important Reproductive Freedom Cases Decided by the Supreme Court (ACLU, 2006)

1965 *Griswold v. Connecticut* 381 U.S. 479
The ACLU filed a friend-of-the court brief in this landmark case in which the Supreme Court struck down a state prohibition against the prescription, sale, or use of contraceptives, even for married couples. In *Griswold v. Connecticut,* the Court held that the Constitution guarantees a "right to privacy" when individuals make decisions about intimate, personal matters such as childbearing.

1971 *United States v. Vuitch* 402 U.S. 62
The ACLU's general counsel, Norman Dorsen, argued this case—the first about abortion to reach the Supreme Court. In *United States v. Vuitch,* a doctor challenged the constitutionality of a District of Columbia law permitting abortion only to preserve a woman's life or health. The Court rejected the claim that the statute was unconstitutionally vague, concluding that "health" should be understood to include considerations of psychological as well as physical well-being. The Court also held that the burden of proof should be on the prosecutor who brought charges, not on the doctor.

1972 *Eisenstadt v. Baird* 405 U.S. 438
The ACLU filed a friend-of-the-court brief in *Eisenstadt v. Baird*, in which the Supreme Court struck down a Massachusetts law limiting the distribution of contraceptives to married couples whose physicians had prescribed them. This decision established the right of unmarried individuals to obtain contraceptives.

1973 *Roe v. Wade* 410 U.S. 113
The ACLU's general counsel, Norman Dorsen, was a member of the team of lawyers representing the plaintiffs in the landmark abortion rights case, *Roe v. Wade.* This case challenged a Texas law prohibiting all but lifesaving abortions. The Supreme Court invalidated the law on the ground that the constitutional right to privacy encompasses a woman's decision whether or not to terminate her pregnancy. Characterizing this right as "fundamental" to a woman's "life and future," the Court held that the state could not interfere with the abortion decision unless it had a compelling reason for regulation. A compelling interest in protecting the potential life of the fetus could be asserted only once it became "viable" (usually at the beginning of the last trimester of pregnancy), and even then a woman had to have access to an abortion if it were necessary to preserve her life or health.

Doe v. Bolton 410 U.S. 179
The ACLU argued Roe's companion case, *Doe v. Bolton,* in which the Supreme Court overturned a Georgia law regulating abortion. The law

(continued)

prohibited abortions except when necessary to preserve a woman's life or health or in cases of fetal abnormality or rape. Among other conditions, the law also required that all abortions be performed in accredited hospitals and that a hospital committee and two doctors in addition to the woman's own doctor give their approval. The Court held the Georgia law unconstitutional because it imposed too many restrictions and interfered with a woman's right to decide, in consultation with her physician, to terminate her pregnancy.

1975 *Bigelow v. Virginia* 421 U.S. 809
In *Bigelow v. Virginia*, an ACLU case, the Supreme Court ruled that states could not ban advertising by abortion clinics. Such bans violate the First Amendment's guarantees of freedom of speech and freedom of the press.

1979 *Bellotti v. Baird* 443 U.S. 622
The ACLU represented plaintiffs challenging a Massachusetts statute requiring women under 18 to obtain parental or judicial consent prior to having an abortion. The Court found the statute unconstitutional because, as it was interpreted by the state's highest court, it gave either a parent or a judge absolute veto power over a minor's abortion decision, no matter how mature she was and notwithstanding that an abortion might be in her best interests. *Bellotti v. Baird* established that all minors must have the opportunity to approach a court for authorization to have an abortion, without first seeking the consent of their parents, and that these alternative proceedings must be confidential and expeditious.

1980 *Harris v. McRae* 448 U.S. 297
In *Harris v. McRae,* the Supreme Court rejected a challenge to the Hyde Amendment, which banned the use of federal Medicaid funds for abortion except when the life of the woman would be endangered by carrying the pregnancy to term. The ACLU was cocounsel in this case and played a pivotal role in coordinating challenges to similar state funding bans. Although the lawsuit challenging the federal ban was unsuccessful, the ACLU and its allies did succeed in the ensuing years in overturning many state funding bans.

1983 *City of Akron v. Akron Center for Reproductive Health* 462 U.S. 416
In *City of Akron v. Akron Center for Reproductive Health,* the ACLU scored an important victory when the Supreme Court struck down all of the challenged provisions of an Akron, Ohio, ordinance restricting abortion. Among other holdings, the Court ruled that the city could not require minors under 15 to obtain parental or judicial consent for an abortion; require physicians to give women information designed to dissuade them from having abortions; impose a 24-hour waiting period after the signing of the consent form; or require that all second-trimester abortions be performed in a hospital.

(continued)

Bolger v. Youngs Drug Products Corporation 463 U.S. 60
The ACLU filed a friend-of-the-court brief in this challenge to a federal law that made it a crime to send unsolicited advertisements for contraceptives through the mail. The Supreme Court held the law to be unconstitutional because it violated the First Amendment's protection of "commercial speech" and impeded the transmission of information relevant to the "important social issues" of family planning and the prevention of venereal disease.

1986 *Thornburgh v. American College of Obstetricians and Gynecologists* 476 U.S. 747
The ACLU participated in this case, in which the Supreme Court struck down, among other abortion restrictions, a provision of a Pennsylvania statute requiring doctors to use abortion techniques that maximized the chance of fetal survival, even when such techniques increased the medical risks to the pregnant woman's life or health.

1988 *Bowen v. Kendrick* 487 U.S. 589
The ACLU represented plaintiffs who challenged the Adolescent Family Life Act, which authorized the use of federal funds to teach the value of chastity in the context of social and educational services for adolescents. Many of the grantees were religious organizations. The Court rejected the claim that the Act, on its face, violated the First Amendment's prohibition of the establishment of religion. It sent the case back to a lower court to determine whether the Act was unconstitutional as administered—whether actual grants made under the Act were used impermissibly to promote religious views or to engage in religious practices.

1989 *Webster v. Reproductive Health Services* 492 U.S. 490
The ACLU participated both in representing the plaintiffs and in coordinating the production of more than 30 friend-of-the-court briefs in *Webster v. Reproductive Health Services*. The case was a challenge to a Missouri law that forbade the use of public facilities for all abortions except those necessary to save a woman's life, required physicians to perform tests to determine the viability of fetuses after 20 weeks of gestation, and imposed other restrictions on abortion. The Supreme Court upheld these anti-choice provisions, opening the door to greater state regulation of abortion. The Court did not, however, accept the invitation of the U.S. Solicitor General and others to use the case as a vehicle for overruling *Roe v. Wade*.

1990 *Hodgson v. Minnesota* 497 U.S. 417
This case was a challenge to a state law that reqired a minor to notify both biological parents before having an abortion. It made no exception for parents who were divorced, who had not married, or who were unknown to their daughters. In *Hodgson v. Minnesota*, the ACLU secured for teenagers the option of going to court to obtain authorization for an abortion, when they could not or would not comply with a parental notification law.

(continued)

1991 *Rust v. Sullivan* 500 U.S. 173

The ACLU represented Dr. Irving Rust and other family planning providers who challenged the Reagan Administration's "gag rule" barring abortion counseling and referral by family planning programs funded under Title X of the federal Public Health Service Act. Under the new rule, clinic staff could no longer discuss all of the options available to women facing unintended pregnancies, but could only refer them for prenatal care. Even though the rule reversed 18 years of policies that had allowed nondirective, comprehensive options counseling, the Court upheld it. (President Clinton rescinded the "gag rule" by executive order shortly after his inauguration in 1993.)

1992 *Planned Parenthood of Southeastern Pennsylvania v. Casey* 505 U.S. 833

This case was a challenge to a set of onerous restrictions on abortion enacted in Pennsylvania. As in 1989, the ACLU fought to prevent the Supreme Court from overruling the core holdings of *Roe v. Wade*. In *Planned Parenthood of Southeastern Pennsylvania v. Casey,* the Court preserved constitutional protection for the right to choose. But it adopted a new and weaker test for evaluating restrictive abortion laws. Under the "undue burden test," state regulations can survive constitutional review so long as they do not place a "substantial obstacle in the path of a woman seeking an abortion of a nonviable fetus."

1997 *Schenck v. Pro-Choice Network of Western New York* 519 U.S. 357

In this case, the ACLU filed a friend-of-the-court brief defending the constitutionality of two provisions of an injunction obtained by abortion clinics in western New York as a remedy against blockades and other disruptive forms of protest. The Supreme Court upheld a fixed 15-foot buffer zone around clinic doorways, driveways, and parking lot entrances. It struck down a floating 15-foot buffer zone around people or vehicles entering or leaving a clinic.

2000 *Stenberg v. Carhart* 530 U.S. 914

In this case, the ACLU filed a friend-of-the-court brief calling on the Court to invalidate Nebraska's so-called partial-birth abortion ban. Sending a strong message regarding the paramount importance of women's health, the Court struck Nebraska's law on two independent grounds: the ban's failure to include a health exception threatened women's health, and the ban's language encompassed the most common method of second-trimester abortion, placing a substantial obstacle in the path of women seeking abortions and thereby imposing an "undue burden."

2001 *Ferguson v. City of Charleston* 532 U.S. 67

In this case, the ACLU filed a friend-of-the-court brief urging the Court to void a South Carolina public hospital policy mandating drug testing

(continued)

of pregnant women. In a 6–3 decision, the Court held that the Fourth Amendment does not permit the state, acting without either a warrant or individualized suspicion, to drug test pregnant women who seek prenatal care in a public hospital. Furthermore, the Court insisted on the importance of confidentiality in the medical context.

> **2006** *Ayotte v. Planned Parenthood of Northern New England* 04–1144
> The ACLU argued this case before the Supreme Court on behalf of the New Hampshire clinics and physician who brought this legal challenge. In a unanimous ruling, the Court reiterated its long-standing principle that abortion restrictions must include protections for women's health. The case began as a challenge to a New Hampshire law that required doctors to delay a teenager's abortion until 48 hours after a parent was notified but lacked a medical emergency exception to protect a pregnant teenager's health. The lower courts struck down the law because of this omission. The Supreme Court vacated and remanded the case, instructing the lower court to consider whether the New Hampshire legislature would have wanted this law with a medical emergency exception. If not, the Court said the law should be struck down in its entirety. No matter what, the Court said the law must be blocked in those cases where teens face medical emergencies.
>
> *Information provided by the ACLU: http://www.aclu.org/reproductiverights/ index.html*

REFERENCES

Abortion and breast cancer. (2003, January 6). *New York Times,* p. A20.

American Civil Liberties Union. (2006). *Timeline of important reproductive freedom cases decided by the Supreme Court.* Retrieved January 2, 2007, from http://www.aclu. org/reproductiverights/index.html

American College of Obstetricians and Gynecologists. (2004, June 2). *Statement on Federal Court "Partial-Birth Act" decision by The American College of Obstetricians and Gynecologists.* News release. Retrieved January 19, 2007, from http://www.acog.org/ from_home/publications/press_releases/nr06–02–04.cfm

American College of Obstetricians and Gynecologists. (2006, September 22). *ACOG Files Amicus Brief in* Gonzales v. Carhart *and* Gonzales v. PPFA. News release. Retrieved February 5, 2007, from http://www.acog.org/from_home/publications/press_releases/ nr09–22–06.cfm

American College of Obstetricians and Gynecologists. (2007, April 18). Statement on the U.S. Supreme Court decision upholding the Partial-Birth Abortion Ban Act of 2003. Retrieved April 18, 2007, from http://www.acog.org/from_home/publications/ press_releases/nr04-18-07.cfm

Boonstra, H., & Sonfield, A. (2000). Rights without access: Revisiting public funding of abortion for poor women. *The Guttmacher Report on Public Policy, 3*(2). Retrieved January 11, 2007, from http://www.guttmacher.org/pubs/tgr/03/2/gr030208.html

Center for Reproductive Rights. (1996). Legislating a tragedy. [Videotape]. (Center for Reproductive Law and Policy, 120 Wall Street, New York, NY 10005.)

Center for Reproductive Rights. (2004, April). *Targeted regulation of abortion providers (TRAP): Avoiding the TRAP.* Briefing paper.

Center for Reproductive Rights. (2005, November 15). *Parental consent and notification for abortion.* Retrieved November 4, 2006, from http://www.crlp.org/st_law_notification.html

Child Interstate Abortion Notification Act (CIANA; Teen Endangerment Act; Child Custody Protection Act). H.R. 748, S. 8, 396, 403. 109th Cong. (2006).

Cramer, E. (2006, July 28). Fighting abortion with false 'facts.' *Palm Beach Post*, p. A10.

Crary, D. (2007, April 18). Abortion ruling will impact states. *Associated Press Online.* New York.

Finer, B., & Henshaw, S. K. (2003). Abortion incidence and services in the United States in 2000. *Perspectives on Sexual and Reproductive Health, 35*(1), 6–15.

Gonzales v. Carhart, 127 S.CT. 1610 (2007).

GovTrack.us. H.R. 748—109th Congress (2006): Child Interstate Abortion Notification Act, *GovTrack.us* (database of federal legislation). Retrieved May 22, 2007, from http://www.govtrack.us/congress/bill.xpd?bill=h109-748

Guttmacher Institute. (2006, September). *In brief: Facts on American teens' sexual and reproductive health.* Retrieved November 4, 2006, from http://www.guttmacher.org/pubs/fb_ATSRH.html

Guttmacher Institute. (2006, November 1). *An overview of minors' consent law.* Retrieved November 4, 2006, from http://www.guttmacher.org/statecenter/spibs/spib_OMCL.pdf

Guttmacher Institute. (2007a). *State policies in brief: Bans on 'Partial Birth' abortion.* Retrieved January 11, 2007, from http://www.guttmacher.org/statecenter/spibs/spib_BPBA.pdf

Guttmacher Institute. (2007b). *State policies in brief: Mandatory counseling and waiting periods for abortion.* Retrieved January 11, 2007, from http://www.guttmacher.org/statecenter/spibs/spib_MWPA.pdf

Guttmacher Institute. (2007c). *State policies in brief: Parental involvement in minors' abortions.* Retrieved January 11, 2007, from http://www.guttmacher.org/statecenter/spibs/spib_PIMA.pdf

Guttmacher Institute. (2007d). *State policies in brief: State funding of abortion under Medicaid.* Retrieved January 11, 2007, from http://www.guttmacher.org/statecenter/spibs/spib_SFAM.pdf

Jones, R., Darroch, J., & Henshaw, S. (2002). Contraceptive use among U.S. women having abortions in 2000–2001. *Perspectives on Sexual and Reproductive Health, 34*(6), 294–303.

National Abortion Federation. (2003). National Abortion Federation 2003 State Legislative Report. Retrieved January 11, 2007, from http://www.prochoice.org/pubs_research/publications/downloads/public_policy/state_bill_report_2003.pdf

National Abortion Federation. *Parental involvement: Patient stories.* Retrieved January 11, 2007, from http://www.prochoice.org/about_abortion/stories/parental_involvement.html

National Abortion Federation. (2006a). *Abortion facts: Crisis pregnancy centers.* Retrieved January 11, 2007, from http://www.prochoice.org/about_abortion/facts/cpc.html#n4

National Abortion Federation. (2006b). *Crisis pregnancy centers: An affront to choice.* Retrieved January 12, 2007, from http://www.prochoice.org/pubs_research/publications/downloads/public_policy/cpc_report.pdf

National Cancer Institute. (2003). *Summary report: Early reproductive events and breast cancer workshop.* Retrieved January 11, 2007, from http://www.nci.nih.gov/cancerinfo/ere-workshop-report

National Network of Abortion Funds. Retrieved January 11, 2007, from http://www.
    nnaf.org/
Sonfield, A., & Benson Gold, R. (2005). *Public funding for contraceptive, sterilization and
    abortion services, FY 1980–2001: National and state tables and figures.* Retrieved from
    The Guttmacher Institute Retrieved January 11, 2007, from http://www.guttmacher.
    org/pubs/fpfunding/tables.pdf
U.S. House of Representatives. (2006, July). Committee on Government Reform-
    Minority Staff. Special Investigations Division. Retrieved January 29, 2006, from
    http://oversight.house.gov/Documents/20060717101140–30092.pdf
Women's Health Action and Mobilization. *Fake clinics: public health hazard. Found in
    Brooklyn Pro-Choice Network.* Retrieved January 11, 2007, from http://www.
    echonyc.com/-bpcn/fakeclinic.html
Wright, A. A., & Katz, I. T. (2006). Roe versus reality: Abortion and women's health. *The
    New England Journal of Medicine, 355*(1), 1–9.

CHAPTER 2

The Impact of Abortion Politics on Therapists

Abortion has been around since the ancient times and has been practiced by women all around the world. It was not until the mid-to-late 1800s that states began passing laws making abortion illegal. By 1910, all but one state in the United States had criminalized abortion except when, in the doctor's judgment, abortion was necessary to save the woman's life. Although it was not until 1973 that abortion again became legal in the United States, abortion was still commonly practiced, and most women knew how to find the local doctor or community practitioner who would help terminate an unwanted pregnancy.

Prior to *Roe v. Wade,* the 1973 U.S. Supreme Court decision that legalized abortion in the United States, women would use any means necessary to terminate a pregnancy that they did not want to carry to term. From using dangerous instruments to obtaining dangerous back-alley abortions provided by people with no medical background, to having abortions performed by more skilled and clean physicians for a hefty fee, women did risk taking their own lives to terminate an unwanted pregnancy. Many women suffered serious medical problems, were unable to ever conceive again, or even died from either trying to self-induce an abortion or going to untrained practitioners, exposing themselves to dangerous unsanitary conditions with unsterilized or homemade instruments, including coat hangers and vacuum cleaner hoses. Pro-choice activists adopted the symbol of the coat hanger with an X through it to underscore the dangers of taking away women's choice to obtain legal abortion.

Two distinct groups of activists oppose abortion: those who assert the sanctity of fetal life and argue that abortion is morally wrong and therefore should be outlawed, and those who argue that having an abortion will harm women at the time of the abortion or at some time later in their lives. Most of the people in the first group belong to traditional religious groups. Some in the second group also belong to the first group and are deliberately using the fear of mental disturbance in the future as a scare tactic. There is some evidence that many women in the latter group have had abortions themselves and now have severe mental distress that they attribute to the abortion. Many may have had emotional difficulties even before they terminated their unwanted pregnancies. Most of them have had other life experiences that could account for their current mental conditions. However, these women, with the help of many men whose motives are not always well understood, have formed local and national groups designed to prove that all women will suffer the same harm as they did.

A percentage of the anti-choice activists are what we call antiabortion extremists. These individuals, who are often members of groups or cults, attempt to use violence against abortion providers to advance their own personal and political agenda. They have taken credit for injuring and murdering health care workers across the country and intimidating and harassing patients who need reproductive health care. The extremists often travel to participate in these violent activities. They work together with other anti-choice zealots and aid each other by offering resources such as housing and funding. Some of the activities of these individual extremists have included bombings of abortion clinics, murdering physicians who perform abortions, and sending anthrax threat letters to clinics (see www.prochoice.org for further discussion of these extremists).

The Army of God, a well-known underground network of domestic terrorists within the anti-choice activist groups, believes in and advocates the use of violence as an appropriate and acceptable means to end abortion. The Army of God has a manual that is basically a "how-to-do-it kit" for abortion clinic violence. It includes information and methods for blockading clinic entrances, butyric acid attacks, arson, bomb-making, and other illegal activities. In addition to strong antiabortion sentiments, this manual also includes antigovernment and anti-gay and anti-lesbian language. An excerpt from the Army of God Manual states that the Army of God ". . . is a real Army, and God is the general and Commander-in-Chief. The soldiers, however, do not usually communicate with one another. Very few have ever met each other. And when they do, each is usually unaware of the other soldier's status. That is why the Feds will never stop the Army. Never. And we have not yet even begun to fight" (www.prochoice.org).

An article by Emily Bazelon in the *New York Times Magazine* (Bazelon, 2007, January 21) described a new national group claiming abortion creates mental harm to women. Typically called abortion-recovery activists, this group is made up of women, most of whom have had abortions. Bazelon's investigative reporting found that these post-abortion recovery groups are growing larger, are spread out in various areas of the United States, and are funded by two major groups: the U.S. government's faith-based counseling grants and the Catholic Church.

The Catholic Church, which operates abortion-recovery ministries in at least 165 dioceses in the United States, and the Federal government finance at least 50 nonsectarian crisis pregnancy centers (CPCs) where women are counseled not to have abortions, often with erroneous information (as we discussed in Chapter 1). Unfortunately, many of the abortion-recovery groups have been the only places for women who have experienced strong emotions post-abortion to go. These emotions are often due to hormonal fluctuations that may naturally occur when terminating a pregnancy, as pro-choice groups do not have such a well-financed network where post-abortion groups are offered. We discuss the post-abortion syndrome literature in more detail in Chapter 6 where we conclude that some women have normal transient emotional symptoms after their abortions but that no data exist to conclude that there is such a post-abortion syndrome.

Bazelon's statistics indicate that of the almost 3 million unplanned out of 6 million pregnancies each year in the United States, approximately half or 1.3 have been terminated by abortion. At the current rate, about one-third of women nationally will undergo the procedure by age 45 and yet only a small group experience long-lasting emotional distress. Nonetheless, currently, this small group has only a few places to seek counseling from nonbiased and well-trained therapists. The information provided in this book is an attempt to encourage and assist counselors and therapists to be able to deliver services to any woman who either must make a choice about what to do about an unplanned pregnancy or help her afterward.

The National Abortion Federation (NAF), the major umbrella organization that provides information, training, and education for the many abortion centers in the United States, maintains a Web site with information for the general public, as well as and links to other pro-choice sites. It is an important source of facts about abortion and the possible risks and complications surrounding the mostly medically safe procedure. Planned Parenthood (http://www.plannedparenthood.org)

maintains approximately 80 abortion clinics and sets standards for pre-abortion counseling, informed consent, and guidelines for post-abortion counseling for those women who will need to talk about their feelings for awhile afterward. Exhale (http://www.4exhale.org) is the name of a hotline that is available for women who have had an abortion and wish to speak with someone about their feelings, usually those that deal with emotional sadness on the anniversary date of their abortion, spiritual conflicts caused by their religious and moral beliefs, and emotional pain from having to keep their abortion a secret from family and friends. We include information from an interview with Aspen Baker, the director of Exhale, in Chapter 6.

While many of the abortion providers have found that women do not attend support groups after their abortions, usually because pre-abortion counseling properly identifies high-risk women and recommends therapy with private therapists, we have found that most private therapists have had little training or knowledge about what are the usual issues raised by women who seek abortion. Our own experiences agree with the literature that most of the emotional difficulties experienced by women post-abortion can be identified before the pregnancy is terminated. Some of the emotional problems can be directly attributed to the politics of abortion with women feeling as if they are caught in a war that is much larger than their own choice to terminate a pregnancy. However, given the rise of these new abortion-recovery centers, most of which provide biased, faith-based counseling, we believe that it is important for women to have options for counseling that is based on psychological theories and science. To do this, it is critical for therapists to educate themselves in the issues of both politics and research that we provide in this book. This chapter deals specifically with the impact of the politics on the psychological state of the women who seek abortions and those who work in the abortion centers.

VIOLENCE TOWARD AND HARASSMENT OF ABORTION PROVIDERS AND THEIR PATIENTS

The threat of violence and harassment continues to persist as an unfortunate component associated with the provision of abortion care today. Providing medical services against this backdrop of disruption has created obstacles to abortion care throughout the country. The environment of abortion providers involved in a war of attrition with antiabortion extremists who attempt to make it difficult for women to obtain needed services limits the number of providers today. There is no other medical specialty that becomes forced to deal with security components as those physicians who choose to incorporate abortion services in their comprehensive health care delivery practices.

Since 1977, NAF, the national and international organization whose mission is to set the standards and guidelines for abortion care with licensing guidelines, has kept statistics on what they call violence and disruption. These incidents are reported by their members in the United States and Canada. In almost 30 years there have been, of abortion providers, 7 murders, 383 death threats, 482 acts of stalking, and 33,030 arrests of antiabortion demonstrators who have broken the law either by trespassing, invasion, or vandalism.

These acts have had a definite impact on the decreasing number of providers today including medical schools who refuse to offer abortion as part of their medical training programs. Although some hospitals oppose performing abortions for religious reasons, many are fearful of the potential of protesting and threats of violence that would impact the other services the hospital provides. Without physicians trained to do abortions, the access problem is intensified by this reality. This contributes to the impact of only 13% of U.S. counties having abortion providers (Henshaw & Finer, 2003). Women throughout the country have to travel many hours, sometimes crossing state lines, to obtain abortions. The difficult travel, combined with the 24- to 48-hour waiting periods and parental consent laws, delays the process of obtaining an abortion and culminates with the financial challenges of and restraints from childcare arrangements and taking additional time off from work.

The majority of abortion providers today have been forced to incorporate extensive security measures to ensure the safety and of their patients and staff. Many facilities pay for armed security guards, have installed metal detector systems, will not allow anyone to bring in large purses or backpacks, and in some cases, will not allow anyone to accompany the patient for fear of safety. Although incorporating necessary safety features is essential, it increases costs to the patients who already faced key challenges in raising the necessary funds for their medical care. Financing is a major deterrent to obtaining an abortion today. As of November 2006, 17 states used their own funds to subsidize abortion for poor women (Guttmacher Institute, 2006). In actuality, however, about half of these states provide little or no funds to cover these services (Sonfield & Gold, 2005). The high rate of uninsured individuals in this country and the fact that only a limited number of insurance companies cover abortion services also create financial hardships for women.

Abortion services have become marginalized in our country in great part due to the factor of violence, harassment, and disruption. The formation of Operation Rescue in 1988 and their so-called refuse and resist tactics in front of facilities providing abortions in Atlanta was given much press coverage during the Democratic Convention that year. Women were clearly unable to access services at that time with the hundreds of Operation Rescue members lying down in front of centers—many even chained themselves to posts and doors. Subsequently, facilities in other states became targets for the same type of attack utilized to prevent abortions and harass patients and providers.

In 1989, the National Organization for Women and an abortion doctor filed a lawsuit alleging a civil conspiracy among the individual members of Operation Rescue, the Moral Majority, Jerry Falwell, Randall Terry, and a local church, which spearheaded the quasi-terrorist tactics used by the clinic blockaders. Shortly before trial, the attorney for Operation Rescue screamed in a busy waiting room of the plaintiff abortion doctor, "You are a dead man," and the doctor promptly withdrew his name from the lawsuit. The National Organization for Women remained in the case, and for the first time in legal history, the civil racketeering laws were successfully used against Operation Rescue. As a result, all of the defendants were held collectively responsible for the payment of $1 to the National Association for Women and over one-quarter of a million dollars to cover their costs and attorney's fees. When the defendants refused to pay and chose to appeal the decision, the plaintiff's attorney threatened to foreclose the church involved with the blockaders and to turn it into a place where low-cost abortions would be made available. When Pat Robertson heard about this, he promptly raised the money to pay the attorney's fees, which he charged to the church, plus interest, as a fund-raising event for his organization.

Due to the precedent Racketeer Influenced and Corrupt Organizations Act (RICO) lawsuit victory, most of the supporters of Operation Rescue defected, and the organization collapsed. As a result, Operation Rescue and clinic blockades became a thing of the past, but later the organization was born again with a different focus and different tactics. However, the rhetoric of Operation Rescue's leader, Randall Terry, and his band of so-called Terryists remained the same. Terry, in print, urged his followers to emulate Jesus by letting a wave of hate and intolerance wash over themselves, and use this hate and intolerance to target abortion providers, as well as all others who did not share their narrow, hateful views.

Although we have discussed the impact of the violence on providers themselves, many providers express concern as to how the violence has affected the women who depend on providers for their care. Most U.S. cities do not have a professional relationship with abortion providers or their centers. Many cities have been targets of lawsuits accusing them of violating First Amendment rights: antiabortion protestors feel they should be allowed to protest freely outside of abortion centers with no constraints. Many of these lawsuits have been costly and have disrupted clinic services, and unfortunately, law enforcement is often reluctant to get involved. Women who come to the centers may find hundreds of antiabortion protestors yelling and screaming, often with bullhorns and other amplification systems, as they enter a facility for abortion services. Often they are greeted by grotesque signs displaying a bloody fetus or are handed clearly distorted and inaccurate information regarding the fetus's development. These antiabortion activists set up cameras outside facilities that perform abortions, and they film patients, record license plate numbers, and research these patients' names. Web sites have displayed their cars, pictures, and personal information. Physicians, nurses, and counselors who work in these facilities are similarly harassed.

The heightened emotions involved in the abortion debate cause potential physical harm to patients. Antiabortion activists often use tactics that have sometimes escalated into violent physical confrontation and destruction of property (Hern, 1991). Additionally, women are often brought to tears and anguish over the rhetoric that is hoped to intimidate them into changing their minds. The lies and misinformation are upsetting and confusing to a woman who might already have great stress, having already made a difficult decision. One abortion provider reports being disturbed over the mean spiritedness of those calling themselves "good Christians" and who argue that they are trying to help and provide better options. This same provider expressed her concern over the lack of respect and sensitivity of protestors toward women and she questioned their lack of regard for those once they are born into this world.

The alternative of adoption is often part of the message of the antiabortion activists, and although for many, adoption is the right alternative, the majority of women who decide to terminate their pregnancy find carrying a pregnancy to term and then, giving the baby away to another couple to raise, would devastate their entire lives. Providers of abortion services do include other options, including adoption, in their counseling and information and they support women's alternative requests with referrals to available programs and information in the community.

When discussing the problems abortion providers face, they talk about their shared concerns for the safety of their families. We interviewed a number of them while preparing this book. One provider talked about the trauma she experienced when signs calling her a "murderer" were left outside of her home where she lived with her two small children at the time. Subsequently, signs were left on the door of her home demanding that she "stop killing children." It is unclear whether the antiabortion activists who did this were aware of the trauma they were inflicting on young children and their mother. Often there is picketing outside a provider's home—mailings sent to inform neighbors of the danger of having a provider of abortions living on the block. Personal information is also sometimes circulated throughout the abortion provider's community, giving phone numbers, names, and ages of their children or their spouses. One woman said that it "wears you down and frightens the children."

We have interviewed a number of children of abortion providers to inquire about the impact the abortion protestors have had on their lives. They all know about and have been terrified by the murders of seven abortion providers and the goals of the antiabortion movement to eliminate those directly associated with abortion care. Many of them have had nightmares in addition to fears and concerns. Another abortion provider shared that she has engaged in numerous conversations with her daughter where her daughter begged her to stop working in this field. Her daughter also attempted to involve other family members in trying to persuade her mother to find safer work as well. The broader mission and commitment to safe and legal abortion continues to create an almost heroic status for many today who are unwilling to back down. While speaking with staff members from a facility in the South who had experienced an arson that destroyed the entire inside of their facility, whether they would rebuild was never a question. In fact, they claimed the silver lining in that nightmare was that hundreds in the community came out in support of their rebuilding. Many shared personal stories of gratitude for being there for them or for their daughters, wives, or friends.

In a further discussion with providers in the southern region of the United States, we saw their day-to-day struggles with continuing to provide abortion care grow more numerous and costly. The harassment often results from the political climate that creates problems for both the providers and the patients. For example, the authority's continuous requests for patient's medical records, despite the confidentiality laws, often create a concern by providers that patients may become so fearful about losing their privacy that they then chose to go to another state for their care, accruing tremendous costs to do so. According to one local provider, many women will not come on a day where there are protestors for fear of encountering a member of their church or place of work. Although the U.S. Congress has passed laws such as the Health Insurance Portability and Privacy Act (HIPPA) to protect privacy around medical treatment, a woman's ability to access confidential medical care is often jeopardized with these situations and when the government does not enforce its own laws.

Many providers have shared their own history of harassment and violence, bomb threats, glue in their door locks, and Web sites that link them to the Nuremberg Files. Although this Web site has been removed, for many years it listed abortion providers whose names would be displayed with a red line through them when they were murdered and a gray line through the name when they were wounded. It was a sort of "hit list" designed to terrify the providers into quitting. Physicians speak of being ostracized from their own medical communities, losing privileges at hospitals close to facilities that provide abortions. Many abortion providers have been rejected from their churches or their country clubs. This backlash has affected the spouses and the children of individuals working in the abortion field as well.

There have been reported incidents of butyric acid leaked into facilities, as well as anthrax hoaxes. These acts of violence have unfortunately closed facilities for a day or even weeks or months. Many abortion providers complain about their lack of success when attempting to rent space or trying to get property insurance. The rates often become prohibitive, which either causes the center to close their doors or forces them to pass the additional costs on to the patients, who often already have a difficult time coming up with the fees.

POLITICS IN THE COUNSELING SESSION

Due to the highly controversial and emotional nature of the abortion issue, it is important to discuss how the politics of abortion can enter into a counseling session. Perhaps the most important issue is for therapists and counselors to recognize and confront their own values and biases in this emotionally charged area.

Here are some suggestions for therapists and counselors to think about, according to Anne Baker (1995), who has counseled women for many years:

- What are your feelings about abortion in general? More specifically, under what circumstances do you believe abortion is OK? Not OK? Why?
- At what gestational stage, if any, would you be against elective abortion? A medically indicated abortion?
- Should abortion be more restricted legally or less restricted in terms of cost, availability, gestational limits, and age of women? What about parental consent? Spousal consent? Why?
- How would it affect you if abortion became illegal? How might it affect your female friends and family members?
- Depending on circumstances, would you ever have an abortion yourself? If not, is it OK for someone else but not for you? Why?
- Have you ever had an abortion? What was your experience? Positive? Negative? In what way? Do you still think it was a good decision? What were your feelings at the time, and how

do you feel about it right now? If you had or have any difficult feelings about your abortion, how have you coped?

- How do you feel about a woman having an abortion who never used birth control?
- How do you feel about a woman having more than one abortion?
- How do you feel about a woman who is morally against abortion but insists upon having one?
- How do you feel about an adolescent having an abortion? A preadolescent? A teen who has not told her parents about the pregnancy?
- How do you feel about a married woman having an abortion?
- How do you feel about a woman having more than one abortion using government funds to pay for the abortions?

If after reviewing the information provided in this book you still feel that your values may interfere with your providing nonjudgmental and good therapy, then, of course, it is your ethical obligation to refer this client to another clinician.

Here are some stories about women who have been interviewed about their choices to terminate a pregnancy. See what you think about them after reading what they have to say. This may also help you to decide if you are able and want to provide abortion counseling to women who are trying to make a choice or who have made a choice and are now questioning their decisions.

Cathy

Cathy, a 20-year-old White woman, was raised in a strict Catholic family. She became pregnant after a brutal rape that left her in the hospital for several days. Cathy had one-and-a-half years of college left and was an active member of the rowing team. She was very angry about the rape but especially about the pregnancy, which she did not want to continue. She felt guilty for having these feelings, as she was raised believing that abortion was wrong. In addition, on her way to school each day, Cathy had to pass by the local abortion clinic. She always took notice of all of the protestors screaming and chanting. She was sure that she could not be one of the women they condemned. For these reasons, Cathy chose to carry the pregnancy to term and give the baby up for adoption. Cathy is now 36 years old. She describes the rape and subsequent pregnancy as "screwing up [her] life." She finally graduated college at the age of 26, after taking almost four years off. To this day, Cathy wishes that she had made the choice to have the abortion. "I regret my decision for many reasons. The pregnancy took its toll on my physical and emotional health. And I still think about where my child is, and I wonder if he will become a rapist like his father."

Maria

Maria, a 34-year-old Hispanic woman, came to therapy because of marital problems. Her husband, Jose, would not come to therapy with her. Six months after beginning treatment, Maria found out she was pregnant. She was surprised because she had been on oral contraceptives for several years. At the time, Maria was not sure if she would remain married to Jose because the problems they had to work out were quite severe.

The therapist and Maria spent several sessions talking about the pregnancy, and Maria became increasingly upset and confused. She told the therapist, "I don't think I want to have this child." Time was spent exploring Maria's options and discussing the good things and less good things about each option. Maria ultimately made up her mind, saying, "I want to have an abortion. After all, my marriage is about to end, I do not have a full-time job and my family does not live in the country. It is not the right time for me to have a child."

Maria scheduled an appointment to have the procedure. She was sure she wanted to terminate the pregnancy. When she turned onto the street where the clinic was located she saw protestors with horrible signs standing on the sidewalk. As she pulled in to the clinic parking lot, the protestors screamed at her, "Don't do this, don't murder your child." Maria was so frightened that she did not park but instead drove away. She was crying and scared. Maria called her therapist and was able to schedule an appointment with her that day.

Several hours later, when she came to see the therapist, Maria was still frightened. Despite her experience earlier in the day, Maria was still set on terminating her pregnancy. The therapist suggested that they call the clinic together to find out about the protestor situation and how it could be avoied. In addition, the therapist asked the client about the possibility of a friend going with her. Maria said that her best friend Rose had offered to go with her, but that she didn't think it was necessary. She decided she would call Rose later that day and let her know that she would like some company.

Maria went back to the clinic 3 days later. This time she was with her friend Rose and prepared for what to expect. She had the abortion procedure. To this day, Maria is happy with the decision she made and feels that it was the only decision for her at the time.

Many women who became pregnant prior to 1973, when abortion was legalized, have horrifying stories of seeking an illegal abortion. Here are the stories of two such women who shared their stories with us.

Annie

Annie was 32 years old when she discovered that she was pregnant. At the time, birth control was not even an option, so she was using the rhythm method. She already had two children, was separated from her husband, and knew that she could not raise a third child as a single mother. Annie was raised Methodist but had attended Catholic school and felt conflicted between her ethics and morals. But becoming pregnant and knowing that she could not care for a third child was part of what changed Annie's mind to feeling that a woman should be able to make her own decision.

The year was 1967 and abortion was not yet a legal option. Annie's friend, Barbara, gave her a phone number to call, that she had herself used, about terminating the pregnancy. Annie called the number and an anonymous person answered the phone. He told her to be on a certain street corner on Friday at 2 p.m. Her friend dropped her off at the designated street corner and from there Annie was picked up by strangers, hidden under a rug in the back seat of the car, and driven to a house. When she got out of the car she was in a garage in a private home. The men took her to the kitchen where she was able to have her pregnancy terminated. Annie recalls being "frantic and scared." She was not given any sedation during the procedure. Everyone around her was speaking Spanish, and so she could not understand what was being said. Annie remembers feeling scared. She lost a contact lens while at the house and so she could not see well for parts of the procedure. As a registered nurse, Annie does report that she believed the person who performed the termination was a physician, so she was glad about that, as she knew that most illegal abortions were not performed by physicians. Annie recalls the procedure being "fast and clandestine." The men brought her back to the same street corner, where her friend picked her up. She was relieved that it was over. Annie was not given any postsurgery medications, and she went back to work the following day. She remarks that it was likely easier for her than it would have been for other women, because being a nurse enabled her to take care of herself, whereas other women may not have been able to do the same. Despite not having believed in abortion prior to her unwanted pregnancy, Annie reported that her decision-making was easy. She knew that she could not have and did not want to have another child. She reported being lucky to have had the support of her good friend who had, herself, undergone a pregnancy termination with the same group.

Annie reported having no regrets about having an abortion. She feels strongly that no woman should have to go through what she did, although she acknowledges how lucky she was to have had a safe abortion as opposed to a back-alley one. For the past 17 years, Annie has worked as a nurse at a women's health center that provides abortion services. She stated that she thinks about the abortion everyday: "Everyday, I think about my experience and am angry that it needed to be done the way that it was, and I am glad that I was able to have the abortion performed by a physician, unlike many other women at the time."

Michelle

Michelle, a White woman, was 19 years old and had a 2-year-old daughter when her husband abandoned her. Soon after, Michelle found out that she was pregnant. "I had no choice, I could not support another child," she said.

It was 1928, 44 years before *Roe v. Wade*. Michelle found a doctor who was willing to perform an abortion for $100. He botched that abortion and soon after Michelle came down with a rampant fever and a painful infection. The abortion was incomplete. Michelle recalls being "frightened." "I felt so alone. It was terrible. I couldn't tell anyone."

Despite the negative experience she had, Michelle said that she has never regretted her decision to have an abortion. She repeated: "I had no choice, I could not support another child."

SUGGESTIONS FOR THERAPISTS
AND HEALTH PROFESSIONALS

Therapists and health professionals who work with women who are considering terminating a pregnancy should be aware of how abortion clinics typically operate. Box 2.1 lists two suggestions that might be helpful for the therapist to discuss with the client.

Box 2.1   Suggestions for Therapists Helping Women Before Their Abortion Procedure. There are Variations From Clinic to Clinic

1. Have the client call the clinic and ask about the protestor situation before going for their appointment.
2. Have someone— a partner, friend, or family member—accompany the woman for support.

The typical pre-abortion counseling provided by most abortion centers includes discussing the options, the procedure to be followed, and the woman's support system, among other issues, to help her be able to make an informed choice about an abortion. The counseling also includes aftercare instructions to be sure the woman will be able to care for her health needs. These instructions are provided in Box 2.2, with further details in Chapter 4.

Box 2.3 lists what one abortion center tells women who call for an appointment on days when there are likely to be protestors.

Box 2.2   Topics That Are Typically Covered in the Pre-Abortion Counseling Session at Abortion Centers (Further Descriptions Can Be Found in Chapter 4)

1. Description of the procedure, possible complications, and after-care instructions
2. Her options
3. Her decision: Why she has chosen abortion, and whether she feels certain about the decision
4. Her support system: Whom she has told about the pregnancy and abortion and their reactions
5. Her feelings about abortion and expectations for coping post-abortion

---

Box 2.3   Most Clinics Will Tell Patients Something Like This on the Telephone When Making an Appointment, Especially if They Call for a Saturday Appointment, Which Is the Main Day Protestors Are There

I want you to know ahead of time that there are often protestors outside the building on Saturday mornings. There will be escorts and a police officer to walk you in comfortably and to ensure your safety. The protestors like to yell and so I want to suggest that you keep your windows up and park and wait until an escort comes to walk you in. One of the main reasons I'm telling you this is so that you are not surprised by this when you come in and to encourage you to bring someone with you for support if you can.

SUMMARY

Abortion counseling is not like other types of health care counseling or therapy because of the politics surrounding abortion. In this chapter we discussed some of the difficulties that these politics cause counselors. We suggest that those health providers who will be counseling should think about their own values before they begin working with women who are considering terminating their pregnancies. Stories of women who have been affected by the political controversy are shared to help highlight their concerns.

REFERENCES

Baker, A. (1995). *Abortion and options counseling.* Granite City, IL: The Hope Clinic for Women.

Bazelon, E. (2007, January 21). Is There a Post-Abortion Syndrome? *New York Times Magazine,* 41.

Guttmacher Institute. (2006). *State funding of abortion under Medicaid: State policies in brief.* Retrieved January 12, 2007, from http://www.guttmacher.org/pubs/spib_SFAM.pdf

Henshaw, S. K., & Finer, L. B. (2003). The accessibility of abortion services in the United States in 2001. *Perspectives on Sexual and Reproductive Health, 35*(1), 16–24. Retrieved January 12, 2007, from http://www.guttmacher.org/pubs/journals/3501603.pdf

Hern, W. M. (1991). Proxemics: The application of theory to conflict arising from antiabortion demonstrations. *Population and Environment, 12*(4), 379–388.

National Abortion Federation. *Anti-abortion extremists.* Retrieved February 5, 2007, from http://www.prochoice.org/about_abortion/violence/extremists.html

National Abortion Federation. *Anti-abortion extremists: The Army of God and justifiable homicide.* Retrieved February 5, 2007, from http://www. prochoice.org/about_abortion/violence/army_god.html

Sonfield, A., & Gold, R. B. (2005). *Public funding for contraceptive, sterilization, and abortion services, FY 1980–2001.* Retrieved January 12, 2007, from http://www.guttmacher.org/pubs/fpfunding/tables.pdf

CHAPTER 3

Assessing Competency and Decision-Making Skills of the Client

How people make decisions about important moments in their lives is part of the study of cognitive psychology. Three major domains must develop in a person to be able to influence how a decision is made: cognitions, or how we think; emotions, or how we feel; and behavior, or how we act. Each choice that is made uses a combination of skills from thinking, feeling, and acting that then influences a decision that then, using a feedback loop, influences how we think and feel and behave, which influences our next decision, and so on.

Some people take a long time to make a decision, whether a major or minor one in their lives. These people may think for a long time about what the consequences mean for them. Sometimes they get stuck and obsess or ruminate and worry about their decision, always wanting more information before they are comfortable in finalizing their choice. Other people may make a decision quickly, sometimes because they know what they want or, in some cases, because they listen to the ideas of someone else. Sometimes they have such strong feelings that they don't want to think rationally about what the decision will mean for their immediate or long-term future. Maybe they are scared. Some have preexisting emotional problems that interfere with using good thinking strategies. Others make impulsive decisions, based more on how they feel at the moment, rather than allowing themselves to rationally think about the problem

49

from all angles. Impulsivity in decision-making often leads to regrets, especially later, when they have time to think about the consequences. But, emotionally, they might not be able to consider all the alternatives at a particular time in their lives, especially when the decision has as many immediate and long-term consequences as does the decision to obtain an abortion.

Counseling can help or hinder people to make good decisions. If counselors clarify and provide accurate information in an unemotional setting and permit a person to think and ask questions, then counseling can help assist in the cognitive decision-making process. If counseling focuses too much on people's emotions, without helping clarify the cognitive part of the decision-making process by carefully examining all the variables and the immediate and long-term consequences of all possible decisions, then it can hinder the woman's later emotional stability.

Counseling should clarify the person's feelings and validate them whether these feelings concentrate only on the anticipated procedure or have roots in earlier life experiences. For example, the woman who has been abused as a child and cannot think clearly about being able to parent her own child will need to understand how her feelings might affect her parenting skills both in the present and future as part of her decision-making process about an abortion. She will have similar and different emotions from the currently battered woman whose fears about her ability to parent her child center around sharing parenting with her abusive partner, not on her own doubts about parenting.

The next few chapters of this book clarify the difference between the emotional and cognitive skills needed to make good decisions and the development of these skills. They will provide a guide for the counselor to assess if a woman is using the right balance of cognitive skills together with her emotions to come to a decision about whether or not having an abortion is the right action for her to take at this time in her life. A good counselor does not have an interest in what decision a woman makes but rather helps her to make the best decision considering all the variables involved. The theories we describe in this chapter will help counselors and therapists become good role models when working with a woman who must make the decision about terminating a pregnancy.

The decision to terminate a pregnancy is one of the most difficult decisions that a woman will have to make during her lifetime. It takes both emotional maturity and stability as well as the ability to think clearly while weighing all the possible consequences. The combination of cognitive skills and emotional stability is often called competency to make a decision. The ability to think clearly and weigh all possible consequences is part of the cognitive skills that people develop as they become adults. There are different theories about cognitive development and, therefore, different ways for a therapist to be able to assess which skills a person possesses at a particular time of development. In this chapter, we attempt to explore the major cognitive theories and how they help women make good decisions during their lives. In Chapter 4, we attempt to provide important, factual information for women to consider as they use their cognitive skills in decision making.

Women who are thinking about choosing an abortion to terminate an unwanted pregnancy must use their cognitive skills and pay attention to their feelings or emotions that also develop at different times of their lives. We discuss emotional development as it affects decision making as described in Chapter 5. It is important for therapists and counselors to understand the nature and quality of cognition when attempting to provide both pre- and post-abortion counseling. Is a particular woman capable of making this important decision? What about teenagers who are not quite women, yet still may have the cognitive abilities to permit them to make the decision without consulting their parents? Even so, most teenagers consult with their mothers and some with their fathers before making the decision to choose an abortion. Those who do not tell their parents usually have good reasons; either they fear the knowledge of their sexual activity and subsequent pregnancy will cause some form of family violence or they cannot bear the pain of disappointing parents with high ideals for them. As was mentioned in earlier chapters, a teenage girl can request a judicial bypass procedure instead of contacting a parent that requires she disclose to a judge her reasons for wanting an abortion and her reasons for not wanting to tell her parents. Most of the time, the judges who hear these cases have permitted the girl to have the abortion.

WHAT ARE COGNITIVE ABILITIES?

The best way to define a woman's cognitive abilities is to look at her capacity for understanding and her ability to reason, solve problems, and make decisions. Four specific areas are suggested by cognitive psychologists: (a) the ability to reason abstractly about hypothetical situations, (b) the capacity to reason about multiple alternatives and their consequences, (c) the capacity to consider additional variables in the decision-making process and combine them in complex ways, and (d) the capacity for systematic and exhaustive use of information. However, in addition to these thinking skills, a person's social and emotional development, usually called personality, will affect the rational decision-making process.

Everyone has a different way of making a decision. In fact, most counselors and therapists are cautioned in their training not to tell clients what decision they think their clients should make because the clients must live with the decision. The therapist and counselor's role is to help the client identify the areas in which a decision must be made and the factors that will go into making such a decision and help the client develop and use the decision-making process that best fits a particular situation. Although it is easy to confuse cognitive processes with intelligence, they are not really the same thing. Most of us know people who are intelligent, who can complete their education at top schools and hold down jobs where they are called upon to make daily work-related decisions, and yet their personal lives are a mess. They have learned to use their cognitive abilities when they function in their job situation but allow their emotions to take over in their personal lives. Adolescents may be very intelligent at school but not well developed socially, causing them to make poor judgments about complex social matters such as what to do about an unplanned pregnancy. However, adolescent girls might also be quite mature socially and able to make an informed decision without the help of any adult. Even so, surveys have found that most girls do consult with at least one parent, relative, or other adult before deciding whether or not to abort an unplanned pregnancy.

It is true that people with few intellectual resources will have a more difficult time making a decision calling for complex cognitive skills, as they have less of an ability to think abstractly or predict future consequences, especially when there are many competing variables to think about. Facing too many variables at the same time, without having a strategy to organize them mentally, may cause a person to become paralyzed, fearing the wrong decision will be worse than no decision at all. The job of the abortion counselor is to help the emotionally paralyzed person develop a strategy to consider each of the variables and put them together, and to encourage her to proceed with the best decision possible when she is ready. A woman who has not decided within the time frame allowed whether to terminate a pregnancy or carry it to term and then places the child for adoption or raises the child herself has also made a decision, albeit passively.

In other cases, an unplanned pregnancy may elicit all the old messages about being a so-called bad girl and getting in trouble by not listening to authority figures. Getting stuck on accepting punishment for making a mistake is not a good cognitive decision, although it might be good for temporary expiation of angry emotions at oneself. A woman in such a situation needs to expand her view from feeling better in the short term to understanding the long-term impacts of a pregnancy on her health and the consequences of raising a child. She also has to figure in her own personal, moral, and religious values. Then, she needs some reality testing about social supports for herself and the child. Or, if she decides to terminate the pregnancy, she must think about how it will be for her to continue the rest of her life in her social community. Will she be ostracized if she talks about it? Can she keep it secret? She needs to take an objective, that is, more factual than emotional, look at how her decision will affect other loved ones in her life. For example, a mother with three other children under the age of five has to add another variable to her decision about whether having a fourth child will negatively affect the time and attention she can give to the three children already in her life.

IMPACT OF SOCIAL VALUES ON MORAL DEVELOPMENT

The controversy that has surrounded the decision to obtain an abortion in order to terminate a pregnancy has caused most women who make this decision additional anguish because of their personal and social values. Many women who believe that abortion is against their own personal and religious values also think about the competing values such as believing that raising a child without sufficient emotional stamina or financial assistance is also wrong. Helping a woman make this decision is far more complex than other health care decisions, but the decision is easier to make once all the variables are carefully examined and short- and long-term consequences are assessed.

What do we mean by personal values? Although some of the social values that affect a decision are discussed in the following chapters, we provide a briefer review of them here.

Personal values include the development of a person's identity, autonomy, and ability to solve social dilemmas. The role of autonomy, self-esteem, and personal identity, often considered part of the volitional area of decision-making, is further discussed in Chapter 6 on emotional development. Here we will focus on the development of the more cognitive or judgmental areas, especially moral values. A number of psychological theories discuss the ability to develop and use a person's personal values to make a moral decision.

Kohlberg's Stages of Moral Development

The most notable theory is that of a Boston psychologist, Lawrence Kohlberg (Kohlberg, 1977), whose research suggested that people learn how to understand social rules and laws including the ability to put the rule of law above one's own social or interpersonal relationships. Kohlberg's work stresses that autonomy and universal application of the abstract principle without modification is the highest level of moral development. He found that the first two stages, wherein people make decisions based on right and wrong, tend to be associated with their consequences. If you do something that is considered bad, then you are bad and punished. Decisions are based on the individual's self-interests or whether or not the person cares about following the externally imposed rules so the person can be considered good or bad by that decision alone.

By stage 3, the individual is said to care about whether or not the rest of the people in the community of friends, family, and social network are pleased by the decision that the person makes. At this stage it is possible for a good person to make what in an early stage would be called a bad decision if the rest of the community agreed with the person's motives. In stage 4, there is more of a focus on following the rules of the community if doing so will benefit the community and not just the person's own needs or motives. Many people who insist that everyone must follow their rules based on their moral standards, whether or not they agree with them, might be considered to be making decisions at a stage 3 or 4 level.

By stage 5, people are said to be able to compromise individual rights so that the community will value as a group. This focus is often difficult to separate from stage 3 and 4 moral reasoning. However, a key fact said to be present here is the ability of the individual to subjugate his or her own rights in order to conform to abstract principles that will sustain the larger social order. Finally, the highest level of moral reasoning, stage 6, is where people are said to be able to follow a universal view of justice that takes into account all the possibilities of viewpoints and values. Here the individual makes rational decisions based on reason and abstract principles that conform to justice, not interfered with by emotions associated with individual rights or relationships. Gender studies, as discussed subsequently, have criticized this model as one that is not consistent with women's adherence to a caring ethic where moral judgments are based on reasoning tempered by compassion for others.

The six stages of Kohlberg's theory are listed in Box 3.1.

Kohlberg's theory would imply that if one's religious or moral values state that terminating a pregnancy is wrong because the individual's rights are disrespected, then it is not possible to go any further. Defining the point that life begins is important here. Without the definition that life begins at conception, then the dilemma raised by the need to choose between the woman's rights and the fetus's rights would not exist. Some counselors with strong religious affiliation take this stance and no other factors are possible to consider. Some legislators want to support this position, while others, including those who have made it possible for women to choose to obtain a safe abortion, accept the right of each

Box 3.1   Kohlberg's Six Stages of Moral Development

Level I   Preconventional Morality

Stage 1   Obedience and Punishment Orientation

Here a person makes a moral decision based on right and wrong consequences. Therefore, if something is bad, then it should be punished because it is bad. So, if an individual gets punished, then it proves that the behavior was bad. In this stage of development, the person sees the rules of what is good or bad as external to himself or herself.

Stage 2   Individualism and Exchange

Here an individual is able to understand more than one right view given by the authorities. Different people can hold different viewpoints. This means that the individual has a choice. Individuals can exchange favors to make choices but the good of the family or community is not perceived. Self-interest motivates the choice at this stage of moral development.

Level II   Conventional Morality

Stage 3   Good Interpersonal Relationships

When an individual reaches this stage, he or she is able to understand the expectations of other people including family, friends, and community values. Good intentions help make choices, especially when there aren't too many conflicting areas. The shift from stage 1 to stage 3 moves from unquestioning obedience to relative understanding tempered by conformity with social relationships or good motives for nonconformity.

Stage 4   Maintaining Social Order

In this stage, an individual is capable of being concerned about society as a whole. Laws should benefit everyone, not just himself or herself. The focus is on obeying laws, respecting authority, and performing duties to keep the social fabric of society intact and continuing to function. Those individuals whose religious values legitimize the Right to Life of a fetus are able to rationalize their insistence that all individuals must follow their rules in order to keep the social fabric of society intact.

Level III   Postconventional Morality

Stage 5   Social Contract and Individual Rights

At this stage, the individual is able to understand that society must benefit himself or herself and not just everyone in general. For example, a

(continued)

dictatorship might keep the social order so that society functions but denies the rights of the individual. The mode of reasoning and the person's ability to perceive morality and rights together identifies this stage of moral decision-making. In this stage, an individual tries to determine what society should value rather than accepting the religious or other group values alone.

Stage 6 Universal Ethical Principles

This is the stage where an individual is able to achieve a view of justice that supersedes the earlier stages. Here one's perspectives go beyond the value of society alone but include a concept of individual rights. Theoretically, one issue that is said to distinguish stage 6 from the earlier stages is the belief that a commitment to justice carries with it the responsibility of civil disobedience if unable to change the social contracts and laws in a democratic way. In both stages 5 and 6, an individual is able to take a more idealized view of how others might coordinate their interests. However, in stage 6, an individual is able to consider how all different parties might think about a particular issue according to the principles of justice before coming to a decision.

individual to make the choice for herself within the legal confines. It is important for the counselor or therapist to recognize that this is a non-negotiable position if someone strictly holds these values. Understanding this conflict helps to explain why people who hold these values believe that no one can have the choice to abort a fetus, no matter what the stage of development. Following Kohlberg's moral decision-making options, only if the law reflected the narrower and more fundamentalist view of conception could a person justify demanding everyone must choose the fetus's right to life over the woman's right to choose becoming a mother.

As might be expected, there are many criticisms of Kohlberg's theory. Perhaps the most important challenge is that the theory may hold up in the research laboratory but it does not allow for the diversity of society's members in real life. Kohlberg's stages of thinking require the acceptance that mental functioning occurs in an invariable sequence of patterns with different functions occurring at each new stage of development. This means that children would always naturally go from stage 1 to stage 2 to stage 3 and so forth and cannot think at more than one stage beyond their current level of moral development. People are said to move to the next stage when the moral dilemmas with which they are faced cannot be decided at the stage at which they are currently. However, the original research used cross-sectional groups of children at different ages rather than a longitudinal study across one child's development. When

Kohlberg tested teenagers and followed them into adulthood, he found some stayed at the stage they were at over a long time, some advanced to the next stage as he predicted, and some had regressed to a lower stage of reasoning.

Another of the major criticisms of Kohlberg's model is that when the studies were repeated in other cultures, a high percentage of adults never got beyond stage 3 thinking. In fact, when Kohlberg broadened his sample, he found that the predominant stage of reasoning leveled off at stage 4 for most of his subjects and only around 25% ever reached stage 6. It should be remembered that most of Kohlberg's original subjects were all boys from a privileged social class, which made generalization to other groups in society less reliable.

In more recent studies, Kohlberg and his colleagues have found that people do not lose the insights they gain as they advance to the next stage but rather learn how to integrate them into their more advanced way to reason. Many of his studies now have similar findings across different cultures in different countries despite different cultural values and assumptions, making it an important psychological theory about moral reasoning, not just moral values. The theory does not deal with moral actions, only with thinking about morality. Thus, it may be possible that after stage 3, people raised in other types of societies, such as rural villages, or those trained in Eastern philosophies, continue to develop moral reasoning but in a direction that Kohlberg's theories do not capture.

Gilligan's Theories on Cognitive Development of Girls and Women

Another Boston psychologist, Carol Gilligan, challenged Kohlberg's theories in her research with girls and women. One of the main foundations of her criticism is based on the fact that only White, privileged boys and men were used in Kohlberg's original studies from which he formulated the theory. The choice of using such a narrow sample and the results obtained from using it correspond to accusations that the study would inevitably lead to the same kind of sex-role stereotyping and cultural biases that have been criticized in many other psychological theories when using a gender-sensitive and multicultural analysis (Herman, 1992; Levant & Kopecky, 1995). His sample of boys and men came from a culture where they were socialized into believing advanced morality is based on rules, rights, and abstract principles whereas girls and women were socialized into the ethic of caring for one another. Therefore, it should be no surprise that they reflected the teachings of their environment rather than principles of psychological development that apply to everyone regardless of gender, race, socioeconomic class, or culture.

Gilligan (1982) found that the highest level of moral development in girls and women occurred when they temper with compassion
their view of what Kohlberg termed universal justice. Originally using
Kohlberg's six stages, developed almost exclusively on interviews with
boys and men, she found that girls and women would frequently be
at what might be termed an additional stage 7, because of their interest in interpersonal feelings rather than reason alone. Gilligan asserted
that this reflects the difference in moral and psychological tendencies
between women and men. She found three stages of moral development that progress from selfish, to social and conventional, to postcon-
ventional morality that includes women's ability to tend to their own
interests as well as those of others. Feminist scholars believe that the
last stage requires an even higher level of moral development as it is
dependent upon women being able to understand the complexities of
relationships as well as rational justice and a reluctance by women to
develop just one view of justice.

Gilligan has developed a research method that is called the Listening
Guide Method, which studies the voice and its resonance to understand
how women approach understanding the real world and their relationships within it. She has collaborated with teachers who teach actors how
to train their voices in the theater. The method is used to assess people's
relations with others while trying to understand the world in which they
live. This emphasis on better understanding the role of the so-called caring ethic for girls and women has been helpful in shining a light on the
interrelationship between cognition and emotion when making complex
decisions such as whether or not to have an abortion.

Considering the fact that most theories about women's psychological development include the need for affiliation along with the need
for autonomy, Gilligan's theories about moral reasoning may be more
applicable to women who are making the decision to have an abortion
than Kohlberg's. Gilligan asked women about decision making in real-life
complex situations, including the decision to have an abortion. Through
these interviews, Gilligan has demonstrated that girls and women move
from consideration of their responsibilities from what they believe is
conventionally expected to adding their own insights into the ethics of
care and responsibility. Under this theory, even those women with strong
religious or moral opinions are able to temper their own decisions by
considering other factors that will affect that person's situation. This may
be why more women than men believe in the right of a woman to choose
whether or not to carry a pregnancy to term. Of course, including these
factors together demands the ability to consider more than one variable
in the decision-making process and to apply compassion to an extremely
complex and difficult decision.

HOW DO COGNITIVE ABILITIES DEVELOP?

The theories about moral development as it applies to cognitive decision making described earlier are based on a Piagetian model, which found one stage invariably led to the next stage of development. Gilligan's work, along with others, suggested that perhaps another way to understand cognitive development is based on domains that develop independently rather than one stage developing at a time across all domains. Gilligan suggested that for moral development it is probable that one domain is the development of logic, justice, and social organization whereas another focuses on development of interpersonal relationships. Perhaps each domain develops at a different rate for men and women, and then the highest task of the adult is to integrate them. Other cognitive development theorists now suggest that our cognitive abilities or intelligence is indeed based on many different domains.

These psychological theories help us understand how cognitive abilities develop and are useful in both understanding if someone has the requisite ability to make complex judgments and in devising a treatment plan to help organize the girl's or woman's thinking strategies to clarify such decisions.

Stage Development Theories

As we mentioned, some cognitive theorists believe that cognitive abilities develop in a predictable way, with each cognitive skill unfolding at a particular stage of development. Piaget (Inhelder & Piaget, 1958) is often seen as the leader in the developmental stage approach. His detailed observations of how the various skills develop suggested young children have more fixed ideas, whereas the capacity to think in an abstract way develops around the age of 12. Once a person is capable of thinking abstractly, then he or she can hold certain information constant while considering other information, and then is able to use or discard that new information to affect and change the original thoughts. Piaget and his followers conducted numerous experiments with children and adults to see when the next stage would occur and found that it was fairly predictable. Thus, by the time a girl is old enough to become sexually active, from her mid-teens to adulthood, a Piagetian theorist would believe that she would be capable of making the decision to voluntarily terminate a pregnancy.

Domain Development Theories

Other cognitive psychologists began to dissect the skills that are required for cognition and developed what is called a domain-focused approach to their understanding. While skills may develop in an orderly and predict-able way in each domain, the various domains develop at different and more unpredictable stages. Thus, a 12-year-old might have good abil-ity to think abstractly about a simple problem but not about one with several moral and personal complexities. However, combining with the stage development theorists, even the domain theorist would expect that by the time a girl is 14 years old, she will have developed sufficient cogni-tive skills to make the decision about an abortion.

Sternberg (2005) is often seen as one of the leaders in the intelli-gence domains school of thought. Believing that intelligence is made up of analytical, practical, and creative functions, Sternberg believes that these three domains of abilities are not fixed and can change, becoming stronger or weaker, through everyday life experiences. Thus, unlike the stage-driven theorists, the domain theorist believes that people can and must rise to the occasion, even if they are not equally balanced in all three areas. By capitalizing on their strengths and identifying and compensating for their weaknesses, successful people both respond to and shape their environ-ment. They learn from their past experiences and achieve success according to their own definition, which is based on their social and cultural envi-ronment. According to Sternberg, successful decisions are made by people who apply their mental abilities toward their personal goals.

ADOLESCENT COGNITIVE ABILITY TO MAKE DECISIONS

Most adults have the capacity to make complex decisions by strategically allocating their mental energy toward finalizing their decision. This is important given the time-limited window for making a decision to ter-minate a pregnancy. However, much controversy surrounds the cognitive ability of adolescents to make similar decisions. Thus, the counselor or therapist working with an adolescent who announces her pregnancy has even more of a responsibility to assure that the adolescent is capable of making such a difficult decision. Although there has been a trend to grant adolescents some limited legal rights, for example, in adjudicating juvenile criminal actions (see *in re Gault, 387 U.S. 1, 1967*), the opposite trend has been witnessed in adolescent abortion cases where minors are required to obtain permission from or notify at least one parent or else be prepared to justify their secrecy by going before a judge in a special bypass procedure. Despite the testimony of psychologists about adolescent competence to make such decisions, the legal field has supported parental notification as a minimum standard. It appears that public policy differs from scientific knowledge in this case. Let's look at what the research data tell us.

The research of psychologist and lawyer Lois Weithorn suggested the same four main abilities adults have can be measured to determine the development of an adolescent's cognitive skills to make good legal decisions. Using vignettes requiring these four abilities—to reason, to think abstractly and hypothesize situations about multiple alternatives and their consequences, to consider and combine multiple variables in various combinations and complexities, and to think about information in a systematic way—Weithorn and Campbell (1982) found that adults and children think about the information provided to them differently, but that both can come to a good decision-making process. Weithorn (1982) suggested that there were three major ways to determine if an adolescent is competent to give informed consent to medical treatments: (a) adolescents may be assessed for a minimum level of competence; (b) adolescents' responses may be compared with a hypothetical, rationally based standard; and (c) adolescents' responses may be compared with allegedly competent adults. Her research has found that minors are competent to make a variety of legal and health care decisions using these criteria. Adolescents in her research were capable of making complex decisions involving appropriate suggestions for protection from child maltreatment, especially when adolescents are exposed to domestic violence in their homes (Weithorn, 2006), and in appropriate steps for preventing delinquents from becoming career criminals (Carter, Weithorn, & Behrman, 1999).

When comparing adolescents' with adults' capacity to make complex decisions, such as seeking an abortion, it has been found that adolescents, at least over 14 or 15 years old, are as cognitively competent as adults, although they may take longer to make the decision and usually seek the support of two to three other adults, if not their parents. Adolescents also are likely to give more weight to the impact of their decision on other people in their life, probably because they are still dependent on them for some support. In fact, testimony at several of these legal cases demonstrated data that most adolescents will discuss all the alternatives with at least one parent, usually the mother, before deciding upon an abortion (American Psychological Association Interdisciplinary Committee on Adolescent Abortion, 1987).

In research by Lewis (1987), she compared adolescents' and adults' decision making about abortion using hypothetical case studies. Lewis found that adolescents knew about as much as did adults about the medical procedure and legal aspects of abortion. Although this was an admittedly small sample, the study is cited for its ability to assess the critical areas of cognition suggested to be necessary to make a complex decision. Ambuel and Rappaport (1992) studied a larger sample of girls from ages 13 to 21. Using an experimental design submitted for funding by the

National Science Foundation, they found that girls over the age of 15 were as competent as adults to make the decision about what to do when faced with an actual unplanned pregnancy. The only group of girls that were seen as less competent to make a decision were those under the age of 15 who refused to consider an abortion as part of their decision-making process.

Worthington et al. (1989) challenged the position of the American Psychological Association (APA) on adolescence competency and posited arguments in support of legislation requiring parental involvement. Although they did not have empirical data to challenge studies finding most adolescents competent to make health care decisions such as those cited by Ambuel and Rappaport (1992), Gilligan (1982), Lewis (1980), and Weithorn and Campbell (1982) mentioned previously, they did question whether a real-life crisis such as an unwanted pregnancy will elicit the same responses as adolescents give to a hypothetical situation. Moreover, they suggest that the state has a compelling legal interest in supporting the strengthening of the family and make the assumption that the girl's parents will be cognitively or emotionally competent to assist her in making this difficult decision. Other psychologists, such as Gruber and Anderson (1990), challenge the Worthington et al. (1989) premises, citing the actual studies of whom adolescents turn to as supportive people to help them make this decision. They include the coconceiver, grandparents, aunts and other relatives, teachers, counselors, physicians, and friends. Obviously, it is impossible to know whether these support figures are able to help the girl reach an independent decision or are merely exerting undue influence on her choices, but the same is true for one or both parents who may insist on her following their own choice. We discuss this issue further in the next several chapters.

LEGAL DECISIONS AND PSYCHOLOGY OF COGNITION

Several major legal decisions concerning the right of adolescents to make a decision to have an abortion have considered information provided by cognitive psychologists, particularly psychologist and lawyer Thomas Grisso, who has developed competency assessment methodology used to assess both adults' and minors' competency in various areas of the law.

In *Planned Parenthood of Central Missouri v. Danforth* (1976) (herein called *Danforth*), four areas were suggested to evaluate decision-making competencies: (a) cognitive and volitional capacity, which includes being able to make a decision without being coerced or acquiescing to others; (b) consideration of risks and benefits including immediate and future consequences; (c) quality and clarity of reasoning; and (d) number and types of factors considered before making the decision. In subsequent legal decisions, *Carey v. Population Services International* (1977) and *Bellotti v. Baird II* (1979), the Court consistently extended the same privacy rights as accorded to adult women and found that competent adolescents could make the decision to seek an abortion without parents having the legal right to veto that choice but had to at least notify in some states and obtain consent in others from one parent. In cases where the girl chose not to notify or obtain consent from a parent, she was afforded the legal right to seek judicial bypass for review of her decision. In reviewing the literature, we were unable to find cases describing any judicial reversals of the girls' choices and therefore assume it is rarely if ever done.

Hodgson v. Minnesota (1990) struck down a part of the Minnesota law that demanded adolescents obtain permission from both parents to get an abortion and required only notification of one parent and created the judicial bypass for those girls who were unable to tell their parents that they were pregnant. Psychologist Gary Melton testified as to adolescent competency and Lenore Walker testified as to probability of various forms of family violence in preventing the girl from disclosing her pregnancy. The APA supported the psychologists' testimony by entering an Amicus Curae Brief in *Hodgson* as well as others that are often cited in the literature (e.g., Bersoff et al., 1989; Odgen & Kappler, 1991). The Amicus Curae Brief often provides scientific evidence to assist the judges in making decisions that should be based on scientific data as well as social conditions; the term *amicus curae* means *friend of the court*. In this case, given the emotional and political controversies that surrounded the challenge to the adolescent notification requirements, the APA was able to persuade the appellate court that requiring parental permission or even notification without protection from abusive parents would not be in the adolescent's or the state's best interests.

The issue of an adult woman's competency was raised in several more cases, such as in *Planned Parenthood of Southeastern Pennsylvania et al. v. Casey* (1992), another important case, which challenged the married woman's competency to make a decision to obtain an abortion without notifying her husband. The arguments in *Casey* rested on both a woman's right to privacy and the law not creating an undue burden on a woman to obtain an abortion within the limitations set by the U.S. Supreme Court in *Roe v. Wade* (1973). In addition to competency issues, most of these cases added another variable to the decision-making process for both teens and women who had to deal with the danger from an abusive parent or partner if their pregnancy or decision to terminate it were to be disclosed.

The issue of competency was addressed by expert witness testimony by psychologists, particularly Gary Melton on the issue of cognitive competency and Lenore Walker on prevalence of family abuse and its impact on girls and women. The APA added Amicus Curiae Briefs in the appeals process in *Thornberg v. American College of Obstetricians and Gynecologists* (Bersoff, Malson, & Ennis, 1985), *Hodgson v. State of Minnesota* (Bersoff & Ogden, 1987), *State of Ohio v. Akron Center for Reproductive Health et al.* (Bersoff, Podolsky, & Schneider, 1989), and *Planned Parenthood of Southeastern Pennsylvania v. Casey* (Ogden & Kappler, 1991) that have also delineated what we knew then about cognitive development and capacity. Using either the developmental or domain approach to cognitive development, as described previously, the APA concluded that adolescents and adult women usually were capable of making this complex decision. Studies indicated that most adolescents will speak to at least three other supportive adults in their lives before deciding to get an abortion even if one of those people is not her parent. Further, the decision not to talk with a parent is usually based on a realistic cognitive appraisal of the danger to herself or her mother. Based in part on the expert testimony, the courts supported the requirement of a judicial bypass in states that required adolescents to obtain parental permission. In *Hodgson,* the argument claimed that requiring two-parent permission or notification was an undue burden given the high number of divorces that cause fathers to be less involved in their teenage daughters' lives.

ASSESSMENT OF COGNITIVE COMPETENCY

The assessment of cognitive competency has been an issue in other health situations and legal cases. The issue of informed consent has a long forensic psychology history. Someone must demonstrate capacity to understand the consequences of any health procedure, usually signing a complicated legal informed consent form. If the person is incapable of giving informed consent, then a guardian or someone with a health care proxy may make the decision. However, how to assess whether or not a person is competent is not clearly delineated in the law.

Informed Consent in the Law

There are several areas of the law that require cognitive competency to give informed consent. The most well-known area because of the publicity given in television shows is the Miranda Warning, or one's competency to understand his or her legal rights to remain silent and obtain an attorney to be present if law enforcement wish to question the person.

Precise psychological assessment for one who has been arrested is important because most legal systems, including that of the United States, require different levels of cognition in order to determine appropriate charges and assess for responsibility to properly apply a sentence should the person be found guilty. For example, someone with mental retardation or other developmental or emotional disabilities that make him or her unable to apply the legal standards using the requisite *mens rea* might be found not guilty by reason of insanity or ineligible for the death penalty based on cognitive difficulties.

There are two well-accepted ways of measuring cognitive capacity in legal settings. The first is based on the psychological research of Thomas Grisso (Grisso, 2004; Grisso & Applebaum, 1998; Grisso, Borum, & Edens, 2005), and the second is based on the psychological research of John Monahan and Henry Steadman, who worked on the MacArthur Foundation Studies on Mental Health and Violence Risk Assessment (Monahan et al., 2001).

Grisso and his colleagues began their work looking at the ability of juveniles to consent to waiver of their legal rights in the justice system. His work on competency extended to health care issues, as well as to other areas where psycholegal issues are raised for both juveniles and adults. Monahan and his colleagues led a 15-year study about violence risk, and part of their work included assessment of competency to stand trial. Both groups of psychologists and lawyers go further in requiring not only an understanding of the people involved in and the purpose of legal standards and the legal system, but also in requiring what is termed a rational understanding of the entire process.

Grisso has developed a series of instruments, called the *Function of Rights in Interrogation,* designed to assess whether a juvenile or an adult defendant is competent to waive Miranda rights. The instrument consists of four parts. The first deals with the defendant stating in his or her own words what each legal right means. The second part of the test asks the defendant to compare each of the statements to other legally relevant statements and see whether they are the same or different. The defendant is then asked to define each term and finally to use his or her understanding in a series of scenarios dealing with right to silence, assistance of counsel, and behavior in a courtroom.

Monahan and colleagues have developed the *MacArthur Competency Assessment Tool—Criminal Adjudication* (MACCAT-CA), an instrument for the assessment of competency to stand trial. It divides cognitive competency into knowledge, appreciation, and reasoning, giving the defendant several scenarios from which they have to show their ability to reason it through and discuss it coherently with their attorney. It has the distinct advantage over other briefer competency assessments in that it actually assesses ability to assist counsel, which other instruments do not.

In order to assess for the cognitive skills needed to make the complex decision about whether or not to seek an abortion for an unplanned pregnancy, Ambuel and Rappaport (1992) assessed six different category types in making the decision: (a) the type of conflict perceived, (b) whether the girl perceived herself as having social support, (c) whether the decision was based on volition or independent autonomy, (d) whether the global quality of her decision was based on applicable reasons and concerns, (e) whether she had considered both short-term and long-term consequences of her decision, and (f) richness, that is, whether her discussion of the variables she considered included the impact on herself, on others involved, and on the unborn child should she decide to raise it, and the psychological impact on herself, others, and the unborn child. These areas were measured using a scale created for each category for this purpose and are similar to those used in studies by Weithorn and others. In the Ambuel and Rappaport (1992) study, however, they actually questioned girls who were pregnant and at a clinic where they had to make a decision about whether to abort or not.

SUMMARY AND IMPLICATIONS FOR COUNSELORS AND THERAPISTS

Several of the legal abortion cases have tried to delay or place blocks in the way of women seeking to terminate their pregnancies. For example, in *Planned Parenthood of Southeastern Pennsylvania v. Casey*, the state law attempted to demand that only a particular type of counseling would occur. This included giving the women erroneous information about fetal development as well as showing them frightening pictures or videos allegedly of fetuses in utero. This tactic is still being used by those who belong to the Right to Life movement in their attempt to outlaw late-term abortions by claiming the fetus can feel pain during an abortion. We described the tactics used by antiabortion activists at Crisis Pregnancy Centers (CPCs) funded by the government in an earlier chapter. It is important for counselors and therapists to be sure that the cognitive knowledge that the girl or woman comes in with is accurate. Even if she doesn't raise the questions, the role of the counselor is to do so.

We sent questionnaires to psychologists and other mental health professionals known to provide therapy services to women via various feminist listservs to which they might belong. Interestingly, in their private practices, most of the responders have only seen one to two women when facing the decision of whether or not to have an abortion, although many of their clients have had successful abortions. In these cases, the psychologists responded that their clients were very knowledgeable and did not need their therapists' factual information about the abortion, including the short- and long-term consequences of their decision, but were able to utilize the therapists' assistance in developing a mental strategy for coping with their decision. It appears that most of the pre-abortion counseling was conducted by workers at the centers where abortions are performed. None of the psychologists reported difficulties that their clients might have had with their decision post-abortion.

Given the small number of responses to our queries, it may be that traditional therapists have not been the people to whom girls and women turn when they need help in making the actual decision to abort or not. However, they may need to talk with their therapists about the consequences on their future mental health even if they have already made a decision to terminate the pregnancy. We believe that given the growing number of CPCs, women and girls who respond to their misleading advertisements may become psychologically confused from the strategies used by these centers to prevent the girls and women from choosing abortion. Therefore, it is important for private therapists to be informed so as to help clear up these clients' confusion.

In the next few chapters we discuss some of the major areas the woman should explore in order to feel comfortable that she has made the best decision. Chapter 4 deals with health care information common to what happens when a woman chooses to have the abortion, and Chapter 5 deals with understanding the typical emotions involved.

REFERENCES

Ambuel, B., & Rappaport, J. (1992). Developmental trends in adolescents' psychological and legal competence to consent to abortion. *Law & Human Behavior, 16*, 129–153.

American Psychological Association Interdivisional Committee on Adolescent Abortion. (1987). Adolescent abortion: Psychological and legal issues. *American Psychologist, 42*, 73–78.

Bersoff, D. N., Malson, L. P., & Ennis, B. J. (1985, August 21). APA files Amicus Brief in *Thornberg v. American College of Obstetricians and Gynecologists*. Retrieved April 12, 2007 from http://www.apa.org/psyclaw/thornburgh.pdf

Bersoff, D. N., Ogden, D. W. (1987, March 16). APA files Amicus Brief in *Jane Hodgson v. State of Minnesota*. Retrieved April 12, 2007 from http://www.apa.org/psyclaw/thornburg.pdf

Bersoff, D. N., Podolsky, S. R., & Schneider, M. D. (1989, September 1). APA files Amicus Brief in *State of Ohio v. Akron Center for Reproductive Health et al*. Retrieved April 12, 2007 from http://www.apa.org/psyclaw/reproductivehealth.pdf

Carter, L. S., Weithorn, L. A., & Behrman, R. E. (1999). Domestic violence and children: Analysis and recommendations. *The Future of Children. Special Issue: Domestic violence and children, 9*(3), 4–20.

Gardner, W., & Scherer, D. T. (1989). Asserting scientific authority: Cognitive developmental and adolescent legal rights. *American Psychologist, 44,* 895–902.

Gilligan, C. (1982). *In a different voice: Psychological theory and women's development.* Cambridge, MA: Harvard University Press.

Grisso, T. (2004). *Double jeopardy: Adolescent offenders with mental disorders.* Chicago: University of Chicago Press.

Grisso, T., & Applebaum, P. (1998). *Assessing competency to consent to treatment: A guide for physicians and other health professionals.* New York: Oxford University Press.

Grisso, T., Borum, R., & Edens, J. F. (2005). *Evaluating competencies: Forensic assessment and instruments.* New York: Springer.

Gruber, E., & Anderson, M. (1990). Legislating parental involvement in adolescent abortion: Reexamining the arguments of Worthington and his colleagues. *American Psychologist, 45,* 1174–1176.

Herman, J. (1992). *Trauma & recovery.* New York: Basic Books.

In re Gault, 387 U.S. 1, 1967.

Inhelder, B., & Piaget, J. (1958). *The growth of logical thinking from childhood to adolescence.* New York: Basic Books.

Kohlberg, L. (1981). *The Meaning and Measurement of Moral Development. Vol. 13., Clark U. Heinz Werner Institute: Worcester: MA*

Levant, R., & Kopecky, G. (1995). *Masculinity reconstructed: Changing the rules of manhood—at work, in relationships, and in family life.* New York: Dutton.

Lewis, C. C. (1980). A comparison of minors' and adults' pregnancy decisions. *American Journal of Orthopsychiatry, 50,* 446–453.

Lewis, C. C. (1987). Minors' competence to consent to abortion. *American Psychologist, 42,* 84–88.

Marecek, J. (1987). Counseling adolescents with problem pregnancies. *American Psychologist, 42,* 89–93.

Monahan, J., Steadman, H. J., Silver, E., Applebaum, P. S., Robbins, P. C., Mulvey, E. P., et al. (2001). *Rethinking risk assessment: The MacArthur Study of Mental Disorder and Violence.* New York: Oxford University Press.

Ogden, D. W., & Kappler, A. M. (1991, October). APA files Amicus Brief in *Planned Parenthood of S. E. Pennsylvania v. Casey.* Planned Parenthood of Southeastern PA v. Casey, 505 U.S. 833, (1992).

Rubin, L., & Russo, N. F. (2004). Abortion and mental health: What therapists need to know. In J. C. Chrisler (Ed.), *From menarche to menopause: The female body in feminist therapy.* New York: Haworth Press.

Sternberg, R. (2005). *Cognitive psychology* (4th ed.). San Francisco, CA: Wadsworth Publishing.

Weithorn, L. A. (1982). Developmental factors and competence to make informed treatment decisions. *Child & Youth Services, 5*(1–2), 85–100.

Weithorn, L. A. (2006). The legal contexts of forensic assessment of children and families. In S. N. Spart & G. P. Koocher (Eds.), *Forensic mental health assessment of children and adolescents.* New York: Oxford University Press.

Weithorn, L. A., & Campbell, S. B. (1982). The competency of children and adolescents to make informed treatment decisions. *Child Development, 53*(6), 1589–1598.

Worthington, E. L., Larson, D. B., Brubaker, M. W., Colecchi, C., Berry, J., & Morrow, D. (1989). The benefits of legislation requiring parental involvement prior to adolescent abortion. *American Psychologist, 44,* 1542–1545.

CHAPTER 4

Facts, Not Myths, About Women's Reproductive Health

It is important to those who are counseling women who are thinking about an abortion to have accurate, current information about abortion. Earlier chapters have delineated the political realities affecting women and girls who go to an abortion center, the laws that continue to rule the legal aspects of abortion, and the cognitive abilities that women and girls must have in order to make a fully informed decision about what to do about an unwanted pregnancy. As is obvious, despite the numerous challenges to the dictum in *Roe v. Wade,* set down 34 years ago, abortion is still legal and medically safe in the United States and other countries, especially during the first trimester of pregnancy. Late-term abortions, usually after 32 weeks, are more controversial, and Congress and certain states have passed laws, insisting that regulations are necessary to protect the safety of the woman and fetus. Most of these laws have not survived legal challenges. On April 18, 2007, the U.S. Supreme Court voted to uphold the Partial-Birth Abortion Act of 2003. While it is still too early to understand the impact of this recent USSC case (*Gonzales v. Carhart,* 127 S.CT. 1610), there is no doubt that it will have serious implications for the provision of abortion services.

All of the legal challenges after *Roe v. Wade* have given the states the right to regulate women's access to obtain an abortion in the third trimester of pregnancy. Other legal challenges, as reviewed in Chapter 1, have included restrictions on financing the abortion, parental notification or consent if the woman is under the age of 18, and whether or not mandatory counseling and waiting periods are in the states' interests. In this chapter, we focus our attention on the information therapists and counselors need to know to help women who are considering having an abortion sort out facts from myths. This is especially important to help counselors and therapists understand what the women are exposed to when, by law, they are given information by state-approved agencies.

Some agencies, in addition to Crisis Pregnancy Centers (CPCs), that publish pamphlets purporting to give women factual information about abortion, distort the information to influence women to not have an abortion. They may publish pictures of fetuses supposedly at different stages of development to try to scare the woman into believing that the gamete (an egg fertilized by the sperm that is beginning its cell division) or fetus (once the gamete has developed mostly human characteristics but still dependent upon the mother's body for continued development) looks like a fully functioning baby by substituting pictures of neonates (newborns). In some cases, the materials may erroneously state medical procedures that are not accurate or public policies that do not exist or are illegal under the law.

The most serious and blatant error made by these so-called factual materials that are required to be available or actually distributed to women seeking abortion is the claim that there is a post-abortion syndrome that causes women psychological distress many years after they have an abortion. In fact, though, no psychological sequelae caused by having an abortion have been scientifically validated. We discuss the available research in Chapter 6. However, some women who have psychological issues prior to becoming pregnant and choose to terminate the pregnancy may have short- or long-term psychological reactions that are similar to what they might have when carrying a fetus to term and giving birth. These emotional issues are complex, and we discuss this further in Chapter 5 and Chapter 6. In this chapter we discuss information to assist counselors and therapists both in answering their clients' questions that require factual information and in helping their clients sort through the myriad of information they obtain, helping them to recognize what information may not be accurate.

UNIVERSAL CLAIM TO WOMEN'S REPRODUCTIVE RIGHTS AND HEALTH

Is the United States the Only Country Permitting Legalized Abortion?

No, the United States is not the only country permitting legalized abortion; in fact, the United States only performs 3% of all the abortions performed around the world. Approximately one-half of the abortions performed worldwide, mostly in developing countries, are not legal or safe. Although the legal right to an abortion is regulated by the laws of individual states and countries, the international community has issued proclamations that call for worldwide respect for women's reproductive rights and health. These proclamations appear in several arenas, most notably the World Health Organization (WHO) and the United Nations Declaration of Women's Rights. The Hyde Amendment that was passed in 1976 by the U.S. Congress and its subsequent additions does not permit the United States to give money to agencies that use those funds to pay for abortions unless the woman became pregnant through rape or incest. This means that poor women whose health services are funded by Medicaid, women with disabilities on Medicare, or even women in other countries whose health care depends on U.S. financial aid are unable to obtain an abortion unless they have their own funding. However, private foundations may do so, or the countries themselves can and do provide access to safe abortions consistent with their own health policies.

Obviously, this policy is a bias toward promoting childbirth, the costs of which are provided through public funding. Legislative battles over funding for birth control have also been part of this debate. Many believe that the so-called abortion wars set the policy for all of women's lives, making it a human rights issue (Brownmiller, 2003). Unless women can control their own reproductive functions, which only last for less than one-third of women's expected life spans today, their ability to choose other areas of their lives, including many careers, is compromised.

The WHO Definition of Women's Health

The WHO, with offices in Geneva, Switzerland, is the organization that studies health around the world, collects statistics on diseases, and issues proclamations on best practices. The definition of women's health that is articulated in the WHO constitution's preamble is often said to be the definition that is most widely accepted. Health is said to be an obligation of all nations, which must foster the health of its citizens. Health is broadly defined as, ". . . a state of complete physical, mental, and social well-being and not merely the absence of disease and infirmity" (WHO, 1948). Reproductive health is considered a part of this definition, and WHO has convened various study groups and issued reports suggesting best practices that include access for women to safe abortions as a fundamental human right. It is estimated that half of all unwanted pregnancies around the world will end in an abortion, with almost 15% ending in the woman's death, usually from an illegal or unsafe procedure. According to

Feitshans (1998), a legal advisor to the WHO Committee of Experts on Reproductive Health at Work, the WHO preamble further states:

> The enjoyment of the highest attainable standard of health is one of the fundamental rights of every human being. . . . The achievement of any State in the promotion and protection of health is of value to all. (p. 94)

The contribution to the overall health of people all over the world as a fundamental human right cannot be emphasized enough. The call for nations to respect human rights of its citizens is loudly heard around the world, with many organizations set up to respect these rights. As the United States belongs to the international community, it must respect and follow the WHO's call to develop strategies to help cure and prevent disease and infirmity among its citizens. This includes promotion of reproductive health and should allow WHO to study issues relating to abortion and other areas of reproductive health even if there is no actual threat of disease present. A 1998 conference to create a new plan for nations to follow outlined the types of reproductive health issues for women that have been raised around the world (Feitshans, 1998). Among the various issues studied at this conference, such as increased exposure of pregnant women to toxins in the workplace, increase in reported cases of violence, rape, and incest, new technologies that permit a variety of reproductive strategies, and issues of termination of pregnancies, countries were challenged to review their policies to meet worldwide standards for women's reproductive health, including access to safe and legal abortions.

Often clients believe that they are committing a sin or engaging in a shameful act when making the decision to have an abortion. It may be helpful for them to be aware that the world community believes it is one of their fundamental human rights to make this decision on behalf of their own needs. Obviously, many countries including the United States have laws that state that the fundamental human right of choice is balanced by the interests of the state, which has been translated into the battle between those who favor choice and those who do not.

United Nations Conferences on the Status of Women

The United Nations (UN) is another worldwide organization that studies issues around health and social status and issues policy statements. The UN Charter also recognizes the human rights of women to good health standards, and the organization provides a forum to discuss ways to achieve this human right. In Article 13 of the UN Charter, the member nations state their aspiration to "promote" the economic and social advancement and "better standards of life, including the promotion of human rights protections" (UN Charter, Art. 13, ¶ 1, as stated in Feitshans, 1998).

In the 1970s, beginning with a conference of delegates held in Mexico, a major conference on population held in Cairo, and concluding, at least at this time, with a conference in Beijing, P. R. China, in 1995, the UN studied ways that nations could improve the status of women in their countries. During the mid 1970s, in the United States, each state held a Conference on Women to select its priorities for women to reach equality and elect a slate of delegates to attend the national Conference on Women held in Houston in 1977. Author Lenore Walker was elected a delegate from Colorado and attended the Houston conference and the subsequent Third UN Conference on Women in Nairobi, Kenya, in 1985. Using what they called platforms of issues, delegates gave reports of the status of women in each of their countries and debated the best practices in these issues at the meetings, and then the UN issued a series of reports together with policy statements designed to encourage member nations to upgrade the status of women toward equality with men. Interestingly, although the U.S. has never ratified the Equal Rights Amendment (E.R.A.) to its Constitution, which would give women equality under the law, other countries and worldwide organizations such as the UN, have made it clear that women and men are not treated as equals, that equality is considered a fundamental human right, and further, that such inequality has many negative consequences. One of those negative consequences is the detrimental impact on women's mental health which can then impact on their self-esteem and ability to seek an education, plan a career, or take other actions to achieve all they can become.

Equal access to health services and the elimination of all forms of violence against women are two of the eight points for action in the Beijing Declaration, which guided the discussions at the U.N. Fourth World Conference on Women (1995) and resulted in the expanded Platform for Action that followed. Both documents were adopted unanimously as part of the "comprehensive plan of action to enhance the social, economic, and political empowerment of women" and include a comprehensive plan for women's health. Not surprisingly, many of the member countries that oppose abortion were reluctant to have reproductive health issues included in the document, especially since they had experience with the power of these documents from the outcome of the Cairo conference (see Hasselgrave & Harvard, 1995) but eventually compromise language was reached, and women's access to adequate health services remains one of the fundamental human rights (Pitanguy, 1995). This is important as it permits the UN divisions to participate in and encourage other worldwide organizations to study the scientific areas that are important in reproductive and other health technologies as they develop.

One of the interesting areas of law that is debated at these scientific meetings is the balance between special protections for women, such as those needed in the workplace to protect pregnant women and their fetuses from toxic substances, and the need to achieve equality of women and men that can be reached by not treating women differently from men. However, just taking the issue of exposure to toxic substances as an example, it is mostly women who work in low-paying jobs, in either the formal or informal labor market, where they are exposed to tedious and unhealthy conditions. But, if women are to be reassigned to other jobs, and there are no other comparable jobs, then their status is not being improved. If employers are legally liable for protectionism, will they then favor hiring men and not women? In either case, women are not really being protected unless there are penalties for employers to create a safe workplace for both men and women, equally. This raises the issue of basic health protections versus special protections for women and the continuing argument that women will never be equal to men unless they control their own reproductive health issues. So, despite the success in the international arena, the future of women's access to acceptable health conditions will continue to be the responsibility of each country (see Bunch, 1995, for further discussion).

Mandatory Disclosure of Health Care Information

The results of several of the legal cases in the United States have required mandatory disclosure of health care information and a 24- to 48-hour waiting period before performing an abortion. Detailed information regarding mandatory disclosure of health care information and waiting periods can be found in Chapter 1; a state by state guide including mandatory disclosure of health care information and waiting periods can be found in Appendix 2. The Informed Consent provisions in *Planned Parenthood of Southeastern Pennsylvania v. Casey* are a good example of requiring exaggerated and misleading information. The American Psychological Association (APA) (Ogden & Kappler, 1991) entered an Amicus Curiae brief that in part stated that the requirement that health care professionals must offer materials that contain "objective information describing . . . the possible detrimental psychological effects of abortion" (18 Pa. C.S.A. p3208 [a] [2]) "conveys the false and misleading impression that abortions are more likely than alternatives to abortion to produce such detrimental effects" (Ogden & Kappler, 1991, p. 20).

Research, as cited subsequently and in Chapter 6, demonstrates that the psychological effects from abortion are rarely negative and that the alternatives to abortion are not always psychologically benign (Russo & Zierke, 1992). Studies demonstrate that potential negative psychological effects may occur from carrying a fetus to term and placing the infant for adoption (Condon, 1986), and postpartum depression has been found to occur in approximately 10% of mothers studied (Harding, 1989). Some women kill their newborn infants or children after they are born as discussed below (McKee, 2006). The National Academy of Sciences (1975) study found no significant harm from legalized abortion. Even former U.S. Surgeon General C. Everett Koop testified before Congress that there is only a "miniscule" likelihood of the development of significant psychological problems related to abortion (Koop, 1989). Given these findings, none of which has demonstrated any greater risk from having an abortion or alternative choices when a woman becomes pregnant, it is unnecessary and suggests bias when requiring counseling other than what is needed for informed consent as is customary and usual in all health care decisions.

WOMEN'S ACCESS TO PROPER HEALTH CARE

Do U.S. Women Have Access to Proper Health Care?

Alice

Alice, a 35-year-old woman with two children, ages 5 and 12, was in the middle of a highly contested divorce from her husband, who had beaten her and kept her locked in their home for many years. Believing that Alice was his sexual property because they were married, her husband would force her to have sex without using any birth control. She had eight abortions during their 15-year marriage in addition to the two pregnancies he permitted her to carry to term. When her youngest child was 3 years old, Alice had what was diagnosed as a mild heart attack or a panic attack after another beating. Their housekeeper called an ambulance. which brought her to the hospital, but her husband signed her out of the hospital against medical advice before diagnostic tests were completed. However, this incident gave Alice the courage to seek legal advice, and she filed for divorce, ultimately losing primary custody of her children. Mourning her losses, Alice found a lover and she became pregnant again during the pending divorce. She discussed her options with her therapist and decided that she would terminate the pregnancy by having an abortion. One of the most important factors that figured into Alice's decision to have another abortion was learning that if she carried this pregnancy to term, the baby would legally belong to her husband, as she was not yet legally divorced when she became pregnant. Only if her husband or her lover challenged paternity in court would she have the legal ability to keep this baby out of the custody issue already being contested. This case illustrates the need for counselors to help the woman learn about the legal issues that might be involved.

Joann

Joann, a 28-year-old married woman with three children, became pregnant for a fourth time while, unbeknownst to anyone, she was addicted to cocaine. Coming from a wealthy family, Joann had access to her own money and was able to afford to obtain and use an increasing amount of the drug. She claimed that she needed the stimulation and energy that cocaine gave her, and it also served as an appetite suppressant so she could keep her thin figure. Joann decided that she neither could emotionally cope with raising another child nor could she tolerate the risk of her baby being born with the effects commonly seen in cocaine-exposed fetuses. These factors were considerations in her decision to obtain an abortion and demonstrates the importance of counselors having accurate information about drug exposure on the various stages of development of the fetus.

Suzanne

Suzanne, a 19-year-old college freshman, found herself pregnant after her first sexual experience with the 19-year-old man she was dating at that time. She was unsure of her feelings for this man, as they had only been dating a short time when they decided to have consensual sex. Although he used a condom, it slipped off while he was withdrawing his penis from her vagina. Suzanne was upset; she had been told by her friends to make the man use a condom to prevent sexually transmitted diseases (STDs) and HIV transmission. She did not realize that condoms could fail to protect her from becoming pregnant. By the time she found out she was pregnant, she and the man were no longer dating each other. After looking at all her options, Suzanne decided to have an abortion.

Cathy

Cathy, a 15-year-old high school freshman, became pregnant after having sex with Steve, her boyfriend of 2 years. Cathy's parents were very strict and if things didn't go the way her father expected, he would yell, scream, hit, and eventually beat up her mother. Only Steve knew how difficult Cathy's home life situation was for her. She never invited girlfriends to her home so they were never exposed to Cathy's father's violence. Both Cathy and Steve decided that they were too young and unable to care for a baby at this time of their lives. Therefore, they decided to abort the pregnancy. When they went to the abortion clinic together, they had to walk through a gauntlet of protestors, screaming at them and taunting them with their signs that had pictures of fetuses at different stages of development.

In each of these cases, Cathy, Suzanne, Joann, and Alice had considered all the relevant alternatives and made a decision to obtain an abortion before they went to their local abortion clinic. Providing factual information for each of them at that time, even if it was absolutely accurate which these brochures rarely are, is unnecessary and burdensome and if it is inaccurate or designed to cause distress could itself to be the factor that causes the woman troublesome negative thoughts and feelings. Lemkau (1988) found that "The sociocultural environment in which women make abortion decisions reinforces ambivalence at best, and at worst introduces negative thoughts and feelings with which women might not otherwise be troubled" (Lemkau, 1988, p. 461).

Alice lived in the southeast region of the United States and did not have access to a clinic. Rather, after an appointment at a gynecology clinic that was located a long distance from her home, she was given all the required information and then referred to a private doctor nearer to where she lived. As it was the same doctor who had performed the last abortion she had, Alice recounted feeling comfortable about going there until she made the phone call to set up the procedure and the doctor sounded different than the last time she had contacted him. When she arrived at the office where the abortion was going to be performed, she stated that the doctor was angry with her for getting pregnant again. Already feeling upset at herself for allowing herself to get into this position again, she felt that the doctor was very rough and rude to her. Of course, there is no way to know if her repeated abortions caused her difficulty in healing this time or if it was the doctor's personal feelings getting in the way of how the procedure was performed. In either case, Alice did not have access to the best health care but, rather, felt forced to follow the advice of the only clinic near where she lived.

What should Alice have expected in terms of health care? First, she should have had access to a competent physician who would not permit his or her own emotions to get in the way of delivering good health care. This might have included some time to find out why this woman had so many abortions. He could have referred her to a family planning counselor or to a specialist in working with trauma victims if Alice reported the domestic violence she experienced by her husband as the cause for the earlier abortions. If Alice had any aftereffects from the last abortion, it might well have been because of the treatment from that doctor, and not the procedure itself.

In Joann's case, it was different. She went to her own physician but didn't tell the doctor about her cocaine use. Rather, she simply said she was depressed and couldn't possibly take care of another child. No questions were asked and the procedure was performed without any problems in the doctor's office, 2 weeks after Joann missed her last period and the pregnancy test that she purchased from her local pharmacy showed positive. Perhaps she might have had a spontaneous abortion if the fetus had been damaged by the cocaine, but perhaps not. Joann was financially able to make her own decision and had access to the resources where she lived.

Suzanne went to the health clinic at her university and told the medical staff there about her unwanted pregnancy and her desire to have an abortion. They immediately gave her a referral to a Planned Parenthood clinic nearby, and within a short period of time, she was given an appointment, underwent brief counseling, and had the procedure done. She was back in class the next day and went on with her life, after being fitted for a diaphragm and taught how to use it as either primary or secondary birth control.

Cathy's experience was not so good. Although she did not want to tell her mother, fearing that both she and her mother would be in danger of her father's violent temper if he found out, the clinic she went to called her mother to notify her of Cathy's choice. Her father was at home, listened in on the conversation, as is common for controlling abusers, and when Cathy came home that evening, she found her mother sobbing in the bedroom with fresh bruises all over her body. Her mother urged Cathy to leave the house to escape from her father's wrath, which she did. However, her father showed up at the girlfriend's house looking for Cathy, dragged her out of the house, and beat up Cathy so badly that she had a spontaneous abortion from the beating. The clinic violated Cathy's privacy and privilege by making that phone call without her permission, and the staff failed to inform Cathy about the judicial bypass procedure whereby she could have applied to the court to have the judge determine if she was mature enough to make the decision to abort the pregnancy without having to tell her mother. It is rare that the judges who sit on the bypass court find the minor girl incompetent to have an abortion, as they usually can articulate a good reason why they do not want to tell their parents that they are pregnant. Obviously, Cathy did not get the access to proper health care to which she was entitled.

These stories are not meant to be an indictment of doctors or clinics. Rather, they illustrate the unnecessary burden these laws have placed on four different women, each of whom had made up their own minds about their inability to go forward with the pregnancy. Other women need the advice and counseling of professionals, and it should be available to them. Alice might not have had so many pregnancies if she had access to appropriate counseling earlier in her life. Her abusive husband kept her prisoner in their own home and controlled her access to accurate information. When Cathy had to walk through the gauntlet of screaming protesters outside the abortion clinic, it predictably would have retraumatized her, given her experiences with a screaming and controlling father who forced her into following his decisions rather than her own.

Elsewhere in this book you will read about the danger at abortion clinics to the staff, the clients, and their property. Obviously, the protesters may be creating more of an unsafe health condition for women than if they found other ways to express their disagreement with the laws that permit women to choose a healthy and safe way to terminate their pregnancy.

What Is a Safe Procedure?

Women should seek an abortion from a state-licensed clinic whose staff participates with the several organizations that help set the guidelines for medically safe abortions. The two most popular groups are the Planned Parenthood Centers and the National Abortion Federation (NAF). Most women probably will experience the routine procedure that is commonly practiced with women who do not have any complications. Many therapists who have not had an abortion themselves and will counsel women should be familiar with these procedures to help women making this choice sort out the accurate objective facts from those that are intended to manipulate or bias the woman in one way or another. Rubin and Russo (2004) describe some of the dangers of misattribution suggested by the literature. They suggest that "attributing the cause of a negative event to circumstances results in sadness. In contrast, attributing the cause to others results in anger, contempt, and disgust" (p. 78). Some women may feel sad after an abortion, but as is described in Chapters 6 and 7, this feeling is natural and usually transitory.

Description of Steps for a Typical Abortion

Day of Appointment

In situations where the abortion is performed during the same day that the woman comes to the facility, several functions are performed in a fairly routine way. The surgical procedure is the least time-consuming part of the process.

1. *Check-in.* When a patient arrives for a procedure, she will check in with the person at the front desk and take a seat in the main waiting room with whomever accompanied them. Usually the clinic requires the patient to be accompanied by another person because driving home might be difficult and it gives her someone to be with in between the various functions. There may be magazines, newspapers, and even a movie playing in the waiting room.

2. *Sonogram.* The first time a patient is called back will be for a sonogram to precisely determine the length of pregnancy. The patient will return to the waiting room.

3. *Laboratory analysis.* Then the patient will be called back to have her lab work done. This will consist of urinalysis, Rh typing, hemoglobin level analysis, and blood pressure screening. She then returns to the waiting room while the lab work is being analyzed.

4. *Abortion counselor.* The next time the patient is called back she will speak with an abortion counselor. The counselor will discuss the patient's options, ensuring that she is certain about her decision to terminate the pregnancy. The counselor will ask about the patient's support system, including who she has told about the pregnancy and her decision to have an abortion and if they are supportive of her decision. The counselor will ask about and address the patient's feelings about abortion and how she will feel after her procedure.

5. *Medical history and informed consent.* The counselor will review the patient's medical history and informed consent forms for the procedure. Unless the patient requests otherwise, the counselor will typically describe what the procedure involves and what to expect when she goes home. The patient will receive both verbal and written aftercare instructions. In addition the counselor will discuss future birth control options for the patient after the procedure. If the patient has any questions, concerns, or problems she is instructed to call the center, which has a 24-hour answering service and on-call physician.

6. *Review of medical history and explanation of procedure and aftercare.* During the counseling session, a trained staff member will review her medical history together with her, explain the procedure to be used and the aftercare instructions, and answer any questions she may have. The woman's guest is invited to share in the informational session only if the woman agrees. However, the guest returns to the waiting area during the actual surgical procedure itself.

7. *Surgical procedure.* The next step in the process is the surgery itself, which is a very safe and simple procedure that usually lasts approximately 3 minutes. It is done in a special room reserved for this procedure so it remains sterile and has whatever medical facilities are necessary.

8. *Recovery.* At the conclusion of the procedure, the woman will then be in a recovery area. If she wishes, at some point, the person who accompanied her will be permitted to stay with her.

9. *Aftercare instructions, birth control, and follow-up information.* Prior to discharge, the woman is given oral and written aftercare instructions and birth control information. A follow-up appointment may be scheduled, or she may go to her own doctor for further medical care.
10. *Discharge and return home.* Within a few hours the procedure is completed and the woman is encouraged to return home and rest for a period of time.

After surgery, patients will remain in the recovery room with our nurses for approximately 30–40 minutes. When she goes home we expect she will be able to return to normal activities within the next day or so. Should she need any additional assistance, trained staff members are always available to speak with the patient and their support system.

What Are the Actual Abortion Techniques Typically Used Today?

There are three major procedures used in an abortion today: (a) dilation and curettage with vacuum aspiration, or D & C, (b) dilation and evacuation, or (D & E), and (c) medical abortion. These procedures are further described in the following sections.

Dilation and Curettage/Vacuum Aspiration (First-Trimester Abortion Procedure).

Commonly called a D & C, the dilation and curettage is the most widely used surgical procedure used today during first-trimester abortions. It is considered a safe, minor surgical procedure that can be performed using general, twilight, or local anesthesia. In this procedure the vagina is widened with a speculum, and a topical anesthetic like lidocaine is applied to the cervix, which covers the opening to the uterus where the pregnancy may have migrated after being fertilized in the fallopian tube. The cervix is widened with a dilating rod, and a tube is inserted to remove the pregnancy by suction. In a procedure that is required to be spread over 24 hours, a natural material called laminaria may be inserted into the cervix, and as the laminaria expands from the fluids in the vaginal canal, the cervix gently opens, permitting a tube to be inserted when the laminaria is removed. This is more often used in second-trimester procedures. A suction instrument is attached to the tube that draws out any foreign material in the uterus. This process may also be called vacuum aspiration. The doctor may then use a surgical instrument called a curette to gently clean the walls of the uterus.

This is similar to the process used after childbirth when the uterus does not expel all its contents or as a way to eliminate the contents of the uterus that might be causing painful menstruation. Prior to the vacuum suction process being used to remove the contents of the uterus, its walls are scraped by the curette and contents are scraped out. The vacuum suction process is a much less invasive method of cleansing the uterus. In fact, Brownmiller describes how women used to train themselves to do a vacuum suction abortion prior to its legalization as a less lethal intervention (Brownmiller, 1999).

Dilation and Evacuation (Second-Trimester Abortion Procedure).

In the second trimester, a dilation and evacuation procedure, commonly called a D & E, may be performed. The first step in a D & E, just like in the D & C, is to dilate the cervix. This is often begun about a day before the surgical procedure by inserting osmotic dilators like laminaria or dilapan. The patient may be given a pain reliever prior to insertion of dilators. The patient goes home with these dilators in place and may be given instructions to take a pain reliever or antibiotic, or both, once at home. The cervix, which is a complex muscle, becomes thicker and harder as the pregnancy progresses so it is a more difficult process the longer the woman waits for an abortion. She usually returns the next day to complete the procedure.

On the second day, the patient may be given a medicine called misoprostol to facilitate dilating the cervix. The patient receives either a local, twilight, or general anesthesia. The laminaria and dilapan are removed, and the contents of the pregnancy are removed using a combination of vacuum aspiration, curettage, and other surgical instruments, as necessary. The D & E procedure is very safe and also is completed in a few minutes.

A less common way that a second-trimester abortion may be performed is through the induction of labor. In this case premature labor may be induced with prostaglandin, a hormone that naturally starts labor in full-term women, and the contents of the pregnancy are passed through the vaginal canal.

Medical Abortion

Medical abortion is the newest method of terminating a pregnancy through chemical and nonsurgical means. Mifepristone was first known as RU-486 and has been used in France since 1988. This pill is most effective when taken between 5 and 7 weeks from the first day of the patient's last menstrual period. Medical abortion involves taking a series of medicines to pass the pregnancy contents at home. The first pill taken is mifepristone, sold in the United States under the brand Mifeprex. Mifepristone stops the development of the pregnancy. The patient may or may not have symptoms after taking this first pill.

At a set time 24–48 hours later, the patient then takes a prostaglandin such as misoprostol. The misoprostol causes the uterus to expel the pregnancy. The patient may be advised to take a prescription-strength pain reliever and an antibiotic. It is very important that the patient follow these directions closely and return to the provider for a check-up to ensure that the process was complete. If the process fails, misoprostol may be readministered or the patient may need to have a D & C to complete the abortion.

Box 4.1 presents a sample of aftercare instructions given after a woman has had a surgical abortion. Although these instructions may vary from center to center, they are usually discussed orally during the counseling session and then given to the woman as she leaves the facility.

Patient instructions for the nonsurgical or medical abortion described previously can be found in Box 4.2.

Box 4.1   Sample of Surgical Abortion Aftercare Instructions

1. Eat something! Start by sipping on a carbonated beverage and have something light to eat.
2. You may have taken your first dose of the medication in the recovery room. If not, take your medications:

    a. Metronidazole (Flagyl): One pill two times daily (or every 12 hours). This is an antibiotic to help prevent infection. Please take this medication with food and finish all of the medication. Do not drink alcohol while taking this medication.
    b. Ergonovine (Methergine or Methyloergonovine): One pill every 4 hours. This drug helps your uterus contract back to it original size. Cramping in your legs and abdomen is a normal side effect of this medication. Please finish all of this medication.
    c. Ibuprofen (Motrin): One pill every 6–8 hours for the first 3–4 days, then as needed. This is a prescription strength nonaspirin pain reliever that can be taken for abdominal cramping.
    d. Birth Control: If we have given you pills, please start them tonight. If you are interested in the NuvaRing you will be instructed on when to begin that when you return for your follow-up visit. Please refer to the information given with your birth control method. Please remember that the first cycle does not protect against pregnancy.

(continued)

Bleeding can range from no bleeding to bleeding like a menstrual period. The Ergonovine you are taking may stop the bleeding temporarily, so you may see an increase in the bleeding when this medication is finished. Bleeding can be irregular and light and may continue for up to 3 weeks.

Cramping is normal after an abortion. Cramping is a sign that your uterus is contracting back to its normal size. The ibuprofen prescribed should minimize your discomfort.

Blood clots are normal after an abortion. Passing clots can actually make you feel better.

Infection prevention is an important part of your aftercare. Your cervix is slightly dilated (open), and to prevent any bacteria from getting into your uterus, please use the following precautions until your follow-up visit (at least 2 full weeks):

1. Use pads, not tampons
2. No intercourse
3. Take showers instead of tub baths
4. No swimming
5. No douching

Activity, exercise, and prolonged standing should be kept to a minimum for the first week after an abortion. If you need a doctor's note for your job or school, please let us know.

Emotional responses may vary after an abortion. Hormonal changes may make you feel sad or moody following the procedure. These feelings usually pass within the first few weeks after the procedure. If you would like to speak to someone after the procedure, please call the office.

Breast tenderness is normal after an abortion. Sometimes within a few days of the procedure your breasts may enlarge and become tender. If this occurs put on a tight bra, apply ice packs to the breasts, and do not touch the breasts. This should only last for a day or two.

Follow-up exams are available at no charge for up to 1 month following the procedure. You may visit your own physician if you prefer.

Complications following an abortion are possible but not probable. Our office is available 24 hours a day to handle your concerns. Monday through Saturday, the office is open and available to answer any of your questions. Our staff is on call 24 hours for medical situations related to the procedure that occur after usual business hours. If you have any of the following conditions, please call the office anytime:

Soaking two maxi pads in 2 hours
Passing blood clots larger than 2 inches
Have a fever over 101° that is not relieved by Tylenol.
Feel faint or weak or have chills
Still feel pregnant after 1 week

(continued)

If you need to call the office, please be able to tell us when you had your abortion, how many pads you have used in the last 4 hours, your pharmacy phone number. If you think you have a fever, please take your temperature prior to calling. We are available 24 hours a day to help you avoid an unnecessary visit to an emergency room, which may result in unnecessary procedures and charges.

Box 4.2   Patient Instructions for the Nonsurgical Abortion

During the nonsurgical procedure you may experience moderate to severe cramping. Your Doctor has prescribed pain medication for you. You must fill these prescriptions at your local pharmacy. These medications may make you drowsy and impair your ability to drive, so please do not operate a motor vehicle while taking these medications. You may also supplement these medications with 500 mg of Tylenol: one to two tablets every 4–6 hours as needed. Be sure to schedule your time for this process appropriately. For example have someone available to help with childcare and reschedule work commitments or important tasks.

1. Today, _____, you have received Mifepristone to stop the development of pregnancy.
2. Today you will start taking Metronidazole (Flagyl) 500 mg twice daily for the next 3 days.
3. _____ morning, you will place four tablets between your cheek and gum. Allow the tablets to dissolve for 30 minutes and then swallow the remaining tablets.

- In approximately 2–7 hours you should start to experience moderate to severe cramping followed by heavy bleeding. The cramping has been described to be similar to bad menstrual or diarrhea cramps.
- The bleeding should be fairly heavy and have some blood clots for a few hours (2–8 hours) and then reduce to a light or moderate flow similar to a menstrual period.
- Too much bleeding is soaking two maxipads per hour for 2 hours in a row and should be reported to (*Name of center and phone number*).
- Light bleeding or spotting may continue for up to 3 weeks. Some women experience light bleeding until their next period.
- Do not take any medication containing aspirin until your follow-up visit.

(continued)

- Do not put anything in your vagina (do not have intercourse, douche, use tampons, take tub baths, or swim) until your follow-up visit.
- If you are breast feeding, do not breast feed for 48 hours after the Misoprostol insertion. There is no data available on the effects of Mifepristone or Misoprostol on a breast-feeding infant.

Please contact (*Name of center*) **immediately** if any of the following occur:

- **Sharp Abdominal Pain or "Feeling Sick"**—Symptoms may include sharp abdominal pain, weakness, vomiting, or diarrhea, with or without fever, more than 24 hours after inserting the tablets (Misoprostol) between your cheek and gum.
- **Fever**—In the days following your process, you have fever of 100.4° or higher that lasts for more than 4 hours.

These are possible symptoms of an infection that require immediate medical attention. Immediate medical treatment can prevent a potentially serious complication.

Surgical abortion is the preferred method of pregnancy termination. Medical abortion carries a higher risk of possible complication (1 in 1,000 versus .01 in 1,000 for the surgical procedure). Consistent with the most recent outcomes, (*Name of center*) recommends the surgical procedure.

Your follow-up appointment is scheduled for _____ **at** _____. **It is imperative for you to keep this appointment even if you no longer think you are pregnant. The only way to confirm the success of this procedure is through an ultrasound.** If you do not return for this visit you will be contacted by phone and certified mail, therefore the confidentiality of your visit may be jeopardized.

The symptoms described above are typical of this process. Your experience may be different from that stated above. If you have any questions or concerns regarding this process, please contact (*Name of center and phone number*). For medical emergencies, we are available 24 hours a day.

Patient signature: _____   Date: _____

Witness signature : _____   Date: _____

WHAT ABOUT WOMEN WHO DO NOT ABORT?

Women Who Abandon or Kill Their Babies

The debate about whether or not to have an abortion usually frames the question around the morality and values and rarely around looking at the alternatives, many of which have dire consequences for women and their children. Let's take a look at the women who kill or abandon their babies. The U.S. Department of Justice estimated that between 1976 and 1994, 13,744 children under the age of 10 were murdered in the United States (Bureau of Justice Statistics, 1997). Of these, 80% were under the age of 5, and almost one-third (31%) were under the age of 1. Many studies have found that these children were most likely killed by one or both parents or de facto parents who were caring for the child at the request of a parent (McKee, 2006). Biological mothers accounted for 30% of the child homicides in the last quarter of the 20th century (Bureau of Justice Statistics, 1997).

Even more staggering are the numbers of babies abandoned by their mothers at birth. In 1998, the latest year for which the U.S. government has statistics analyzed, an estimated 31,000 infants were abandoned by their mothers in hospitals or other public places. This was a 40% increase over a 7-year period (U.S. Department of Health and Human Services, 2004). The mortality rate for abandoned babies is quite high. In 1998, almost one-third of the babies found were dead. This is probably an underestimate given the numbers of mothers who were not known to be pregnant, who gave birth alone, and who buried or otherwise disposed of the babies' bodies. In one study, approximately two-thirds of the dead babies were accidentally discovered in trash cans or on the beach, none of whom were reported missing, confirming the intent of the new mothers to abandon the babies (McKee, 2006).

Recently, states and cities have attempted to protect these babies by passing legislation that permits mothers to leave newborn babies at safe places such as fire stations or hospitals without threat of discovery or prosecution. The babies that have been left there were adopted by families that wanted a child. This appears to be a satisfactory alternative for some mothers who are unable to care for their babies for a variety of reasons. It is not known how many of them might have opted for an abortion had there not been barriers in their way.

Studies indicate that the prospective mothers' attitudes toward their pregnancies will affect whether or not they emotionally bond with their babies. More on the capacity for emotional attachment is addressed in Chapter 5, but for here it is important to note that the research suggests that a large proportion of unwanted pregnancies will result in an inability of the mother to form an attachment with the baby, resulting in some form of child abuse or maltreatment even if it does not reach the point of homicide (Davis, 1994; David, Dytrych, & Matejcek, 2003; McKee, 2006). Obviously, family planning clinics are the first line solution to this dilemma, and there are many groups across the world that fund these clinics. Unfortunately, the U.S. laws, especially the Hyde Amendment, refuses to fund any family planning clinic that also provides abortions, making it even more difficult for women who know they cannot raise a child to obtain contraception that would prevent the pregnancy from occurring.

Adoption

We have not discussed the option of adoption as that is an area where there is enough information to fill the pages of another book for mental health counselors. Suffice it to say that many women who have gone through both an abortion and adoption believe that the emotional impact of the abortion is shorter and less emotionally devastating than giving up their child for adoption. The worry about the health and happiness of the child often follows the woman forever, especially on the anniversary of the child's birth each year. Many women carry the secret of childbirth and adoption to their graves, fearful of upsetting the life they made afterward.

The search of adoptees for their parents and parents for their adopted children fill the Internet, and detectives who specialize in this area flourish. This raises fear in the hearts of the adoptive parents who worry that they will lose the love of the child they have raised all these years. It is also worrisome for some mothers who do not want the child they placed for adoption to find them. There is a strong movement to open adoption records so that family health information at a minimum can be shared. Some suggest that adoptive parents and mothers who have placed their children for adoption should have regular contact, whereas others, particularly the adoptive family, feel that would be too intrusive. In any case, this area is still quite unsettled and needs more study as each of the parties, the child, the mother (and maybe the father), and the adoptive parents all have different needs that must be reconciled.

Common Reasons Women Give for Terminating Unwanted Pregnancies

According to research, women who terminate an unwanted pregnancy repeatedly give more than one reason for wanting to do so, with some reasons being more common than others. Most often their reasons include inadequate finances and inability to assume the responsibility of a child at that particular time. Sometimes, the woman has no other children, whereas in other cases she may believe that another baby will harm her ability to parent her other children. Another frequent reason given is the fact that having a baby at that time would sufficiently change the woman's life in an unwelcome way. Relationship problems, including issues around domestic violence and child abuse, are another frequently cited reason for favoring termination, including cases where the pregnancy occurred because of rape or incest. Health problems in the fetus, the woman, or the coconceiver also are frequently discussed as reasons to abort.

WOMEN'S NEED FOR A HEALTHY ENVIRONMENT WHEN PREGNANT

Numerous toxic substances can cause severe birth defects in the developing fetus should a pregnant woman be exposed to them. International and local laws regulate the workplace environment to protect pregnant women from chemicals or other commonly shared airborne substances known to be teratogens (substances that can cause fetal damage). But some substances are not known to cause damage until many people are harmed. Some of these substances are accidental spills such as those that occurred in the former-Soviet nuclear plant near Chernobyl or intentionally released like in the atomic bomb that the United States dropped on Hiroshima, Japan, during World War II. The list of suspected teratogens is sometimes so long that it is a wonder how anyone who leaves the house has a normal baby. And sometimes the home is an environmentally unsafe place, such as when there is asbestos in the insulation or other chemicals that may leak from dysfunctional heating systems. Biological toxins and germs are also known to be detrimental to fetal development. Simple childhood diseases such as measles can cause deformities, especially of the sensory and circulatory systems. In other cases, exposure to sex-linked genetic factors may also make a woman fairly certain about the decision to abort, especially if it is known that the fetus carries the gene for the genetic disorder. Advanced technology makes testing for certain diseases quite simple and not very intrusive today.

Of course, this is assuming the pregnant woman has a home in which she lives. Women who live or work on the streets have no protection from the elements. They often are poor and have very little resources, poor nutrition, and no prenatal medical care. Chronic diseases and airborne contagious infectious conditions all contribute to possibly compromise the fetal development in seen and unseen ways. But, the damage to the fetus may be moderated by other factors if such exposure is known. For example, the mother's exposure to HIV infection or the infant's exposure to the mother's possible HIV infection may be controlled through certain procedures taken during the delivery should the woman choose not to have an abortion. This information may be very important to those women when considering their choices. Abortion counselors should inquire about any exposure to toxic substances and help the woman understand what the possible effects might be on the baby and would be moderators should she choose not to terminate the pregnancy.

Even more salient for today's lifestyles are the toxic substances that fetuses are exposed to by the mother. Despite all the warnings about alcohol, street drugs such as cocaine and heroin, and prescription drugs, pregnant women who ingest them are exposing their fetuses to possible harm. Kubasek (1999) suggested that government estimates show 11% of pregnant women use illegal drugs during their pregnancies with the average cost per drug-exposed infant being around $1 million. These estimates usually do not include infants exposed to prescription medicines that later turn out to have negative impact on the developing fetus. In an attempt to prevent pregnant women from intentionally using drugs known to be teratogens, most prescription medications are labeled if they are known to have produced damaging effects in animal or human research. Prescribers are trained in knowing these drugs and what these labels mean so that they do not intentionally prescribe them to women who are known to be pregnant. However, in many cases, such as women who use antidepressant medications on a regular basis, by the time they find out they are pregnant, the damage may have been done.

The U.S. government adopted a policy of prosecuting women for prenatal drug abuse thinking the threat of prosecution might deter them from using illegal drugs, usually cocaine and heroin, during pregnancy. These prosecutions, using already established child protection criminal laws, hinged on two factors: first, that the viable fetus has the same legal status as a child (Barnes, 2005), and second, that the detention of these women would protect the fetus from the detrimental effects of the drugs. These policies were not well conceived even though the government's concern may be appropriate. In fact, of the 240 women from 35 states who have been prosecuted, only the State Supreme Court of South Carolina in a case called *Whitmer* upheld the conviction because of legal challenges to the limitation of the woman's freedom to reproduce and the inapplicability of a fetus being a victim of the various criminal laws that were cited (Kubasek, 1999).

From a psychological standpoint, many of these prenatally drug-exposed babies have problems with attachment and bonding issues resulting in their inability to be comforted when irritable, which in their first year or so of life can be close to 24 hours per day. Their language skills have been found to develop more slowly and they show difficulties in attachment to mothers or other caretakers, which later affects their interpersonal relationships with other children and adults. However, many of these babies are born into homes where they are exposed to other factors that are known to negatively affect their development, such as domestic violence, poverty, and racial discrimination. Thus, the exposure to the illegal drugs may not be the only factor causing their developmental problems. Surely, incarcerating their biological mother and placing the neonate in what could be a series of foster homes will not prevent these developmental issues from occurring and may indeed actually create or worsen their development (Walker, 1994).

PREPREGNANCY GENDER ISSUES

Another reason a woman may seek an abortion is to choose the sex of the baby. Sometimes parents want to select the sex to avoid known genetic sex-linked disorders, whereas others want to select the preferred sex. This latter reason is often thought to be less acceptable than others because the woman is not choosing whether or not to have a child but rather is using abortion as a way to select the sex of the child. It is assumed that if the fetus is a girl and the parents want a boy, then they will abort the girl and try to have a boy in the next pregnancy. As has been seen in some countries, such as China, under its one-child-per-family policy, sex selection is quite gender biased, with more families preferring to have boys than girls. However, in the Western world, reproductive technology is fairly sophisticated, and prepregnancy sex selection is more possible prior to impregnation. For example, it is known that X-chromosome-bearing sperm are somewhat heavier than Y-chromosome-bearing sperm. X-bearing sperm will produce a girl and Y-bearing sperm will produce a girl when mated with an ovum bearing two X chromosomes. For some time now, fertility clinics have known how to sort out the gametes and embryos according to gender, but now the technology is making it possible to sort out the sperm so gender can be determined in the petri dish prior to fertilization or implantation of the gamete or embryo in the woman's body (Davis, McKee, & Robertson, 1999).

Obviously, there are a number of arguments against using prepregnancy sex selection but most of them involve ethical and moral values. Research in countries that already use sperm-selection techniques have found that parents who choose this technique for preferences, even if for policy reasons such as in China, their resulting children are more likely to be raised in a sex-role-stereotyped environment rather than being able to make choices about education, career, family life, leisure activities, and so on. This argument extends to selection of other genetically linked characteristics such as skin, hair, and eye color, or even intelligence. This type of genetic engineering is frowned upon for the same reasons. In fact, the research demonstrates that the expectations that are associated with gender for those parents who choose to control it are usually paramount. Even so, there is some indication that these technologies will be better used than repeated abortions. Another argument against using prepregnancy sex selection is the cost. At this time the cost is something like $2,000 for each procedure, and it is unknown how many procedures will be needed until fertilization and implantation occur.

There have been some who have opposed the new reproductive technologies by arguing that somehow tampering with sperm selection may change the scientific nature of the DNA or genetic structure of the resulting fetus and subsequent child. There is no scientific validity to that argument. The genetic sex selection often done today is to use in vitro fertilization techniques in order to deselect male sperm in those couples where hereditary transmission of chromosome-related diseases is more likely to be transmitted to boys and not girls. It is still a lot of work, and usually only done when there are other fertility problems, but gender can be determined in the fertility clinic rather than by random selection and using abortion until the right gender is obtained.

MATERNAL–FETAL CONFLICTS

Another reason for wanting an abortion is when there are maternal–fetal conflicts, usually because of medical complications (Cherry, 1999). In these cases, various types of technology may be used to discover that the fetus is not developing normally or perhaps that its development threatens the health and life of the mother. The conflict arises when the pregnant woman refuses medical care for the fetus because it compromises her own health. For example, if a fetus is found to have spina bifida, which causes malformation of the spinal column, it may be correctable through fetal surgery. However, this surgery also involved an invasive surgical procedure through the woman's abdomen. Does she have the legal right to choose an abortion, which is a much less invasive procedure, over the maternal–fetal surgery? What if she refuses to have the surgery?

Nocon (1999) interprets the American College of Obstetricians and Gynecologists (ACOG) policies as a mandate to advocate for the mother when the maternal–fetal conflict occurs. However, the American Medical Association and the American Academy of Pediatrics both have a different policy, supporting the physician obtaining a court order to force the woman to protect the fetus if the risk to the mother is minimal and the invasive procedure would clearly prevent substantial and reversible harm to the fetus. Interestingly, in his discussion, Nocon also raises the issue of a woman who refuses to take AZT therapy and a cesarean delivery even though she knows she is HIV infected and knows that cesarean delivery is safer for to avoid transmission of HIV to the baby but more dangerous to her own health (Nocon, 1999). Furthermore, the timing of starting

AZT therapy may compromise her own immune system's response. Here, mandatory testing can discover that the pregnant woman has the infection and the procedures can help eliminate the spread of the infectious disease. While the issue of choice of terminating this pregnancy may not be relevant in this type of case if the testing has been done during the last trimester of pregnancy or this woman wants to terminate a subsequent pregnancy, it is possible that the woman may be compelled to take the treatment and cesarean delivery because it is a compelling state interest to stop the transmission of HIV and AIDS.

DISPUTES ON FROZEN EMBRYOS

Yet another reason for considering an abortion surrounds the legal issues that arise when a married couple decides to get divorced and there are frozen embryos available for implantation from a prior in vitro fertilization or assisted reproductive technology (ART). Most state laws covering the responsibility for parenting a child attribute such responsibility to the parents. When a marriage is dissolved, or in the process of dissolving, the parental responsibility may be apportioned according to a stipulated agreement or by court order. However, the fetus is considered the responsibility of both parents even if the father or mother is not the coconceiver or the gametes are implanted into someone else, or both, unless the paternity is challenged. Given these new reproductive technologies, issues over ownership of the frozen gametes and embryos have been sent to the courts to resolve creating an interesting law that appears to be based on the jurisprudence of abortion starting with the individual's right to choose not to procreate (Daar, 1999).

The first case upon which most of the subsequent cases followed was called *Davis v. Davis* and occurred in Tennessee. The Davis couple had been using IVF for an ART procedure and had obtained a number of frozen embryos for future implantations, as the first two were unsuccessful. After the second unsuccessful attempt, they decided to divorce. Ms. Davis wanted to continue trying to become pregnant and raise the child by herself, whereas Mr. Davis did not want to be a parent whether married or not so they put the issue before the courts. The case went all the way to the Tennessee Supreme Court, which established a three-part test in its opinion (Daar, 1999). First, the Court should ask what the parents want to do with the frozen embryos and follow their recommendations, if they agree. Obviously, they wouldn't be in front of the Court if they did agree, so this is not usually sufficient. However, it could be useful if one party died and prior to his or her death, made his or her preferences known. Second, the Court must look to the parties' prior agreements, especially those prior to conception. And, third, if no agreements are available, then the party wishing to avoid procreation should prevail, assuming the other party has a reasonable possibility of achieving parenthood in some other way. If not, then a balancing test should be used weighing the right to procreate with the right not to procreate.

Although these tests may be sufficient to determine legal ownership of the embryos, Daar suggests that the *Davis v. Davis* three-prong test may be unfair to women who undergo the IVF and ART procedure, which is quite invasive, long, and painful. In fact, under *Roe v. Wade,* after conception only the woman controls whether or not the embryo will become a child, at least during the first trimester. If the woman's only opportunity for procreation lies in using the reproductive-assisted technologies, then she may be denied the choice of whether to go further with her embryos, depending upon the man's decisions. Other court decisions have modified the initial one in *Davis v. Davis,* suggesting that the woman has sole right to determine the disposition of the frozen embryos within a reasonable time period after the IVF procedure (see, for example, *Kass v. Kass*). As this is a developing area of reproductive technologies and the law, it will be interesting to see where these legal decisions go in the next few years.

FAMILY VIOLENCE ISSUES

Finally, we come to the one theme that is clear in all the issues we discussed here: the high percentage of women and girls seeking abortion who are exposed to domestic violence. Although domestic violence cuts across all demographic groups and affects women and girls who are rich or poor, educated or not, occurs in all races, religions, ethnic groups, and cultures, its impact around reproductive health is hardest on the poor woman who has limited or no access to safe and legal health services. Although it is true that isolation is one of the factors found in families where domestic violence occurs, even if the women can get away for a brief period of time, the lack of adequate services limits their options. Girls who have been exposed to abuse or have been actually abused themselves are at a particular disadvantage, as Cathy was in the case presented in Chapter 2. These girls are unable to protect their mothers and themselves from the angry wrath of their violent fathers. And, if their coconceiver is also abusive, they are at an even greater risk for harm. These girls are at higher risk for abandoning, abusing, or even killing their unwanted babies as discussed previously.

Despite the public information detailing the high risk of violence in the family, the general public still questions the frequency with which it occurs and the reasons why women don't leave the abusive situation

(Walker, 2000). The research demonstrates that girls who are likely to seek an abortion without telling their parents usually give their fear of causing abuse to themselves or their mothers. When these girls stated their fears of the abuse that would result if they had to obtain consent or notify their parents about their choice to terminate the pregnancy, they obtained a judicial bypass; few if any girls' requests are turned down for lack of competency. Sadly, it is the abuse victim who is the most vulnerable to manipulation by anti-choice abortion groups who misattribute the woman's reactions to the abortion experience to anger and distress at the abortion rather than the anger and distress that resulted from domestic violence. In fact, post-traumatic stress disorder (PTSD) is a common component of Battered Woman Syndrome and Battered Child Syndrome, so misattributing these symptoms to a post-abortion syndrome simply confuses the issue (Rubin & Russo, 2004; Russo & Denious, 1998; Walker, 1994, 2000).

Domestic violence cases pose a great threat when the woman has a child together with the abuser. Rarely can these relationships become violence free, and, therefore, they usually terminate in divorce or dissolution. Unfortunately, the most dangerous time for a battered woman is at the point of separation. It is important for her safety to terminate the relationship quickly and carefully, paying close attention to any escalation of the violence. Unmarried couples generally go their separate ways without needing interference from the family court laws. Married couples without children who can figure out how to divide up their assets also can terminate the marriage without too much difficulty. But, couples who have one or more children together are often caught up in the quagmire of the U.S. family court system. Some couples become involved with dependency courts if the violence affects the children and Child Protective Services becomes involved. Mothers are in danger of losing their children to state custody, often trapping them in dangerous situations with the batterer having access to their children. This continues for those who are ordered into custody evaluations with mental health professionals who do not understand the impact of domestic violence on the safety and well-being of children (Kuehnle & Walker, 2003).

Protective mothers typically lose custody of their children when they attempt to control the batterers' access to the children or refuse to share parental responsibility because of the perceived danger (Bancroft & Silverman, 2002; Jaffe & Geffner, 1998; Jaffe, Lemon, & Poisson, 2003). It is not unusual for fathers to use the children to continue their access to the mothers, and the abuse continues. Parental Alienation Syndrome (PAS) is a typical allegation used against protective mothers, and the custody and access to these children can last for years in the courts (Walker, Brantley, & Rigsbee, 2004). It is no wonder that women who are in abusive relationships decide to abort the pregnancy rather than bring a child into this difficult and dangerous situation.

SUMMARY

In summary, the information this chapter has reviewed makes it clear that the reproductive health care for women in the United States and in other countries is compromised by laws that do not take into account the reality of women's lives, despite the acceptance of reproductive health as a human rights issue in international organizations. Reproductive health as a human rights issue includes women's access to accurate information and funding for health care procedures and contraception in addition to access to safe abortion services, if needed. The types of procedures typically used in safe and legal abortion centers are carefully detailed in this chapter to correct the misinformation that is apparently being given by CPCs and other anti-choice groups. Therapists and health care professionals need accurate information to assist women in making their own decisions about pregnancy planning.

REFERENCES

Bancroft, L., & Silverman, J. G. (2002). *The batterer as parent: Addressing the impact of domestic violence on family dynamics. Sage Series on Violence Against Women.* Thousand Oaks, CA: Sage.

Barnes, A. (2005). Update on abortion law. In A. Barnes (Ed.), *The handbook of women, psychology and the law* (pp. 147–177). San Francisco: Jossey-Bass.

Brownmiller, S. (1999). *In our time: Memoirs of a revolution.* New York: Dial Press/ Random House, Inc.

Bunch, C. (1995). Beijing, backlash and the future of women's rights. *Health & Human Rights, 1*(4), 450.

Bureau of Justice Statistics. (1997). *Homicide trends in the United States.* Retrieved on February 5, 2007, from http://ojp.usdoj.gov/bjs/homicide/homtrnd.htm

Cherry, A. L. (1999). Maternal-fetal conflicts, the social construction of maternal deviance, and some thoughts about love and justice. *Texas Journal of Women and the Law, 8,* 245–259.

Condon, J. T. (1986). Psychological disability in women who relinquish a baby for adoption. *Medical Journal of Australia, 144,* 117–119.

Daar, J. (1999). Panel on disputes concerning frozen embryos. *Texas Journal of Women and the Law, 8,* 285–293.

David, H. P., Dytrych, Z., & Matejcek, Z. (2003). Born unwanted: Observations from the Prague Study. *American Psychologist, 58,* 224–229.

Davis, H. P. (1994). Reproductive rights and reproductive behavior: Clash or convergence of private values and public policies. *American Psychologist, 49,* 343–349.

Davis v. Davis, *842 S.W.2d 588* (Tenn. 1992).

Davis, D., McKee, G., & Robertson, J. A. (1999). Panel on pre-pregnancy sex selection. *Texas Journal of Women and the Law, 8,* 267–283.

Feitshans, I. L. (1998). Is there a human right to reproductive health? *Texas Journal of Women and the Law, 8,* 93–133.

Gonzales v. Carhart, *127 S.CT. 1610* (2007).

Harding, J. J. (1989). Post-partum psychiatric disorders: A review. *Comprehensive Psychiatry, 30,* 109–110.

Haslegrave, M., & Harvard, J. (1995). Women's right to health and the Beijing Platform for Action: The retreat from Cairo. *Health & Human Rights, 1,* 461–471.

Jaffe, P.G., & Geffner, R. (1998). Child custody disputes and domestic violence: Critical issues for mental health, social service, and legal professionals. In G. W. Holden, R. Geffner & E. N. Jouriles (Eds.), *Children exposed to marital violence: Theory, research, and applied issues* (pp. 371–408). Washington, DC: American Psychological Association.

Jaffe, P. G., Lemon, N., & Poisson, S. E. (2003). *Child custody & domestic violence.* Thousand Oaks, CA: Sage.

Kass v. Kass, *696 N.E.2d 174* (N.Y., 1998).

Koop, C. E. (1989). *The Federal role in determining the medical and psychological impact of abortions on women: Testimony to the House Committee on Government Operations,* H.R. Rep. No. 101–329.

Kubasek, N. (1999). The case against prosecutions for prenatal drug abuse. *Texas Journal of Women and the Law, 8,* 167–181.

Kuehnle, K., & Walker, L. E. A. (2003). *Children exposed to domestic violence* (Home Study Continuing Education Program). Sarasota, FL: Professional Resource Press.

Lemkau, J. P. (1988). Emotional sequelae of abortion: Implications for clinical practice. *Psychology of Women Quarterly, 12,* 461–472.

McKee, G. R. (2006). *Why mothers kill: A forensic psychologist's casebook.* New York: Oxford University Press.

National Academy of Sciences. (1975). Legalized abortion and the public health. Washington, DC: Author.

Nocon, J. (1999). 1999 Symposium remarks: Panel on maternal-fetal conflict. *Texas Journal of Women and the Law, 261,* Lexis Nexis Academic.

Ogden, D. W., & Kappler, A. M. (1991, October). APA files Amicus Brief in *Planned Parenthood of S. E. Pennsylvania v. Casey.*

Pitanguy, J. (1995). From Mexico to Beijing: A new paradigm. *Health & Human Rights, 1,* 454–460.

Rubin, L., & Russo, N. F. (2004). Abortion and mental health: What therapists need to know. In J. C. Chrisler (Ed.), *From menarche to menopause: The female body in feminist therapy* (pp. 60–90). New York: Haworth Press.

Russo, N. F., & Denious, J. (1998). Understanding the relationship of violence against women to unwanted pregnancy and its resolution. In L. J. Beckman & S. M. Harvey (Eds.), *The new civil war: The psychology, culture, and politics of abortion* (pp. 211–234). Washington, DC: American Psychological Association.

Russo, N. F., & Zierke, K. (1992). Abortion, childbearing, and women's well-being. *Professional Psychology: Research and Practice, 23,* 269–280.

United Nations. (1996). *Platform for Action and the Beijing Declaration.* New York: United Nations Department of Public Information.

U.S. Department of Health & Human Services. (2004). *Administration for Children and Families News: Abandoned babies—Preliminary national estimates.* Retrieved February 5, 2007, from http://www.acf.dhhs.gov/news/stats/abandon.htm

Walker, L. E. A. (1991). Abused mothers, infants, and substance abuse: Psychological consequences of failure to protect. In P. R. McGrab & D. M. Dougherty (Eds.), *Mothers, infants and substance abuse: Proceedings of the American Psychological Association Division 12, Midwinter Meeting, Scottsdale, AZ., January 9–10.* (pp. 106–139). Georgetown University Press: Washington, D.C.

Walker, L. E. A. (1994). *Abused women and survivor therapy.* Washington, DC: American Psychological Association.

Walker, L. E. A. (2000). *The battered woman syndrome.* New York: Springer Publishing.

Walker, L. E. A., Brantley, K., & Rigsbee, J. (2004). A critical analysis of Parental Alienation Syndrome and its admissibility in the family court. *Journal of Child Custody, 1*(2), 47–74.

World Health Organization. (1948). *Frequently asked questions.* Retrieved on February 5, 2007, from http://www.who.int/suggestions/faq/en/index.html

CHAPTER 5

Gauging Your Client's Emotional Regulation and Good Decision Making

INTRODUCTION

In Chapter 3 we discussed the cognitions or thinking skills necessary to make a decision about whether to terminate a pregnancy by abortion. Most health care decisions cannot be made only using objective information since emotions also play into the decision-making process, particularly in an area of health care as controversial and political as abortion. Therapists and health care counselors who counsel women and girls going through this high-stress time need to understand both how emotions develop and how they work, including how emotions affect our cognitive skills. In this chapter, we attempt to review emotional development from a normal perspective and then discuss some of the more common problems that may be affected by the stress of a difficult emotional period.

HOW DOES THE BRAIN AND NERVOUS SYSTEM CONTROL EMOTIONS?

The human brain and nervous system is a wondrous and intricate system that is too complex to describe in this book. However, it is important to understand some basics about how it works in order to understand the interaction between cognition, or thinking, and emotions. The study of brain behavior, or neuropsychology, suggests that our nervous system is mostly regulated by electricity and chemistry. The electrical impulses carry the messages from the body to the brain and back again. This is facilitated or hindered by the biochemicals including neurotransmitters and hormones created or released by the nervous system.

The nervous system is divided into several sections: the central nervous system (CNS) with the brain, the peripheral nervous system (PNS) with the nerves that extend throughout the body, and the autonomic nervous system (ANS), which regulates our emotions and life-sustaining activities such as breathing, blood pressure, and other systems that we don't think about. The ANS regulates the production of the neurotransmitters and hormones that help the different parts of our nervous system all work together. In this section, we discuss how the brain and ANS normally work to regulate our emotions.

Nerve Cells

The basic cell in the nervous system is the neuron. Many neurons bundle together to form nerve cells, which are located almost everywhere in our body. Unlike other cells in our body, once nerve cells die, they usually cannot be replaced. However, other neurons may be able to take over their functions. Stem cell researchers are finding new ways to stimulate the regrowth of some of these nerves, which could cure many of the debilitating brain disorders, particularly those found in the aging population. Unfortunately, such stem cell research has become controversial because it uses embryonic tissue from fetuses that have been spontaneously or therapeutically aborted before the cells are completely formed. One major fear is that this research will increase the number of therapeutic abortions that occur in order to harvest the cells needed for the researchers' laboratories. Should this quest for science become an industry, it could create a demand for women willing to become pregnant simply to have an abortion so their fetal embryonic tissue can become harvested for science or even medicine, if it is found to be successful. Obviously, the potential here for exploitation of women will have to be monitored as the research becomes more widely available. At this time, government funding to support new research is unlawful, although private funding is possible.

Autonomic Nervous System

Our emotions are regulated by the ANS, the part of the nervous system that functions automatically, which means emotions are more difficult to control than are our thinking skills, which are regulated by the neurons in our CNS. Psychologists and other health professionals who have studied neuropsychology generally focus on the cognitive areas of the brain and not the emotional part of the nervous system. However, recent additions to the psychology curriculum in psychopharmacology have focused directly on how the emotional system functions.

Neurotransmitters and Their Impact on Emotions

There are several major biochemicals and hormones, called neurotransmitters, that affect the electrical impulses as they travel through the nervous system. Some of the more commonly known neurotransmitters are serotonin, norepinephrine, and dopamine. Neurotransmitters are found at synapses, or places where the electrical impulse jumps from one nerve to another. Some help the impulse before it passes to the next neuron, whereas others help cleanse the fluid in the synapse afterward so it is ready for the next impulse to arrive. These chemicals are produced at different places in the body and may be stored at the site where they do their job, ready to be released when needed, or they may travel through the blood system and be available for the proper cells to use when activated. They are carefully regulated by the brain as only tiny amounts of the chemicals are needed to perform the actions. If too much of one is manufactured, it may flood the system so it doesn't work efficiently, and if not enough is manufactured, it could negatively affect the system also. Enough of a neurotransmitter may be manufactured but not properly released and that could also affect the system. More than one of these biochemicals and hormones may act together to form the correct neurotransmitter for a particular reaction. In some cases, the body regulates how much of the neurotransmitter is produced based on how much of it is used. So, if emotions are swinging up and down at a rapid rate, which is common under stressful situations, then up- and down-regulation is occurring all the time, placing a stress on the physical integrity of the body as well as the mind.

Research suggests that there are circuits that are formed by these various neurotransmitters that are guided by the DNA from each person's genetic material (Stahl, 2000). Difficulties with these circuits appear to occur simultaneous to expression of certain groups of emotions labeled as mental disorders. For example, mood disorders, which includes major depression, involves too little serotonin in the synaptic fluid. This is usually due to the inability of the body to provide enough serotonin at the synapse so that the nerve impulse is slowed down. It could be a deficiency in the manufacture of serotonin, too little stored or released at the synapse, or it could be that too much serotonin is removed from the synaptic fluid after an impulse passes through. The serotonin available may not be able to do its job due to interactions with other biochemicals that are present. Medication that regulates the reuptake of the serotonin at the synapse can help the nervous system work more efficiently. The most commonly used class of medication is called selective serotonin reuptake inhibitors (SSRIs) since they work directly on serotonin.

Other medications may also work on a number of different neurotransmitters. As in the example of mood disorders such as depression, it may be that norepinephrine, which also plays a role in our emotions, is not regulating properly. Two other classes of medication, sometimes called selective norepinephrine reuptake inhibitors or tricyclics, may also be used. Newer medications, called atypical or secondary antipsychotics also have an influence on emotional disorders, as they affect different mechanisms of action than the original antipsychotic medications and have fewer side effects. Sometimes, when someone usually diagnosed with bipolar disorder has major mood swings with both depressed and manic moods, mood stabilizers or medications that are also used to control seizure disorders may be added to the medication regime. It is becoming more common for those with these serious emotional dysregulation disorders to be regulated by medical psychologists trained as psychopharmacologists who use an integrated approach with psychotherapy and various psychotropic drugs.

All of these medications produce side effects that might be overcome by getting used to them slowly. Sometimes people try to live with the side effects because the medication is important for proper functioning. Sometimes these medications are necessary to continue to regulate a person's emotions, and stopping them will cause serious emotional distress. Unfortunately, it is unknown how many of these medications may also have a teratogenic or toxic effect on the developing fetus, and therefore many should not be taken when a woman is pregnant. Some women who use these prescribed medications and who unintentionally become pregnant, wish to have an abortion as they do not want to take the risk that their fetuses are damaged by the medication.

Toxic Medicines

Psychotropic medications that help to stabilize people's emotions get classified into the same system that is used for all medications to determine the toxic effects they might have for pregnant women and fetuses. A-level drugs have been tested on humans and have been found to be safe for exposure to fetuses (no psychotropic medications are on this short list); B-level drugs have been safe when tested with animals but no testing has been done in humans; C-level drugs have had problems in animal tests but no testing has been done with humans; D-level drugs have been shown to be unsafe in both animal tests and in humans; and X-level drugs are known to cause problems in fetal development.

The development of the embryo and fetus may be affected depending upon the stage of development and the impact on various systems that develop at a particular time. Box 5.1 indicates the known timetable for development of the fetal systems.

Most psychotropic drugs used to regulate emotions are in the C level, so their impact is not really known on the developing fetus. However, some are on the D and X lists, and they do have some known adverse impact. These medications are known to pass through the brain–blood barrier that protects fetuses from other toxicities, so it is important to understand what potential impact they might have on the developing fetus. All medications that are used as mood stabilizers such as lithium and depakote are thought to be the most toxic, causing cardiac problems in the developing fetus or possible facial cleft palate if taken within the first trimester. Antianxiety drugs called benzodiazepines, which are marketed under the brand names of Valium, Xanax, and Ativan, for instance, are known to cause neurotubular abnormalities within the first trimester also. Paxil, one of the SSRIs, has also been found to cause these deficits in the developing fetus.

Most doctors recommend that women try to go off these medications when they are planning to get pregnant. However, there is a discontinuation syndrome that may develop, so it is advised to do this slowly, with a doctor's assistance. If a woman becomes pregnant unintentionally, then she may have already been taking the medication before she knows she is pregnant. At that point, it is up to the woman to decide whether she wants to terminate the medications that are keeping her emotionally functional or terminate the pregnancy for fear of damage to the fetus.

Box 5.1   Stages of Fetal Development

Phases in Development	Number Weeks After Conception
CNS	2.0–5.0
Face	2.5–7.0
Ears	2.5–6.0
Eyes	2.5–6.0
Palate	4.0–10.0
Arms and Legs	4.5–12.0
Hands	4.0–7.0
Heart	2.0–8.0
Gut	4.0–7.0
Kidneys	3.5–8.0
Genitourinary	2.0–12.0

An ultrasound or testing for alpha-fetoprotein levels may help find out if there are any abnormalities. If women choose to go forward with the pregnancy, it is usually recommended that they discontinue the psychotropic medication slowly several weeks prior to birth so that the neonate is not adversely affected during the first few weeks of life.

These decisions are not easy ones for women or doctors to make. The possible risk to the woman for not taking the medication is that her depression, anxiety, psychotic, or manic behavior may worsen and the dysregulation in her production of neurotransmitters will also affect the fetal development. The woman's relationship with her partner and other family and friends in her support system may worsen. She may develop an impaired mother–infant attachment or serious postpartum depression should she keep the pregnancy and give birth. And, she may become actively suicidal. On the other hand, if she continues using psychopharmacological agents, especially high doses on a regular basis during the pregnancy, there may be risks to the development of the fetus. Medications used during organogenesis (weeks two to eight of fetal development) may be particularly teratogenic, causing major or minor congenital abnormalities in physical or functional areas. In the last trimester, there can be all kinds of neurobehavioral sequelae, similar to that seen in fetal alcohol syndrome or cocaine-exposed babies, such as prematurity, low birth weight, developmental delays, learning problems, and neuropsychological deficits.

Fetal Exposure to Alcohol and Illegal Drugs

The use of alcohol and other illegal substances during pregnancy exposes the developing fetus to neurological and other problems that have been studied despite difficulties in obtaining a good scientific sample from which to make conclusions that will generalize to other populations. Most of the pregnant women and subsequent babies born to them that are studied come from lower socioeconomic groups with poor nutrition, lack of access to good health care, disenfranchisement from the majority culture, and other unhealthy and unsafe lifestyle problems, in addition to the exposure to various drugs, called polysubstances in the published articles. Therefore, it is difficult to know how much of the impact to attribute to the prenatal exposure to alcohol and other drugs, particularly cocaine and crack, that have been studied. Most children born into poverty are known to suffer disproportionately high rates of low birth rates, malnutrition, anemia, lead poisoning, and other childhood diseases whether or not their parents have been using these substances.

The nationally funded studies over the years have found that approximately 20% of women of childbearing age use alcohol and other drugs during pregnancies. Many state that crack is the most prevalent drug causing fetal problems, although fetal alcohol syndrome from expo-sure to alcohol during gestation is still a common problem. The average pregnant cocaine user is around 25 years old, with two living children, and has had three to four abortions, some of which were miscarriages and others were terminations. Approximately three-quarters of the preg-nant cocaine abusers use other drugs and alcohol. Interestingly, cocaine is mostly used by African American and White women and not Hispanic women (Dougherty, 1991).

A number of serious complications have been found in some cocaine-exposed pregnancies including spontaneous abortions, placen-tal problems, and hypertension. Cocaine-exposed babies have been born with a variety of birth defects including brain, heart, and other vascular abnormalities, and they are known to develop nervous system abnor-malities. Some are identified as cocaine exposed as infants when nothing can console them and they cry all the time. One of the most important interventions for these babies, particularly those who must detoxify and go through cocaine withdrawal at birth, is to form attachments by bond-ing early with their mothers. Speech and language development may be delayed in these children, making such attachment to others difficult.

Fetal alcohol syndrome babies, who are exposed to alcohol during their mother's pregnancy also have many problems that plague them throughout life. They have physical stigmata that sometimes identify them, and many have neurological complications including attentional problems. Like the cocaine-exposed babies, they are more irritable, have identifiable crying patterns that are different from nonexposed babies, and may be difficult to console. They also need to attach to significant caretakers, which is difficult given their irritability. Although their lan-guage skills are not as compromised as in cocaine-exposed babies, an unusually large proportion of them are affected by emotional dysregula-tion for their entire lives. Some have a greater propensity to poor judgment and violent behavior. A high proportion of criminals are known to have both fetal alcohol syndrome and in-utero cocaine exposure. However, it is important to remember that it is probably not just in-utero exposure to these substances but also the unfortunate lifestyles of their mothers dur-ing pregnancy that contribute to their later difficulties.

Environmental Impact on Emotions

As we discussed in the previous section, the impact of poverty and minority status for women in their communities causes many problems for the women and their children. Homelessness, exposure to disease with poor access to health care, violence in the streets and their homes, poor nutrition, lack of proper rest and sleep, fatigue from taking care of other children or working long hours in difficult and stressful conditions, worry about immigration or minority status, and exposure to HIV are only some of the problems that low- or no-income women who become pregnant must deal with.

Teens who come from these homes and become pregnant have additional problems including lack of family support, lack of interest on the boyfriends' or coconceivers' part in helping them, and lack of education or training necessary to earn money to support themselves all make life difficult for them. Their decision to abort a pregnancy may be the only way they can escape the poverty cycle they have grown up with in their own family. However, for many of them, they want to be different from their friends and families, which may cause them conflict about their decision to terminate a pregnancy. These teens may not get support from their families and even if they can get enough money to get an abortion, they still have to build up the courage to notify their parent or go before a judge, which is burdensome, delays their seeking care in a timely manner, and causes them unnecessary stress. If they come from a culture where abortion is not acceptable, then they find themselves in a conflict between values learned at home and their own personal goals to escape from poverty.

Although the middle classes in the United States tend to permit their teenage children to live at home well past the legal emancipation age of 18, in other cultures or ethnic groups, this does not occur and children are treated as adults by the time they graduate from high school no matter what their age. In some families, especially those in cultures where education is not as valued, teenagers drop out of school before the age of 16. Girls from dysfunctional families where one or more parents is using alcohol and other drugs commonly experience abuse in the home. Girls who are no longer in school may become pregnant and choose to terminate the pregnancy especially if the coconceiver and his family are not willing or able to support the teen and a baby. Some girls from this environment recognize that completing their education is the only way out of this poverty cycle and choose to obtain an abortion. If they come from abusive homes, they may not be able to get parental permission in consent states or proof of notification in other states. Going through the judicial bypass procedure becomes another obstacle for these girls to overcome.

EMOTIONAL DEVELOPMENT

Self-Esteem, Self-Confidence, and Self-Efficacy

Developmental psychologist Susan Harter (1997) has studied the development of self-esteem in young children. Self-esteem is defined as the global evaluative dimension of the self and is thought to be divided into five domains that can be measured: (a) scholastic competence, (b) athletic competence, (c) physical appearance, (d) peer acceptance, and (e) behavioral conduct. Children develop self-esteem from the emotional support and social approval that they receive from parents, other adults, and peers. Self-esteem increases when individuals are faced with a problem and try to cope with it rather than avoiding dealing with the problem. Harter suggests that self-esteem begins to develop within the first year of life as the child learns that he or she is competent to solve problems. This development continues as people's feelings of competence increase in the important domains and the social support from others is present. The more social approval people receive, the more competent they feel about their ability to make decisions that affect their lives.

Coping Skills

The more people interact in challenging activities in their lives, the more likely they will meet with obstacles to success and even failures. Thus, an important part of emotional development is learning to use coping skills. This means facing a challenge nondefensively with an honest or realistic cognitive appraisal and then figuring out what strategies to employ to manage the challenge. Emotions may get in the way of realistic cognitive appraisals for many different reasons. Developmental psychologist E. Mavis Hetherington (2003) has studied stress and coping strategies in children and families for the past 20 years. She also found a sequential development of the emotional domain as people develop their beliefs about their own competency in getting through life.

EMOTIONAL DYSREGULATION

The study of how we regulate our emotions and override the ANS that tries to regulate them involuntarily has become more popular in the last decade, particularly focusing on stress and how it affects our neurotransmitters and immunological system. Earlier scientists such as Richard Lazarus studied people's coping responses to stress (Lazarus, 1991; Lazarus & Folkman, 1984). Most people have tolerance for a particular amount of stress but develop physiological and psychological problems when their stress levels get too high. When stressors are temporary, emotions reregulate when the stress passes and people go back to their usual functioning. High levels of stress usually occur during a crisis that may alter our lives. Certainly, pregnancy and anticipation of a child can be a positive or negative crisis in someone's life. In some cases, a pregnancy may bring up both positive emotions, negative emotions, or ambivalence.

Lazarus's studies show that it is not simply the event itself that causes the emotional reaction but rather people's appraisal of what the event means to them. His studies scientifically documented at least 18 different emotions that can be produced and that explain a person's physical, emotional, and physiological state. It is the meaning that the person gives to the event that will make the difference in recovery from health problems. In one study conducted by Lazarus and his colleagues, he found that people who refused to believe that a serious medical problem was as severe as it really was recovered much more quickly than those who did have this type of coping strategy. He found an individual's patterns of appraisal or how the individual evaluated the impact of an event on his or her well-being actually made the difference.

These findings are very important when considering the addition of high stressors placed on women who seek abortions when they visit an abortion center where there are demonstrators outside. Given this theory, it is not surprising that those women who seem to have an emotional reaction to the abortion procedure have been exposed to counselors in Crisis Pregnancy Centers (CPCs) or others who have convinced them to expect a negative emotional reaction.

Posttraumatic Stress Disorder

Other people may develop diagnosable emotional problems from too much repeated stress or one major life-threatening stressor. This is called posttraumatic stress disorder (PTSD) and is identified by changes in the way people think, feel, and behave. It is common in those who have experienced major disasters such as hurricanes or earthquakes that caused life-threatening damage; war-related traumas such as the devastation that occurred on September 11, 2001, in New York City when the World Trade Center buildings were hit by enemy airplanes and collapsed; and repeated traumatic events such as those experienced by child abuse victims and battered women. First responders who help those who experience traumatic events may also develop secondary PTSD from indirect exposure to the stressors.

There are several identifying symptoms of PTSD, including intrusive recollections of the traumatic event even when it is not occurring, hypervigilance, fear and anxiety about one's safety, and a numbing of emotions and avoidance of people or places that remind the person of the original trauma. These emotions are being moderated by cortisol-releasing factors and the neurotransmitters released by the ANS to try to reregulate and stabilize our emotions. It is not known exactly how these emotional mood swings affect cognitive decision making, although it is probably a function of the strength of the stressor, the person's perception of its personal impact, and the person's emotional and cognitive abilities prior to the crisis or trauma. We still do not know what impact exposure to trauma and crisis, especially if it is on a repeated basis, will have on the developing embryo and fetus.

Dialectical Behavior Therapy and Mindfulness in Regulating Emotions

One of the areas that appears to be important in reregulating emotions after a period of dysfunction is called mindfulness training (Hayes, Follette, & Linehan, 2004; Spradlin, 2003). Here the person is taught to pay specific attention to what is happening in the instant moment rather than focusing on past events or worrying about the future. Mindfulness training appears to be helpful for those people who have developed PTSD and accompanying dissociative disorders that cause someone to be reexperiencing the trauma or blocking it from one's mind through dissociation. Staying focused on the present helps people concentrate on making good decisions because it regulates their emotions so that they cannot interfere with thinking patterns. Since interpersonal relationships are often disrupted when the person is unable to regulate emotions, mindfulness training can also help the person begin to develop support systems to help them through future crises. We discuss this further in Chapter 7, where we describe techniques useful in intervention programs with women whose emotions do not reregulate easily after an abortion.

Impact of Anger and Anxiety on Health

Sometimes stress levels do not go back to the original levels after a crisis or traumatic event passes. People may develop a Type A personality style, which reflects a type of continuous reactions to stress. High-level business executives and others who are constantly under stress from their jobs may have personalities that are consistent with Type A criteria.

Spielberger et al. (1991) studied the impact of specific emotions such as anxiety and anger on our ability to make decisions and our subsequent development physical illnesses such as cardiovascular disease and cancer. He found that it is not just the intense Type A personality that can cause cardiovascular disease but also the time urgency associated with having to make decisions and get the job done quickly. Cancer patients, on the other hand, may have been living under a stressor for a long time prior to developing cancer, which occurs when the DNA in the cell nucleus is unable to replicate the normal cell and instead produces malignant overgrowth, causing tumors. The exact mechanisms of action by which cancers develop are not well known except in a few cases. However, the neurotransmitters associated with too much stress are believed to have a role in removing protective factors or promoting uncontrolled cell growth.

FACTORS IMPACTING WOMEN'S EMOTIONAL DEVELOPMENT

The development of the emotional domain for women is generally thought to be dependent upon women's relationships with other people. The more a woman pays attention to other people, the more likely she can control her own relationships. Jean Baker Miller and her colleagues at the Stone Center at Wellesley College have developed a psychological theory demonstrating how women's relationships with each other and others who are significant to them contribute to women's mental stability because paying attention to relationships helps women concentrate on their emotions. Miller and her colleagues have called this phenomenon a relational theory of psychotherapy, and they have been working on developing a psychodynamic theory and clinical intervention program for those women who have inadequate or insecure relationships.

Impact of Child Abuse on Emotional Development

Where children experience emotional, physical, or sexual abuse during their early childhood years, they often grow up with issues in the emotional domain, especially since they are not always mentally present using denial, repression, and sometimes dissociation as frequent defenses against feeling the emotional pain from both the abusive behavior and the inconsistent parenting they received. Children who grow up in homes where one or both parents have alcoholism or abuse other substance also experience the emotional effects from inconsistent parenting. Many of these children learn to become their parent's parent, which may be called being overparentified. They often grow up feeling anxious unless they are taking care of other people. However, they quickly become exhausted and may alternate an excessive sense of responsibility together with spacing-out, or dissociating, or simply not being present. These women may be unable to parent a child and yet are unable to make the decision not to go forward with the pregnancy should they find themselves pregnant. Some resolve this dilemma by not focusing on the reality of a pregnancy so by the time they do acknowledge the pregnancy, it may be too late for a safe abortion. Others become so frightened at the thought of having to make a decision to abort or not that they put it off until they are forced to do something quickly because of the time delay.

Incest and Child Sexual Abuse

The sexual abuse of girls is a worldwide problem that creates many different problems for the victims throughout their lives. The legal system is rarely able to stop the incest in most cases, especially when the child is very young. Protective mothers are usually rendered impotent by the legal system so the child has no option but to accommodate to the abuse. The behavior itself creates such intense and sometimes ambivalent emotions that the child becomes less believable than the incest perpetrator by professionals, especially if the perpetrator is the father, step-parent, or brother. It is impossible to do justice to the topic here other than to remind the reader that no matter what girls say about their current emotions, children do not have the legal right to consent. Incest is as much of a crime as are other forms of exploitation and abuse, and when a pregnancy results it robs the young woman of her childhood and can irreparably damage her relationship with her mother and her father.

Young women who become pregnant as a result of incest are in a special category when it comes to emotions. It is important to remember that these young women have learned that the person who is responsible for their nurturance, love, and care also will take advantage of them through manipulation, fear, coercion, and maybe even physical abuse that accompanies the sexual abuse. Most of these girls understand that the sexual relationship with the incest perpetrator is dangerous and must be kept secret. They rarely discuss the sexual abuse with anyone, which is part of the accommodation pattern. This may affect their ability to form close personal friendships with other girls their age. It also makes it very difficult for the girl to report a pregnancy, partly because she may not realize that she is pregnant, especially if she hadn't yet begun to menstruate, or because she is afraid to trust anyone with her secret, fearing the disastrous consequences she has been warned about.

Judith Herman (1992), in her book, *Trauma and Recovery*, found that adults who were physically, sexually, and psychologically abused as children may grow up to have emotional problems that get in their way of developing good interpersonal relationships and stable life skills. Many of these people cannot regulate their own emotions very well. When they get angry it is so intense that they cannot recover their equilibrium easily. The same happens when they feel happy or sad. Those that have frequent mood swings may eventually be diagnosed as having a bipolar mood disorder but others could develop a personality disorder, usually borderline personality disorder when they flip back and forth between being unfailingly trusting and vitriolically angry. Herman noted that many of these people actually demonstrated a complex form of PTSD rather than these other diagnoses. As they struggle to control their intensely felt emotions that interfere with their cognitive decision making, they may make a premature decision to have an abortion and then are sorry afterward. In some of these cases, the woman is so emotionally distressed that her perception of reality becomes distorted often after the abortion. Women who demonstrate emotional distress at the time of the abortion are usually sent home to make sure if the abortion is what they really want. These women would be expected to have a difficult time modulating their emotions no matter what they decide to do.

Linehan's dialetical behavior therapy helps people who have not adequately been able to develop their emotional domain by giving them another chance to do so. One of her most important techniques is called mindfulness, which teaches people to learn to focus and attend to the matter at hand, even when it stimulates excessive amounts of anxiety (Hayes, Follette, & Linehan, 2004; Spradlin, 2003). Sometimes meditation also helps train someone's mind to attend and focus at appropriate times rather than to dissociate, fantasize, or simply daydream rather than deal with reality.

Stranger Rape

Women who become pregnant by strangers usually consider terminating the pregnancy for many different reasons. First, they are not emotionally stable after the incident to be able to think about raising a child. Second, they may fear that they will never be able to disassociate the child from his sexually abusive father. Third, they may fear that the father's aggressive behavior is an inheritable trait. Fourth, they may fear that the drugs given to them after the rape may have been harmful to the child. In addition, these women may, for many of the other common reasons, feel that having a baby at that time is unacceptable given their life circumstances. It is important to remember that rape victims typically suffer from some form of PTSD and need time and support to get past the event.

Some women who seek an abortion are fearful of raising a child in the community where they live because of the violence on the streets, whether it involves gang wars or other violence that the women cannot control. These women may not have money, or other factors may prohibit her from leaving that community. Many times these women hope to leave the community at some point and plan to become pregnant and have a child then. Counselors who do not live in such urban areas may not understand these women's issues, but it may be an important factor for some women when making their decision.

Grief Reactions

Being able to grieve a loss is another emotionally learned behavior. Here the context is very important because the woman may be mourning a fantasy of what might have been if circumstances had been different, not necessarily a baby. The ability to grieve a major loss, particularly someone who was loved, has been subjected to much research. It has been found that the typical five stages of grief can be applied to women who have an abortion. Initially the woman doesn't believe she is pregnant, nor can she think clearly about what to do about it. She then goes into the yearning period where she is willing to make bargains to try to make it all go away. The third stage is anger, and a woman who does not permit herself to grieve may get stuck here. A fourth stage, depression, may exacerbate an already existing condition of depression. The fifth and final stage is acceptance and doing whatever has to be done to meet her goals.

In recent research into grief reactions, psychologists found that acceptance was the most commonly endorsed item and yearning was the dominant negative grief indicator from 1 to 24 months after the loss. Most abortion centers find that grief reactions among women who have had abortions clear up within 6 months post-abortion even without professional intervention. This is probably because women who are more likely to demonstrate behaviors that indicate they are struggling with emotional issues will probably be sent home to think about the procedure before continuing.

EMOTIONS SPECIFIC TO TERMINATION OF PREGNANCY

Given the various theories discussed in this chapter, it is important for a counselor to pay attention to the expectations and anticipated emotions that women who undergo abortions may experience. Most important is the assessment of the woman's emotional stability, which is done by examining her emotional history and her current emotional state. Obviously, those women who have become pregnant by a stranger or by a family member through incest or rape will need special care, as it can be anticipated that they are still dealing with the emotional aftermath of the incident.

Madonna–Whore Split

Typical issues that come up in discussions with women making the choice of whether or not to terminate their pregnancies include their attitudes toward motherhood in general. Often women who believe that motherhood is sacred and that once a woman becomes a mother, she is no longer able to go out, party, and have fun will question if they are ready to settle down. Others may have envisioned a particular age at which it is appropriate for them to settle down and therefore think they are too young to become a mother. They may be right. These notions come from religion and are best explained through literature that explores what is called the Madonna–whore split and psychological theories such as the Freudian notion of penis envy. For example, Freud believed that women were jealous of men's penises and therefore could make up for their lack of the penis by becoming pregnant with a male child. In fact, Freud went to such lengths to develop a part of his theory devoted to believing that women's fantasies about pregnancy with a male child would actually cure them of hysteria. The name of the disorder, hysteria, which includes women's dramatic behavior that is often designed to get people, especially men, to pay attention to them, actually means wandering uterus, which obviously stops wandering once it contains a male fetus. Although this theory is not as widely held today among most psychoanalysts, it still does have some influence in the field.

Social Stigma

The social stigma for some women who become pregnant when not married has been significantly reduced in the United States, although other cultures still widely accept that pregnancy outside of marriage is considered shameful. In particular, unmarried Indian and Middle Eastern women believe that they will be stigmatized if others know that they have engaged in premarital sex, which a pregnancy obviously announces. Women from varying cultures have different reasons for fearing stigma or shame if they get pregnant outside of marriage. In some cultures, unmarried pregnant women may even risk the threat of death for disgracing the entire family. These attitudes will affect a pregnant woman's decision to obtain an abortion and may make them feel that they have no other choice. Most of them will not turn to their families for support as they know it will not be forthcoming. Thus, they are at high risk to have emotional difficulties post-abortion but it must be remembered that they are at high risk to have emotional difficulties even if they carry the pregnancy to term.

Religious Values

Women who hold strong religious values may also have strong emotions about having an abortion for two reasons. First, they may believe that aborting a fetus is morally wrong, but secondly, they may believe that they will be stigmatized in their community if their pregnancy outside of marriage is discovered. Others may have similar ambivalent feelings, especially if they believe they cannot raise another child at the time. Health concerns somewhat mitigate the ambivalence, especially if the woman is married and has other children. Many Catholic women in the United States today have expressed feelings that indicate resentment of the fact that the Church is headed by a celibate man who is refusing to consider birth control or abortion for those who can't or won't raise any more children.

Other Issues Creating Emotional Ambivalence

There are numerous conditions that can create emotional ambivalence for women who are considering an abortion. We discuss some of them in Chapter 6. However, it is important to be concerned with the woman's personal conflicts around her body image and other medical issues. Some women, particularly those with a history of eating disorders including anorexia, fear getting fat and cannot tolerate the idea of a pregnancy. Some women, such as those with careers in modeling or acting and other areas where appearance is paramount, may feel they have to terminate their pregnancies in order to keep their careers but still feel guilty that their reasons are insufficient and thus they experience some ambivalence.

Women with medical problems that make pregnancy dangerous to their health may really want to have children but choose to have abortions and not take the risk. These feelings also create some ambivalence. However, for these women with medical problems, there is a health risk associated with carrying a fetus to term, and women with certain medical conditions such as some cancers, heart conditions, neurological disorders, diabetes, or hypertension, among other conditions, could have serious complications that might even be life-threatening if they do not terminate the pregnancy. Women who need certain medicines that are known to be toxic to the developing fetus are also in this group. Most go through with the termination with normal feelings of sadness and perhaps anger associated with the limitations their illnesses place on their lives.

Some women think about terminating their pregnancies because they fear they will not be good mothers. Some of these women may have been exposed to poor mothering themselves, which gave them too much responsibility for their siblings. Others recognize that they cannot meet the needs of the children they already have. They may feel they are too young or too old or that they have too many other responsibilities or not enough money to support themselves and a child. However, these women do love children and feel badly that they want to terminate their pregnancies. This is especially true for women who are having marital problems or recognize the fact that their coconceiver is not going to be there for them. Some women who are in a battering relationship become aware that their partners' abuse to them and possibly toward children will be so problematic that they decide to terminate the pregnancy. In some of these cases, the man insists that the woman get an abortion and they do so with both reluctance and ambivalence. Most of these women express relief after the procedure is over.

SUMMARY

In summary, in this chapter we discuss the various theories of emotional regulation and its impact on a woman's ability to make a competent decision about terminating a pregnancy with an abortion. We first discuss how the brain and nervous system affect our emotional and cognitive behavior. It is important to understand how emotions are controlled by the neurotransmitters that are manufactured and released by the ANS. Women who are diagnosed with mental illnesses can still make a good decision about terminating a pregnancy as long as they take the time to work through the emotions that have the potential to affect decision making. Toxic medications can interfere with fetal development, and women whose health depends on these drugs must understand the implications discussed in this section. This is also true for women who engage in risky behaviors such as using alcohol and street drugs while pregnant. Pregnancy tests can often reveal potential birth defects that may cause the woman to decide to seek an abortion.

The regulation of emotions is a developmental process, and the discussion of how self-esteem, self-confidence, and self-efficacy unfold may help the therapist to understand how the woman's emotions will affect her ability to know if she made a good decision. The ability to cope with stress and how it affects emotions is also an important area to understand. There are new interventions for women with emotional dysregulation caused by too much stress. We also address issues faced by victims of rape and child sexual abuse. Finally, we also explore the types of situations that can cause women to have many different emotional reactions at the same time, or feelings of ambivalence.

REFERENCES

Dougherty, D. M. (1991). Drug use among pregnant women: The scope of the problem. In McGrab, P. R. & Dougherty, D. M. (Eds). *Mothers, infants and substance abuse: Proceedings of the American Psychological Association Division 12, Midwinter Meeting, Scottsdale, AZ, January 9–10.* (pp. 1–33). Georgetown University Press: Washington, D.C.

Harter, S. (1997). *The construction of the self: A developmental perspective.* New York: Guilford.

Hayes, S. C., Follette, V. M., & Linehan, M. M. (2004). *Mindfulness and acceptance: Expanding the cognitive behavioral tradition.* New York: Guilford.

Herman, J. (1992). *Trauma and Recovery: The aftermath of violence—from domestic abuse to political terror.* New York: Basic Books.

Hetherington, E. M., & Kelly, J. (2003). *For better or worse: Divorce reconsidered.* Boston: W. W. Norton.

Lazarus, R. (1991). *Emotion and adaptation.* London: Oxford University Press.

Lazarus, R., & Folkman, S. (1984). *Stress, appraisal, & coping.* New York: Springer Publishing.

Spielberger, C., Spielberger, C. D., Crane, R. S., Kearns, W. D., Pellegrin, K. L., Rickman, R. L., et al. (1991). Anger and anxiety in essential hypertension. In C. D. Spielberger, I. G. Sarason, Z. Kulcs, & G. L. Van Heck (Eds.), *Stress and emotion: Vol. 14* (pp. 265–283). New York: Hemisphere/Taylor & Francis.

Spradlin, S. E. (2003). *Don't let your emotions run your life: How dialectical behavior therapy can put you in control.* Oakland, CA: New Harbinger.

Stahl, S. M. (2000). *Essential psychopharmacology: Neuroscientific basis and practical applications* (2nd ed.). New York: Cambridge Press.

CHAPTER 6

Is There a Post-Abortion Syndrome?

INTRODUCTION

Probably no other area of psychology is more controversial than whether or not having an abortion is a trauma that causes long-lasting emotional harm. Anti-choice activists have created a term called post-abortion syndrome (PAS) without any scientific data to support their position. Approximately 15 years ago (Koop, 1989), the U.S. Surgeon General issueda report that supported the scientific entities stating that abortions by themselves do not cause physical or emotional harm. Since then, anti-abortion activists have attempted to use data from large-scale studies without proper scientific analysis to support their conclusions. This is of concern because most of their analysis does not control for the very factors that are associated with those women who are at highest risk for emotional distress. Reviews of these new studies continue to show that having an abortion does not cause mental illness and in particular, there is no syndrome such as PAS. Women who have emotional problems after an abortion are likely to have had them prior to the abortion. Russo (in press) recently reviewed the new literature and like her predecessors concluded that in contrast to having an unwanted child, "having a legal abortion appears to be a relatively benign experience, particularly if it occurs in the first trimester." Women who have a history of psychological problems are

119

at higher risk to demonstrate these psychological problems after a pregnancy is resolved, whether it is terminated by an abortion or by childbirth. Misattribution of these psychological problems, often caused by a variety of life experiences, biochemical changes during pregnancy, and other factors such as the expectations set up by misinformation and scare tactics used by abortion protesters, can prevent a woman from getting proper assistance to alleviate distress from these emotional problems. It takes well-trained and experienced counselors and psychotherapists to help women sort out all these factors.

The most common factors, as discussed in this chapter, include pre-existing psychiatric conditions and a history of physical and sexual abuse. If just these two factors were controlled in the studies that claim to have found PAS in women who choose to have an abortion, then the results would demonstrate that they are no more likely to suffer from depression, anxiety disorders, psychotic problems or suicidal behavior than those women who choose to carry the pregnancy to full term. And, data from studies of what happens to unwanted children, indicate that they are far more likely to grow up with severe mental problems, probably reflecting their mothers' unhappiness. For example, the Prague study found that 35 years later, as adults the unwanted children were more likely to engage in criminal behavior, be on welfare, and receive psychiatric services (David, 2006).

Despite the politicized nature of the debate about women's access to abortion between the pro-choice and anti-choice movements, no methodologically correct empirical research studies have demonstrated the existence of PAS or any serious emotional abuse that can be directly attributed to an abortion. As we described in Chapter 4, the number of women who terminate unwanted pregnancies around the world is around 46 million, which, according to the most recent World Health Report (WHO) (2005), is approximately 25% of all reported pregnancies. The difference in physical health is striking when abortions are legal and safe as compared to those countries where women seek illegal and unsafe means of terminating unwanted pregnancies. According to the WHO, over 40% of the abortions performed around the world are done under unsafe conditions and result in approximately 68,000 maternal deaths. In the United States, since abortions have become legal under *Roe v. Wade,* abortions carry a lower risk of death than do childbirth, appendectomy, or tonsillectomy (American Medical Association Council on Scientific Affairs [AMA], 1992). Consequently, anti-abortion activists have concentrated on emotional harm as a reason to legislate policy against abortion.

Abortion has been legal for over 30 years in the United States. It is estimated that approximately 20% of all American women of childbearing age have already had an abortion (AMA, 1992). It is clear that if there were such a constellation of long-lasting symptoms associated with the procedure, the anti-choice activists would have found it. Remarkably, few women do develop transient emotional issues after an abortion, especially given the barriers to getting to safe abortion centers, but the research shows that even these emotions are indeed temporary and fade after a few days to weeks. Those few women who may have longer-lasting emotional symptoms have been found to have other factors that are associated with these emotions, including previous history of emotional difficulties or physical or sexual abuse, or other life circumstances that could produce similar emotional difficulties. Again, the strongest predictor of adverse symptoms following an abortion is the woman's mental health before the abortion. This is closely associated with the woman's prior exposure to physical or sexual abuse and the woman's lack of resources or support, often due to poverty (Adler et al., 1990, 1992; Dagg, 1991; Posovac & Miller, 1990).

So the question must be asked, "Why is the construct of PAS still being raised if there are no data to support it?" Just a few months prior to this book being published, the *New York Times* Sunday Magazine ran its cover story on PAS (January 21, 2007). Unfortunately, those women who are at most risk for mental health problems may be counseled into misattributing their emotional distress as associated with abortion rather than the actual source of their distress. Russo (in press), in her examination of the evidence described how the public and policy makers are being misled. In this chapter we review the major scientific literature published both to try to figure out why the idea of a PAS just won't go away and to help therapists, counselors, and other health care professionals better understand the literature.

FRAMING PAS

The idea of PAS was first proposed by Dr. Vincent Rue in the early 1980s. Working with Anne Speckhard, Rue described PAS as a disorder similar to post-traumatic stress disorder (PTSD) and characterized PAS using similar symptoms including "flashbacks, denial, lost memory of the event, [and] avoidance of the subject" (Rourke, 1995). Although Rue did not perform scientific studies to determine whether or how often such symptoms appeared in post-abortion women, PAS as a theory gained legitimacy by some in the psychological community in spite of the fact that the trauma of war or sexual or physical abuse is hardly analogous to that of terminating an unwanted pregnancy. Additionally, Rue identifies a wide range of other symptoms of PAS such as "helplessness, sadness, sorrow, lowered self-esteem, distrust, regret, relationship disruption, communication impairment, and restriction and self con-demnation" (Rue, 1995). By including all of these other negative feelings among the indicators of PAS, Rue defines the disorder in such broad terms that it could apply to virtually anyone whether or not they have terminated a pregnancy. Other studies of questionable methodology had mixed results, either failing to support or further garnered PAS as a psy-chiatric disorder, creating divisive fodder for both prolife and pro-choice advocates, adding to keeping abortion a highly politically charged issue rather than a part of women's reproductive health (Adler et al., 1990, 1992; Koop, 1989).

More recently, anti-abortion activists began to use data from large surveys to try to demonstrate that detrimental emotional effects were attributed to abortion. Reardon and his colleagues were the major authors of this type of research (Coleman, Reardon, Strahan, & Cougle, 2005; Cougle, Reardon, & Coleman, 2005). They isolated several variables from these studies including reported rates of depression, anxi-ety, psychotic disorders, and suicidal behavior and tried to demonstrate that women who had abortions were more likely to develop those symp-toms as were included reports of these disorders in the studies. However, they frequently eliminated high-risk women from the sample that they reanalyzed by creating categories that avoided using women with previ-ous histories of sexual and physical abuse or by using definitions and measures of these mental health problems that were not consistent with the *Diagnostic and Statistical Manual of Mental Disorders* (DSM-IV-TR) (American Psychiatric Association, 2000) categories or other well-known nosology systems. In addition, they did not separate women who had one abortion from those who had repeated abortions without accounting for the fact that repeaters often have more life experience problems with fewer resources to deal with them. Russo (in press) pointing out that abor-tion is confounded with the experience of unwanted pregnancy, concluded that studies, such as those of Reardon, Cougle, Coleman, and their col-leagues, "do not have the proper controls to address the issue of whether a pregnant women will increase her mental health risks should she volun-tarily choose to have an abortion to avoid an unwanted birth. Previous mental health problems, including the aftermath of previous and ongoing violence in one's life, do not go away whatever the chosen option."

The Surgeon General's View

Pressured from Right to Life leaders, former U.S. president Ronald Rea-gan directed Surgeon General C. Everett Koop to investigate the nature of post-abortion sequelae in 1987 (Adler et al., 1992; Koop, 1989). After comprehensive consultations with experts and interest groups of philo-sophical, social, medical, or professional ties to both sides of the abortion issue, as well as exhaustive review of nearly 250 studies related to post-abortion psychopathology, the Surgeon General failed to find method-ologically sound or objectively conclusive support for neither pro-life or pro-choice beliefs (Koop, 1989).

When comparing the medical procedure of abortion to full-term child birth, Koop noted both produced some adverse mental health effects, but in "low incidence" (Koop, 1989). Both the Public Health Service and Koop found that "abortion does or does not cause or contribute to psy-chological problems" (Koop, 1989). With regard to long-term physical effects documented to be associated with abortion—including infertility, cervical damage, or even low birth weight in future pregnancies—the Surgeon General cautioned that any of these could be associated with other aspects of women's reproductive health history, with or without abortion or pregnancy.

Finally, because of the prevalence of methodological problems in scientific literature, the Surgeon General recommended the initiation of a prospective study to review the mating outcomes of child-bearing women to obtain more rigorous finding related to post-pregnancy and post-abortion sequelae in "planned and unplanned, wanted and unwanted" pregnancies (Koop, 1989).

PAS and the American Psychological Association

The American Psychological Association (APA) has been involved with understanding the psychological implications of abortion since 1989, when an expert panel was convened to review women's response to abor-tion as evidenced in scientific literature (Adler et al., 1990, 1992). Beyond review of the history, practice, and demographic prevalence of abortion, the APA panel found serious theoretical biases and methodological flaws in abortion research (Adler et al., 1992). Early research was founded on psychoanalytic theory, which predicted severe sequelae in self-selected participants who were reporting post-abortion psychopathology. Heavily reliant on case study methods that lacked generalizability to all women experiencing abortion, this type of research erroneously produced sweep-ing conclusions denoting negative long-term effects (Adler et al., 1992). Later research, which incorporated the more objective stress and cop-ing perspective, framed abortion as a trauma or stressful event in which mediating or moderating variables could alter the impact of its experience, and has more reliability and validity (Adler et al., 1992). But even with a less initially biased theoretical position, limited or clinical samples, data collection of questionable accuracy, reliability or validity, and a lack of context development within the research led the APA panel to caution that no substantive conclusions that could be made from the body of scientific literature about abortion, much like the findings and recommendations by Surgeon General Koop in 1989 (Adler et al., 1992). In a press release (January 31, 1997), the APA stated "social scientists have known for years that the availability of legal abortion is not associated with long-term psychological distress in women who use it."

Even given the foresight of methodological issues in the literature, the APA panel came to a number of empirically supported conclusions about women's legal abortion experience in the United States (Adler et al., 1992). In general, they found that abortion in the first trimester of pregnancy may not produce psychopathology, even if the women endure both positive and negative emotions during the course of the abortion experience. Positive emotions, such as relief, were more consistently found in post-abortion women, while both socially based (e.g., guilt or shame) or internally based (regret, doubt, etc.) negative emotions were less prevalent (Adler et al., 1992). Additionally, psychological distress was found to dissipate from a high level just prior to abortion to a much lower level directly after the procedure for most women; alternatively, distress levels would drop within a period immediately following abortion to weeks following (Adler et al., 1992).

The APA panel did acknowledge that some women do experience greater post-abortion difficulties than most. But instead of confirming a direct connection between abortion and negative psychological sequelae, they delineated specific demographic, medical, decision process, social support, attribution, and coping expectancy factors that contribute to such distress (Adler et al., 1992). For example, Adler and her colleagues also found that younger women and those culturally or religiously sanctioned against abortion are more likely to experience negative responses. More recent analysis supports these early findings and variables such as earlier and more unwanted pregnancies, less access to support and financial resources, preexisting medical and psychiatric histories, sexual abuse and domestic violence histories, late-stage abortions, and impulsivity are all found in women who are higher risk to develop emotional problems after abortion. However, these women are more likely to develop emotional problems whether or not they have an abortion. Russo (in press) continues to finds similar results in the more recent large-scale survey data despite the methodological flaws.

Women who wait until the second trimester to have an abortion have been found to experience more negative sequelae than those who aborted during the first trimester. The medical procedure used in second trimester abortions is more "prolonged and painful," which may relate to increased postprocedure distress (Adler et al., 1992). However, an interaction of a lack of social support and resources to deal with pregnancy and unstable relationships, as well as internal conflict, mitigate a postponed abortion to later in pregnancy, which could in turn lead to greater post-abortion distress.

Perceived and actual social support during and after the abortion experience was also found to affect women's responses. Women in the study who showed higher levels of perceived support had more favorable reactions to an abortion procedure (Adler et al., 1992). However, accompaniment by a male partner or even a strong relationship with a male partner after an abortion has been shown to relate to greater feelings of regret or increased depression (Adler et al., 1992). Pre-abortion cognitions were also found to affect post-abortion outcomes by the APA panel. Self-blamers, as well as those who expected to cope poorly with an abortion, have been found to be significantly more depressed, experience more negative moods, anticipate more negative consequences, or have more physical complaints than nonblamers or those with more positive coping expectancies (Major et al., 1985; Major & Cozzarelli, 1992). Interestingly, a study by Mueller and Major (1989) found that women who had a more optimistic outlook and felt greater self-efficacy in handling their feelings after the abortion did much better than those who believed all the misattributions that have been put forward by the anti-abortion activists. These results are predicted by the model put forth by Lazarus and his colleagues, as described in Chapter 5.

In its conclusion, the APA panel substantiated the view that abortion itself was generally not related to severe psychological distress and that most women, though experiencing a range of emotions, were generally positive in the abortion aftermath. Overall, the APA panel suggested that "severe negative reactions are rare, and they parallel those following other normal life stresses" (Adler et al., 1992). Such findings only further challenge the validity of PAS as a legitimate psychopathological disorder.

The American Psychiatric Association (Dagg, 1991) and the American Medical Association (AMA) (1992) have also strenuously objected to the claim that abortion leads to psychological damage and have issued their own reports stating that PAS is not a psychiatric disorder. Despite these scientific data, the U.S. policies are giving grants earmarked to faith-based groups to fund the Crisis Pregnancy Centers that distribute unscientific information causing women not to choose an abortion to terminate an unwanted pregnancy or to misattribute any emotional difficulties they may be experiencing after an abortion to that procedure rather than the appropriate sources. Unfortunately, it may be the most vulnerable women with the fewest resources who fall victim to this unsound national policy. These results make it clear that, for the sake of women's mental health, they should not be exposed to biased and erroneous information, which could create expectations of emotional distress. In reality, an abortion is rarely the cause of any potential negative effects. The continued expectation of Post Abortion Syndrome when none exists may doom some women to distress that otherwise would not occur.

In 2007, the Pope was quoted during his trip to Latin America as telling poor women that they will suffer dire consequences if they have an abortion and that politicians who supported its legalization would "go to hell." While this is understandable politics to most people, it may well be the most vulnerable who are harmed by this policy.

PAS AND ABORTION RESEARCH: A REVIEW
OF THE LITERATURE

The more recent disavowal by professional associations and federal health agencies to acknowledge the existence of PAS comes in light of earlier research purporting the claim that psychological distress is a concomitant to abortion. In reviewing historical literature, Brockington (2005) demonstrates a long-standing scientific tradition of connecting abortion, miscarriage, so-called criminal abortion, or even "fetal death in utero" to psychological instability. However, his methodology is flawed. Brockington cites minimally sampled studies (12 to 30 cases) of organic, psychogenic or shame-related, or manic psychosis stemming from an abortion incident that occurred between 1745 and 1917 (Brockington, 2005). The researcher goes on to cite studies comparing psychiatric admission rates between women who either took part in abortion or childbirth in California, noting higher rates of admission of the former. He used a sample of California Medicaid clients for this analysis without controlling for the factors that govern women who use the state Medicaid system including low incomes, frequent moves preventing longitudinal comparisons, and receiving funding other than Medicaid to pay for medical care among others. Further, he does not account for wanted or unwanted pregnancies in the comparison group. Although psychiatric admission rates were found to be significantly higher in post-abortion women, Brockington fails to consider the fallacy of causal implications in any of the studies he reviewed. In other words, correlational studies imply that two or more things happen around the same time but do not assess for cause and effect. By claiming that it was the abortion rather than measuring any of the other life-experience factors, medical factors, or previous psychiatric and abuse histories, Brockington's data can easily be misattributed to the abortion and not the other factors.

Beyond flawed attribution or causal links, past studies on abortion are riddled with inaccuracy. Methodological issues include: Muddy conceptualization and lack of control of relevant variables; inappropriate procedures used in sample selection, lack of or inappropriate comparison groups; outcome measures lacking clinical significance; inappropriateness statistical analyses; and misattribution of causal effects. Studies reporting abortion to increase risk of clinical disorder have multiple and fatal flaws (Adler et al., 1990; Adler et al., 1992; Russo, in press). The best predictor of mental disorder after abortion is pre-existing disorder, which is strongly associated with exposure to sexual abuse and intimate violence (Russo, in press).

Some examples of methodologically flawed research include Speckhard's 1987 study of post-abortion stress, which used only a clinical sample of women experiencing psychological distress, suggesting self-selection and diminishing generalizability. Other studies, such as that of Illsley and Hall (1976) utilized surveys that limited the scope of their questions to virtually eliminate any positive responses. As continuously substantiated, many abortion studies such as these are plagued by biased sampling (Friedman, Greenspan, & Mittleman, 1974; Hatcher, 1976; Senay, 1970; Talan & Kimball, 1972; Wallerstein, Kurtz, & Bar-Din 1972), and methodological or analytical errors (Smith, 1973) that render their conclusions spurious by many current researchers of abortion (Adler et al., 1992; Coleman et al., 2005; Major, 2003; Russo & Zierk, 1992). Even with the more rigorously designed studies, the population of women who have experienced abortion have been shown to conceal information, and studies on topics related to abortion have been plagued with attrition (Reardon, 2002).

Studies of Contextual Issues and Relationship to Abortion Outcome

Increased methodological improvements in recent abortion studies, including the use of comparison and control groups, continues to demonstrate that the psychological distress experienced after an abortion experience is similar to childbirth (Koop, 1989) or benign and infrequent (Adler et al., 1992). Research exists that supports the view that abortion does not negatively affect various aspects of women's mental health and that contextual factors have greater impact on psychological distress regardless of women's abortion experience. A comprehensive review of more current abortion literature has identified the important preexisting conditions and risk factors that relate to post-abortion distress so that attempts may be made to prevent it from being experienced.

In one of the most widely acclaimed studies of women's well-being in light of abortion experience, Russo and Zierk (1992) found no "widespread abortion trauma" in a national sample of over five thousand women ($N = 5,295$). In fact, those women who reported that they had one abortion actually had higher levels of global self-esteem than other women. Also significant is that this study found that the total number of children had a negative effect on women's well-being. Women's income level, employment, and education were also positively related to well-being (Russo and Zierk, 1992). It was not suggested that abortion itself is related to greater well-being, although others have hypothesized that for some women who cannot raise a child at a particular time in their lives that may be true. According to the authors, because childbirth among women ages 14–30 was associated with lower levels of well-being, and multiple abortions were associated with a greater number of children, those who participated in a single abortion may have had the opportunity to delay childbirth; increase education, income, and employability, and lessen the total number of children they may have.

Another large-scale study of women's well-being in relation to abortion, this time with over four thousand women ($N = 4,336$), also supported the earlier findings that having an abortion did not by itself have an independent relationship to well-being in women, regardless of race or religion (Russo & Dabul, 1997). Much like the previous study, the variables of education, income, and having a work role also were independently and positively related to well-being. In both studies, socioeconomic factors were found to play a greater role in women's mental health than did having an abortion, which either had no relationship with well-being or diminished mental health with more birth or abortion experiences (Russo & Zierk, 1992).

In a more recent study on abortion and mental health in young women, Fergusson, Horwood, and Ridder (2006) concluded that abortion in young women may be associated with increased risks of mental health problems. However, although the study did adjust for a range of confounding variables, it did not account for important variables as those previously mentioned such as educational level and social support. In addition, it did not account for contextual factors associated with the decision to have (or not have) an abortion, so it is possible that the mental health effects found are not a result of the abortion but instead the effects other contextual factors associated with getting an abortion or to the effect of an unwanted pregnancy on mental health. These factors could include women who were coerced into getting an abortion without being able to make their own choice. One of the key factors found in previous studies is the ability of women to make the choice after using the cognitive and emotional skills described in chapters 3, 4, and 5. Using the results of a study that does not account for the women's control of the situation is tantamount to stating that childbirth produces serious emotional consequences using only the studies of women who abandon or kill their babies, most of whom were unable to overcome the barriers to abortion, so they carried the babies to full term.

Women With Anxiety Disorders

Using data from the 1995 National Survey of Family Growth (NSFG), Cougle et al. (2005) examined survey records of women for risk of generalized anxiety to see if having an abortion or giving birth to a child during their first pregnancies made any difference to their mental states. Approximately two-thirds of them ($N = 1,813$) carried their first pregnancies to term while approximately one-third ($N = 1,033$) had an abortion. They excluded both women who reported a period of anxiety prior to their first pregnancy as well as women with subsequent abortions. Although the entire group who chose to have an abortion demonstrated significantly greater prevalence of anxiety than the entire group of those who had the child, the subsection of women over 20 years old in both groups showed less divergent levels of anxiety, and the entire sample had rates 5% higher than the general population (Cougle et al., 2005).

These results indicated that it may be that first pregnancies, and not abortion, are more likely to be related to anxiety. Additionally, although the authors cautioned that no causal relationship was sought in the data, nor were any post-delivery or post-abortion measures collected, it is easy for those not familiar with the difference between correlational and causal statistical analyses to misattribute abortion as the cause of anxiety disorders such as general anxiety disorder (GAD) from this study. In fact, this same misattribution has been seen in legal arguments proposed by those interested in restricting access to abortion (Rubin & Russo, 2004; Russo, in press). At best, the findings suggest abortion may be more stressful for younger women and that generalized worry may be a form of cognitive avoidance. However, while both of these possibilities could be considered as risk factors for post-abortion distress, this study, like others, did not assess for any causal factors (Adler et al., 1992; Coleman et al., 2005).

Several other serious methodological errors in collecting the data for this study make it difficult to truly assess levels of anxiety in pregnant women. First, there were no standardized tests used to measure post-abortion anxiety. Second, the measures of anxiety that were used were substantially higher that those found in other surveys, because the measure of anxiety used by the National Survey of Family Growth (NSFG) did not correspond to the criteria used in the *Diagnostic and Statistical Manual of Mental Disorders* (*DSM-III-R* or *DSM-IV*). In addition, despite the availability of rape history information, exposure to violence was not assessed (Steinberg & Russo, 2007). This last flaw is critical given the high risk that exposure to rape and other forms of violence can cause posttraumatic

stress disorder (PTSD), which is an anxiety disorder. It is entirely possible that Cougle and his colleagues were actually measuring PTSD from
physical and sexual abuse and not anxiety from the abortion. In fact, had
this been a better designed study, the findings might well have been that
women with PTSD who had an abortion may have fewer anxiety symptoms and greater relief than those who carry the pregnancy to term.

Steinberg and Russo reanalyzed the NSFG data because of the
limitations in appropriate sampling weights. In reanalyzing the data,
the authors controlled for rape history, age at first pregnancy outcome,
race, marital status, income, education, subsequent abortions, and subsequent deliveries. In doing so, there was no relationship found between
relationship between abortion of the first pregnancy and subsequent
anxiety symptoms.

Steinberg and Russo then analyzed National Comorbidity Survey
(NCS) data to examine the relationship between abortion of the first
pregnancy to GAD, social phobia, and PTSD. Although the mental health
outcomes are well defined in the NCS, unwantedness of pregnancy is
not identified. Even with this delivery group advantage, ever-pregnant
women who reported having an abortion did not differ in rates of GAD
or social phobia from such women who never had an abortion. Women
who experienced abortion had substantially higher rates of PTSD, however. Logistic regression analyses found these rates accounted for by the
higher rates of violence in the lives of women in the abortion group.
Steinberg and Russo (2007) concluded that the elevated rates of anxiety
found in Cougle et al. likely reflect elevated PTSD symptoms that were
unidentified due to inadequacies of the NSFG data set.

Other Factors Affecting PAS

There have also been studies that attempt to assess for other moderating factors (i.e., factors that affect the magnitude and direction) in
post-abortion sequelae. In addition to age, socioeconomic status, social
support, and interpersonal relationships, Coleman et al. (2005) also cited
the woman's emotional attachment to the fetus, as well as her perceiving
the fetus as already human, could also negatively affect self-esteem and
increase levels of guilt, anxiety, and depression. Some of the scripts that
therapists and counselors are required to read to women could well cause
the emotional impact rather than the abortion procedure itself.

Controlling for these factors is an important step in gaining an
accurate understanding of what may cause undesirable effects after a
woman has had an abortion. For example, in one study, Russo and
Denious (2001) at first found greater depressive symptoms, diminished
life satisfaction, and a greater likelihood of experiencing rape, child

physical or sexual abuse, and partner violence in a sample of women who had experienced abortion ($N = 324$) when compared to those a sample of women who had not ($N = 2201$). But after Russo et al. (2001) controlled for all aspects of violence histories, having the abortion itself had no effect on mental health variables. Other researchers also found that a history of violence may be related to post-abortion distress-related moderating factors such as social support and unstable relationships (Coleman et al., 2005) but, again, their analysis has been criticized as methodologically flawed. Additionally, interpersonal pressure, which could be another way to label controlling behavior, from a male partner has been found to significantly predict continuous post-abortion distress 6 months and 2 years after an abortion (Broen, Torbjorn, Bodtker, & Ekeberg, 2005). Here it is important to note that the literature on domestic violence and controlling partners would be more likely to cause the woman's emotional distress rather than the misattribution to the abortion.

Mediating factors relate to the pathway in which abortion and a corresponding positive or negative response can be altered (Coleman et al., 2005). Another such variable is the assessment of how well a woman can attach to other people, called the attachment model. Cozzarelli, Sumer, and Major (1998) found that women who identified themselves with a more positive attachment model (i.e., secure) showed higher self-esteem in comparison with those who identified with other attachment models. In turn, higher self-esteem was correlated with perceived social support, lack of conflict with a male partner, and self-efficacy. The secure attachment model was also positively and significantly correlated with lower post-abortion distress and well-being, suggesting self-esteem and secure attachment as important mediators in lessening the possible negative responses to abortion (Cozzarelli et al., 1998).

Resilience was another personality factor related to diminish post-abortion distress. Women with greater resilient personality resources—self-esteem, perceived control, and optimism, were more likely to use cognitive appraisals related to coping and lowered stress and thereby were better able to cope with and feel satisfied with their decision after an abortion (Major, Richards, Cooper, Lynne, Cozzarelli, & Zubek, 1998). Additionally, those better able to cope used acceptance and positive reframing to deal with their abortions, as opposed to avoidance, venting, religious coping, or support seeking (Major et al., 1998). Coping, positive cognitive appraisal of a woman's ability to cope with abortion, or both, and feelings of self-efficacy have been viewed as most proximal to her post-abortion coping and distress (Cozzarelli, 1993; Major et al., 1998). We discussed the various cognitive strategies women use to make the decision about whether or not to choose an abortion in Chapters 3, 4, and 5.

What Can Counselors or Therapists Do to Help Women Post-Abortion?

As is evident from the aforementioned studies, women who have had some emotional support before and after they have an abortion make a better emotional adjustment, regardless of their pre-abortion emotional status. Rubin and Russo (2004) provide a framework for therapists to become competent in such counseling. Chapter 7 describes this framework while adding information about feminist and trauma treatment from other literature.

An empirical study by Mueller and Major (1989) lends support to validating such treatment by fostering positive coping expectations but also lowering self-blame attributions prior to abortion. Women ($N = 283$) who were randomly assigned to the attribution alteration counseling group experienced less negative moods, whereas those assigned coping expectations counseling showed diminished levels of anticipated negative consequences. The effects were significant when compared to a control group immediately after abortion but did not remain salient in a 3-week follow-up. However, the results of this experimental study proposed that it may be possible to lower post-abortion distress by altering cognitive mediators related to the abortion experience.

It is also important for therapists to avoid a preconceived notion that abortion will necessarily have a detrimental effect on women, particularly in light of the above-mentioned research. Most women who have an abortion state that their predominant emotions are positive and include feelings of relief, not negative feelings. Women who are at highest risk for emotional distress are also most vulnerable to the misinformation put forward by those with a political agenda to restrict access to legalized abortion. As Steinberg and Russo (2007) point out, focusing on abortion may be "inappropriate because it is not abortion that increases risk, but focusing on abortion may distract attention from factors that do. Women who experience violence—regardless of pregnancy outcome—are the ones who are at higher risk and who need assistance." Although their remarks are in the context of research on abortion and anxiety, the point applies to the range of negative outcomes that may be found in women in therapy who have abortion histories. They also observe, "It is important that clinicians explore the effects of violence in women's lives to avoid misattribution of the negative mental health outcomes of victimization to having an abortion (Steinberg & Russo, 2007)." To do otherwise may be to impede full exploration and understanding of the origins of women's mental health problems and prolong their psychological distress.

Therapists can help women to adjust and move on with their lives using a variety of intervention techniques. In Chapter 7 we discuss a treatment model that can be used with women who enter therapy after having terminated a pregnancy.

FEELINGS FOLLOWING AN ABORTION PROCEDURE

There is no right way to feel after an abortion. Women report complex feelings following an abortion ranging from relief, happy, and grateful to confused, sad, and guilty. The positive feelings following an abortion come from women who feel confident that their decision to have an abortion was the best decision they could make under their circumstances. Following an abortion, women often feel much better physically because the nausea and fatigue from their pregnancy goes away shortly after the procedure.

Women who have mixed feelings sometimes look back at what life would have been like, imagine the sex of the baby, and so forth. However, they usually come back to the feeling that they made the best decision for them given the difficult circumstances. Other times women may feel sadness and guilt after their abortion procedure. They may not know how to cope with these emotions, making them feel even worse.

CASE STUDIES

Laura

Laura is a 22-year-old White woman who had attended psychotherapy for approximately 6 months, which ended about 1 year before when her schedule became "hectic." Laura called to make an appointment to return to treatment stating that she had recently had an abortion and was feeling guilty about it. When she came to the office she reported crying and feelings of sadness. She reported that these symptoms had worsened 3 weeks before, after her pregnancy termination. Since the pregnancy termination, Laura reported that her guilt about her decision had been causing her to feel badly about herself.

Laura was raised in a traditional Catholic family that attended church regularly. She was taught that abortion was "murder." When Laura learned she was pregnant, she had just gone back to school, working toward her B.A. She felt like she was finally getting her life on track. She stated that having a baby, without help emotionally and financially, would have been too difficult for her. She lives on her own and would have been looked down upon for having had sexual intercourse outside of marriage.

The most important thing for me to do when Laura came back to my office was to be empathic and allow her to express her feelings of guilt and sadness. I gave Laura permission to cry. We then began to explore her decision to have an abortion. Laura had a long list of reasons of why having the abortion was the right thing for her to do. I reinforced her decision, by reflecting back her reasons that helped her make the decision to terminate the pregnancy. Laura stated that she thought very long and hard about what to do. She was conflicted because she had been raised not believing in the abortion option but knew that if she carried the pregnancy to term, she would not be able to continue school and did not know how she would afford to raise a child without a job or a degree of any kind.

I asked Laura to imagine what her life would be like if she had a child. She began crying heavily and through her tears she was able to tell me that she didn't think she could be a mother yet. She felt she was too young, had too much she wanted to do in her life, and would not have any support.

Being empathic, listening, and helping Laura reflect on her decision proved helpful to her. When she commented that "G-d will never forgive me for what I did," we were also able to explore her religious beliefs and she expressed her prior belief that G-d does forgive. However in her circumstance she was having difficulty truly believing this. Reflecting on past experiences can be a good tool to use as well. I asked Laura to think about other times in her life when she asked for forgiveness and how she got past it then.

Laura continued to be extremely critical of herself. She was having difficulty forgiving herself. Together we discussed in what ways it was serving her to be so critical of herself and what it would mean for her to just let go. Letting go would be giving herself permission to feel better. I asked Laura to imagine for a second how her life would be, how her feelings might change right then, if she actually forgave herself.

Ashley

Ashley was 21 years old when she became pregnant. She was in an abusive relationship with a man who was using drugs frequently. She decided that she would be unable to care for a child and was glad that abortion was a legal option for her. Ashley remembers her experience as being "great." She stated that the environment of the clinic she was in was very comfortable, supportive, and she was kept well informed. Ashley was certain that she was making the right decision at the time.

Ashley is now 28 years old and pregnant, approximately 1 week away from delivery. Ashley stated, "I know I made the best decision at that time for where I was in my life spiritually, mentally, and physically."

Jen

Jen, a 40-year-old White woman, complained of generalized anxiety. When taking a comprehensive history, Jen stated that when she was 16 years old she became pregnant after having unprotected intercourse with her boyfriend at the time. When she told her boyfriend she was pregnant, he told her that he was not ready to be a father and that if she didn't have an abortion he would leave her. Jen thought that this was her first and only true love and did not want to lose him. She does not remember the details, but believes that she was confused and just went along with what her boyfriend wanted her to do so she could keep him in her life. Within days of Jen terminating her pregnancy, her boyfriend left her anyway.

Jen reported feeling guilty about the abortion and stated that she did not feel she had a choice. She is now regretting the abortion and wishing she had kept the child.

Therapy began by establishing rapport with Jen and establishing a safe, compassionate, nonjudgmental, and trusting environment for Jen. The therapist normalized her feelings. The therapist and Jen explored what life would have been like for her if she had carried the pregnancy to term. Jen clearly stated that she could never have given the child up for adoption, and that she, therefore, would have kept the child. She pointed out many ways in which her life would have been changed if she had continued with the pregnancy. She acknowledged how difficult life would have been for her.

The therapist spent some time helping Jen reflect on where she was mentally at age 16 versus where she is now at age 40. Jen acknowledged that she was clearly at a different place mentally and emotionally. She was in a place where it was hard enough to take care of herself and deal with school and her social life. Jen realized that her decision making and what was important to her then was much different than what was important to her now. She freely discussed how although things were different then, she still can't imagine having been able to care for a child on her own.

The therapist asked Jen what it has been like to hold on to this for all of these years. Jen openly discussed her distrust in men and her inability to sustain relationships with men. After more exploration and processing, Jen expressed that she may not have been holding on to the baby she gave up, but instead she was giving herself a reason to feel resentful toward men. The therapist and Jen discussed how her boyfriend leaving her after she had the abortion really affected her trust in men. Another goal of therapy became helping Jen trust men more and feel safer with a man.

Alice

Alice, a 22-year-old African American female, came to treatment after having terminated a pregnancy that was a result of her being raped. She explained that she had been a virgin and was raised believing that both premarital sex and abortion were wrong. Alice worked as a waitress at a popular restaurant and took night classes at the community college. One evening, after work, she was walking to her car, which was parked behind the restaurant, and was grabbed from behind. Her attacker covered her mouth and told her that if she said a word he would kill her. He threw her in the bushes and raped her. Alice reported feeling ashamed and like a slut after the attack. She doesn't remember getting into her car and driving home, but somehow she did.

Alice did not tell anyone about the rape. A few weeks later Alice did not get her period when she was supposed to. She had always menstruated regularly so she began to feel nervous when she did not. After taking a home pregnancy test, Alice discovered that she was pregnant. She became quite distraught and spent several weeks obsessing over how this happened and over the idea of having a baby. Alice decided that she could not continue the pregnancy. She stated that she was not ready for nor could she afford a child. In addition, she would be looked down upon for being pregnant despite the circumstance. Alice decided to terminate the pregnancy. She did not tell a soul.

Two weeks after her termination, Alice began to fall apart. She began crying regularly, had trouble getting out of bed, felt helpless, and had flashbacks of the rape, and she was unable to go back to work and avoided the entire street on which the restaurant was located.

What is apparent in Alice's case is that while the abortion could certainly be part of her distress, especially because she did not initially believe in abortion, what is most obvious is her problems were clearly associated with the rape. Therapy should acknowledge her feelings surrounding the actual abortion decision and procedure, which can include guilt and loss, among other emotions, but the focus of therapy will likely be on helping her with the effects of the rape including possible PTSD, given her stated symptoms.

A POST-ABORTION COUNSELING TALKLINE (EXHALE)

In the summer of 2000, five women with a variety of cultural backgrounds and a range of religious beliefs started Exhale, a post-abortion counseling telephone talkline. Their goal was to provide a place for women who wanted a place where they could talk freely and confidentially about their abortion. Since that time, Exhale has received over 5,000 calls from women all over the world. The average call lasts for 15 minutes, and although some women will call back if they don't feel they have had enough help, only about 15% are repeat callers. Most of the women are very clear and resolved about their feelings but want the opportunity to talk with someone about their experience. One of the founders of Exhale, Aspen Baker, spoke with us about the talkline and the kinds of calls they receive. According to Baker, a majority of the calls to the talkline come from women who have recently had an abortion. Most are looking for someone to talk to regarding their feelings about the abortion, as many do not have anyone in their life who knows. This in itself creates some feelings of frustration and anger. Baker stated: "People assume that women who call us are upset or have a problem. We have not seen that as the case." Rather, most of the women who call just want to talk, mostly just to clarify their feelings about the abortion. Aspen reported that much of what the women at the hotline do is to provide validation to the woman for what she is experiencing.

Some women call because they are confused about what they are feeling and have questions about how having an abortion might have affected them. Baker stated, "For example, a woman might call and say that she has been pro-choice all of her life and is a hard-core feminist, but recently had an abortion and is confused. She wants to know if these feelings make her not pro-choice or not a feminist. Or another example is of a woman who was raised very religious and not believing in abortion. She had an abortion and wanted to know: "Will G-d ever forgive me? And am I ever going to be able to forgive myself?"

Baker reported that repeat callers are rare, but they do get some. "A woman may call the day after her abortion and then again one week later and maybe again one month later, and then she will never call again."

When we asked Baker about her advice for therapists, she spoke about the importance of listening to the clients and respecting their judgments, rather than expressing disapproval or dismissing their feelings. Some women who call the hotline have seen therapists before and said they were disappointed in the therapists' reactions to their choosing to have an abortion. Baker had some interesting comments about things therapists said as reported by the women using the hotline. Some said their therapist inserted their own opinions about abortion as they were trying to discuss their own options about an unplanned pregnancy. On one hand, a therapist who is anti-abortion may have disagreed with the woman having an abortion and expressed this judgment, making the woman feel quite badly. On the other hand, a therapist who is strongly pro-choice may not have taken the woman's feelings of sadness and grief as seriously as the woman may have liked.

Baker commented that at Exhale, they try to stay out of the politics and focus on empowering the woman. Although the pro-choice movement has been concerned that anti-choice activists will attempt to twist the need for a place for women to talk as evidence of what they call PAS, the fact that most women only need to call to talk once is proof that the emotions associated with having an abortion for these women are short lived. Baker stated that she believed that it is important to provide a supportive service for those women who need to talk.

Baker stated that at Exhale, each woman is treated as an individual with special attention paid to how her culture, race, or religion might effect her emotions. "For example, a religious woman, depending on where she is at may be questioning her relationship with G-d after having had an abortion. She may wonder, can I go to church? Will G-d forgive me? To help these women, Exhale counselors are trained to use a lot of I statements."

As an example, a counselor at the talkline might say, "I believe that G-d will forgive you." Baker commented that "as counselors, we *validate* her religious beliefs and faith. Forgiveness is something that's real and feels necessary for her. So we tell her we believe it's possible. We help her integrate that experience into her life, because for this woman, her religion is an integral part of how she organizes her life. We draw upon what's positive and bring strength to these women."

REFERENCES

Adler, N. E., David, H., Major, P., Roth, B. N., Russo, N. F., & Wyatt, G. (1992). Psychological factors in abortion: A review. *American Psychologist, 47*(10), 1194–1204.

Adler, N. F., Adler, N. E., David, H. P., Major, B. N., Roth, S., Russo, N. F., et al. (1990). Psychological responses after abortion. *Science, 248,* 41–43.

American Medical Association Council on Scientific Affairs. (1992). Induced termination of pregnancy before and after *Roe v. Wade:* Trends in the mortality and morbidity of women. *Journal of the American Medical Association, 268,* 3231–3239.

American Psychiatric Association. (2000). *Diagnostic and statistical manual of mental disorders* (4th ed., text revision). *(DSM-IV-TR).* Washington, DC: Author.

Brockington, I. F. (2005). Post-abortion psychosis. *Archives of Women's Mental Health, 8*(1), 53–54.

Broen, A. N., Moum, T., Bödtker, A. S., & Ekeberg, Ö. (2005). Reasons for induced abortion and their relation to women's emotional distress: A prospective, two-year follow-up study. *General Hospital Psychiatry, 27*(1), 36–43.

Coleman, P. K., Reardon, D. C., Strahan, T., & Cougle, J. R. (2005). The psychology of abortion: A review and suggestions for future research. *Psychology and Health, 20*(2), 237–271.

Cougle, J. R., Reardon, D. C., & Coleman, P. K. (2005). Generalized anxiety following unintended pregnancies resolved through childbirth and abortion: A cohort study of the 1995 National Survey of Family Growth. *Journal of Anxiety Disorders, 19*(1), 137–142.

Cozzarelli, C. (1993). Personality and self-efficacy as predictors or coping with abortion. *Journal of Personality and Social Psychology, 65*(6), 1224–1236.

Cozzarelli, C., Sumer, N., & Major, B. (1998). Mental models of attachment and coping with abortion. *Journal of Personality and Social Psychology, 74*(2), 453–467.

Dagg, P. K. (1991). The psychological sequelae of therapeutic abortion—denied and completed. *American Journal of Psychiatry, 148,* 578–585.

David, H. P. (2006). Born unwanted: 35 years later: The Prague Study. *Reproductive Health Matters, 14*(27), 181–190.

Fergusson, D. M., Horwood, L. J., & Ridder, E. M. (2006). Abortion in young women and subsequent mental health. *Journal of Child Psychology and Psychiatry, 47*(1), 16–24.

Friedman, C., Greenspan, R., & Mittleman, F. (1974). The decision-making process and the outcome of therapeutic abortion. *American Journal of Psychiatry, 131,* 1332–1337.

Hatcher, S. (1976). Understanding adolescent pregnancy and abortion. *Primary Care, 3,* 407–425.

Illsley, R., & Hall, M. H. (1976). Psychological aspects of abortion: A review of issues and needed research. *Bulletin of the World Health Organization, 53,* 83–103.

Koop, C. E. (1989). *Surgeon General's report: The public health effects of abortion.* 101st Cong., 1st sess., Congressional Record. Washington, D.C.: U.S. Congress.

Major, B. (2003). Psychological implications of abortion—highly charged and rife with misleading research [editorial]. *Canadian Medical Association Journal, 168*(10), 1257–1258.

Major, B., & Cozzarelli, C. (1992). Psychosocial predictors of adjustment to abortion. *Journal of Social Issues, 48*(3), 121–142.

Major, B., Mueller, P., & Hildebrandt, K. (1985). Attributions, expectations and coping with abortion. *Journal of Personality and Social Psychology, 48,* 585–599.

Major, B., Richards, C., Cooper, M., Lynne, M., Cozzarelli, C., & Zubek, J. (1998). An integrative model of adjustment to abortion. *Journal of Personality and Social Psychology, 74*(3), 735–752.

Mueller, P., & Major, B. (1989). Self blame, self-efficacy, and adjustment to abortion. *Journal of Personality and Social Psychology, 57*(6), 1059–1068.

Posovac, E., & Miller, T. (1990). Some problems caused by not having a conceptual foundation for health research: An illustration from studies of the psychological effects of abortion. *Psychology & Health, 5,* 13–23.

Reardon, D. C., & Cougle, J. R. (2002). Depression and unintended pregnancy in the National Longitudinal Survey of Youth: A cohort study. *British Medical Journal, 324,* 151–152.

Rourke, M. (1995, July 19). 'Forgive—but not forget', *Los Angeles Times,* Life & Style, p. E1.

Rubin, L., & Russo, N. F. (2004). Abortion and mental health: What therapists need to know. *Women & Therapy, 27*(3–4), 69–90.

Rue, V. (1995). Post-abortion syndrome: A variant of Post-Traumatic Stress Disorder. In P. Doherty (Ed.), *Post-abortion Syndrome—Its wide ramifications.* Dublin: Four Courts Press.

Russo, N. F. (1997). The relationship of abortion to well-being: Do race and religion make a difference. *Professional Psychology: Research and Practice, 28*(1), 23–31.

Russo, N. F., & Dabul, A. J. (1997). The relationship of abortion to well-being: Do race and religion make a difference? *Professional Psychology: Research and Practice, 28,* 23–31.

Russo, N. F., & Denious, J. E. (2001). Violence in the lives of women having abortions: Implications for practice and public policy. *Professional Psychology: Research and Practice, 32*(2), 142–150.

Russo, N. F., & Zierk, K. L. (1992). Abortion, childbearing, and women's well-being. *Professional Psychology: Research and Practice, 23*(4), 269–280.

Senay, E. C. (1970). Therapeutic abortion. *American Academy of Child Psychiatry Journal, 11,* 511–536.

Smith, E. M. (1973). A follow-up study of women who request abortion. *American Journal of Orthopsychiatry, 43,* 574–585.

Steinberg, J., & Russo, N. F. (2007). *Abortion and anxiety: What's the relationship?* Unpublished manuscript (under review).

Talan, K. H., & Kimball, C. P. (1972). Characterization of 100 women psychiatrically evaluated for therapeutic abortion. *Archives of General Psychiatry, 26,* 571–577.

Wallerstein, S., Kurtz, P., & Bar-Din, M. (1972). Psychological sequelae of therapeutic abortion in young unmarried women. *Archives of General Psychiatry, 27,* 828–832.

World Health Organization. (2005). *World Health Report 2005: Chapter 3.* Retrieved February 5, 2007, from www.who.int/whr/2005/en/

CHAPTER 7

A Model Program for Post-Abortion Counseling

As demonstrated in the previous chapters, some women may experience emotional reactions following an abortion procedure. Whether or not these emotional problems are misattributed to the abortion itself or understood to have been associated with other life circumstances, it may be the point at which the women will make contact with a counselor or therapist. This chapter is intended to assist counselors or therapists who wish to begin treating these women using the abortion experience as a launching pad for the treatment to begin.

As we state earlier in this book, prevention of serious emotional reactions is usually possible with good pre-abortion counseling. However, even when women receive good counseling at the time of the abortion, many factors can influence women's ability to cope post-abortion. Most notable is the influence the politics of abortion may have had on the woman, including her own lack of confidence in the fact that most of the initial feelings accompanying any medical procedure including abortion usually pass very quickly. Some safe abortion centers are experimenting with offering short-term post-abortion support groups so that women have someplace to go other than the Crisis Pregnancy Centers (CPCs) that are springing up around the country. Some may have a talkline such as Exhale, as we described in Chapter 6. Competent counseling should be available to these women so that they can explore their emotions in a supportive and nonjudgmental atmosphere.

Given the World Health Organization estimates that one out of three American women will have an abortion by the time they are 45 years old (World Health Organization, 2005), it can be anticipated that most women who have an emotional reaction will go to their own therapists or counselors to talk about their feelings. Some women choose to have an abortion due to their own medical conditions or those that they have discovered through genetic testing in the fetus. These women may need a particular kind of counseling that deals with their feelings about the medical conditions as well as the need to terminate a pregnancy whether or not it was intended. Others need help in dealing with their feelings about an unintended pregnancy but at the same time will need to explore any underlying mental health problems that might have been there all along, perhaps even contributing to the unintentional pregnancy.

Of course, unintended pregnancies occur due to many different factors including contraceptive failure during consensual sex with loving partners. These women rarely have emotional issues requiring counseling unless they are very young, in a nonsupportive relationship, or come from a very religious or unaccepting community. However, there are many life circumstances including prior mental health issues that could be a problem for women who might respond very well to counseling and therapy. Women often have been silenced and do not talk easily about abusive experiences, especially if incest or other childhood sexual abuse had occurred but has been buried for many years. Some of these women are not assertive enough to insist that a partner use contraceptives and therefore become pregnant. A current abusive partner is another high risk for unintended pregnancy. In this chapter we discuss the risk factors that may influence a woman's emotional reactions after abortion, preventive counseling techniques, and model post-abortion groups to support women through this period. In addition, we discuss the qualities that have been found helpful for those who work with women exploring pregnancy termination.

RISK FACTORS

As we described in Chapter 6, studies have identified certain risk factors that may influence post-abortion emotional reactions (Rubin & Russo, 2004). Most abortion centers affiliated with the National Abortion Federation (NAF) have had, by carefully screening the women prior to performing the procedure, many years of reported positive outcomes for the women who seek their services. Some abortion centers request that women complete forms that will assess for certain risk factors so that preventive counseling methods may be employed. One such form is provided in Appendix 1. In Box 7.1 we list the factors that may increase the

Box 7.1   Factors That Increase the Probability of Difficult Coping After an Abortion

1. Feeling extreme guilt, shame, or loss; expecting to regret that she ever had the abortion; not having an effective strategy for coping.
2. Feeling pressured into having an abortion for someone else's benefit (usually male partner or parent).
3. Believing that abortion is "killing her baby," the exact same thing as murdering a newborn.
4. Believing that God won't forgive and doubting her own ability to forgive herself, prolonging deep guilt and shame.
5. Feeling undecided or ambivalent about whether or not the abortion is best but proceeding with the abortion anyway.
6. Finding thoughts of abortion very troubling but dealing with them by going back to old habits: blocking the thoughts out of her mind completely or drinking and using drugs rather than seeking emotional support.
7. Feeling no emotional support from her male partner or parent if they know about the pregnancy and having little or no support from any other friend or family member.
8. Having a personal history of doubting past decisions and using "if only" thinking. "If only I had the baby, my boyfriend would have stayed . . . my mother would love me . . . my life would have turned out better," and so forth.
9. Having untreated depression, bipolar disorder, borderline personality disorder, schizophrenia, or other emotional illness and not taking the medication or receiving proper treatment for the disorder.
10. Belonging to a church or believing in a religion that emphasizes a punishing God, sin, and judgment rather than a loving God, forgiveness, and redemption.
11. Blaming someone else rather than taking responsibility for making the decision.

Information taken from the Hope Clinic Web site: http://www.hopeclinic.com/ ProfessionalServices.htm

probability of difficult coping after an abortion, as found by the Hope Clinic.

The most important risk factor identified as increasing the possibility of difficulties in coping with emotions after pregnancy termination is the woman's attitude toward the abortion prior to the procedure. As we discuss in earlier chapters, it is natural for a woman to have many different feelings at this time. Her cognitive skills and emotional development will allow her to deal with complex feelings, make a choice that seems right for her even if it is not perfect, and then, go on with her life. However, it is important to find out how she has made the decision to seek an abortion as this will help understand her feelings afterward. For example, women who cannot resolve feeling pressured into having an abortion by someone else usually fear that they may regret the decision. Women who go forward with an abortion even though the reasons for doing so are not clearly understood by them may have more difficulty in coping than those women who make the choice voluntarily, even if they wish they didn't have to do so. Religious women who have learned that abortion is wrong, a sin, or murder, and who believe that neither God, nor their family, friends, nor even they themselves will not forgive, may also have more of an emotional struggle than those who accept that there is a loving and forgiving God, even when they commit a sin.

The goal of pre-abortion counseling is to reduce these risk factors by helping the woman to make a decision about her pregnancy with which she is comfortable and able to live. Most abortion centers will not go ahead with the procedure until it is clear that this is the woman's own choice, that she has not been pressured by anyone to make this decision, and that she has some emotional support afterward. Sometimes, the counseling can be accomplished during the initial visit, especially if the woman's ambivalence or fears are allayed by providing information about the actual procedure itself. We provide information about the most common procedures used in abortion clinics in Chapter 4 so that therapists and counselors may educate themselves if they are not familiar with what actually occurs when women seek to terminate a pregnancy. They can then pass on this information to their clients. Other times, especially if the woman discloses a diagnosable mental illness such as a major depression or bipolar mood disorder, a personality disorder, or even schizophrenia, provided the woman is sufficiently aware of the choice she has to make, that woman may need more counseling sessions before the procedure is done. In some cases it is clear that termination is the only possible outcome, usually because of the danger to the woman's health if she continues the pregnancy. As we described in Chapter 5, women with serious and persistent mental illnesses or others who must take potentially toxic medication to maintain their health may be in this group. These women will require counseling of a different nature in order to come to peace with the reasons to make the choice to go forward with the abortion even though under different circumstances they may not have chosen the procedure.

The experience of over 30 years of pre-abortion counseling suggests that giving the woman some time to explore her feelings, helping her to feel in control of her situation, and providing empathy and support through the procedure and afterward will help women avoid any lasting negative effects from the abortion itself. Some women prefer to educate themselves prior to the procedure, and they may be directed to the several Web sites that are discussed in this book, especially the NAF Web site (www.prochoice.org). It is possible that some women will not disclose their true feelings despite the pre-abortion screening methods. They may have to deal with their feelings afterward. Women who have previously been provided biased or inaccurate information may need education to correct the misinformation as well as a safe space to explore their feelings. Women who were forced to enter an abortion center while moving through a gauntlet of shrieking protestors also need accurate information along with the assurances of safety. This is difficult work as it raises so many feelings in most people. In Chapter 8, we provide descriptions from interviews with various health professionals who have been working with women who seek an abortion. Their reactions may help women who want to have an abortion go through the sometimes loud and angry protestors to get into the clinic for the procedure.

COUNSELOR AND THERAPIST QUALITIES

Those counselors and therapists who are reading this book may be wondering if they are capable of providing pre- or post-abortion counseling. Although this is an individual decision, it is probably appropriate to consider some of the beliefs and feelings presented in Box 7.1 to see if you have any cognitive beliefs or emotional feelings that will make it difficult if not impossible for you to provide empathetic, understanding, and nonjudgmental services for women who come to see you, whether in an abortion center or in your own therapy offices. It is important to understand that you may become a target for those people who believe that abortion is wrong, is a sin, or even murder and who also believe that they have the right to prevent women from making the choice. Openness, cognitive flexibility, and a willingness to accept the complex array of emotions that accompany abortion services are also qualities that are necessary for someone who is providing abortion counseling. There is no room for dogmatic or rigid thinking in this arena, as it will only make it more difficult for the women before or after the procedure. True believers, either those who insist all women must have an abortion or no woman should have an abortion, do not make good counselors or therapists.

COUNSELING PROTOCOLS

Although there are no known programs for counseling or therapy after a woman has had an abortion that have demonstrated what is being called evidence-based treatment, the clinical experience of abortion providers together with the clinical and research experience of feminist therapists over the past 30 years suggests that there are six basic areas that will provide most women with good emotional support if they have some difficulty in resolving their feelings within a short period of time post-abortion. The experience of the abortion centers that provide post-abortion counseling suggest that therapy groups will be sufficient for most women. However, those women who have a major mental illness or those who have their own personal therapists to help them resolve emotional difficulties, as discussed in previous chapters, may choose to be seen in in-dividual therapy rather than in a group to work out some of their feelings after the abortion has been completed. In those rare cases where women have emotional reactions long after the termination has been done, these same areas may be appropriate to assist the woman's healing whether in individual or group treatment. It is important to remember that the research has found that most of these women probably have risk factors that would make them likely to have the same long-term effects even if they carried the pregnancy to term. Women who are severely distressed were probably distressed before they got pregnant and are more likely to have been sexually abused and currently have an abusive partner. This is an extremely crucial point for the therapist to remember. Therefore, this woman would be having problems even if she had not had an abortion and may even attribute her problems to something else.

Group Counseling

If a group is formed, then it is usually good to have two counselors or therapists present so one can attend to what is going on with other women in the group and the other can focus on the woman who is doing the sharing at that moment. Usually 6 to 12 people make up a good num-ber to establish group process on a weekly basis. More than 12 people in a group may not permit good group process from developing, whereas the same is true for too few women in a group. However, it is important for each counselor to find her or his own stride. Most group leaders have been women, although there are no data stating that gender is essential. However, it is rare that men feel comfortable enough with women's strong and complex emotions at this time, so they tend to self-select away from abortion counseling unless they already have a professional relationship with the woman. Most counselors and therapists who have facilitated group therapy suggest that 2 hours per session per week is the optimal amount of time as that leaves sufficient time for the various sections dur-ing the group. However, 1.5 hours may be sufficient or maybe all the time that is possible in some places. Closed groups are thought to be better than open groups as the introduction of new women in and out of the group may interfere with group process. However, other counselors do not find the entrance of new people disruptive, and in those cases there is no reason to not adopt that structure, especially if there are not enough women to keep running more groups.

The typical group structure is as follows:

15–30 minutes   Check-in

Each woman has time to describe her feelings since the last session.

If homework is given, then this is a good time to check how it went.

30 minutes   Didactic session

Information is provided by the counselor or therapist and discussed by the women.

30 minutes   Group process

Women talk about where they may be in relation to their life and resolving their feelings about the abortion. Women are encouraged to move on with their life during this section, hopefully by other women in the group, after modeling by the facilitators.

10 minutes   New homework assignment
20 minutes   Group closure

Initial Interview

Women must be screened before selected to go into a group format. Some women, especially those who have serious mental illnesses, will not be able to cope with the group format and may need to be seen individually. During the initial interview basic information should be obtained, including various histories usually obtained during counseling and therapy interviews, any medication issues, and circumstances of and amount of time since they had the abortion. Counselors or therapists must interview the women to see if they can tolerate and grow from the group or if they will need individual sessions.

Initial Assessment

When clients first come for treatment, they report what they believe is their reason for seeking psychological treatment. This is called the presenting problem. The therapist listens to the client's presenting problem and gets a history of the problem as the client sees it. It is not uncommon for the real problem to be obscured by what the client presents initially so it is important to obtain a comprehensive biopsychosocial assessment, which includes getting an accurate social, psychological, medical, family, sexual, and relationship history. Usually more than one session will be needed to gather all the relevant data, and information will continue to evolve throughout treatment.

Although therapists should attempt to find out how the client feels about the information revealed, many clients are unable to express their emotions initially. For some clients, they are confused by a number of different and sometimes contradictory feelings. Other clients are ambivalent—they feel differently at different times. Still others have not allowed themselves to try to understand their complex feelings. This is especially true for clients from diverse cultural backgrounds. Paying attention to the different ways that the client expresses herself (or doesn't say anything) will help the therapist in formulating the priorities in the treatment plan.

If the client is coming in for group therapy, the assessment should still be done individually to ensure that the client is a good fit for the group. Many of the women will want both group and individual therapy. A good biopsychosocial interview at the point of initial intake will make these transitions easier. In some cases women may have so many individual problems aside from the abortion issue that they will be too disruptive for a group initially. It may be best to work with these women individually until the therapist believes that they are ready for the group experience. Women who have suicidal ideation or behavior, including self-destructive behavior such as cutting, impulsivity, or other forms of self-abuse are usually not able to explore their feelings in a group and will probably need individual treatment. Group therapy can be an important part of the healing process for those women who are willing and able to participate. It permits the woman to understand the range of experiences of a variety of different women to the same event, the abortion, and it helps the woman feel less shame because others have made similar decisions. It is important to structure the group members so that they all can permit the group process to develop. This means that no one woman can dominate the group, all women can feel comfortable to share their feelings with the group, and there is enough time for all of the group members to have their turn at presenting as well as listening to other presentations.

TREATMENT MODULES

The following is a suggested treatment protocol. All of the units outlined can be used as a guide for both individual and group treatment. An outline of the protocol can be seen in Box 7.2

Box 7.2   Outline of Individual or Group Session Content

Unit 1 Disclosure of Emotions
Determine the woman's presenting problem. Give the women some time to talk about their emotions, their circumstances, and so forth.
Assess comprehensive social, psychological, medical, family, sexual, and relationship histories.

Unit 2 Understanding Cognitive Skills
Explore the woman's decision-making surrounding having an abortion. How was her decision made? What information did she have before the abortion? What information does she have now?
Share accurate information with the woman using Web sites or literature.

Unit 3 Achieving Emotional Stability
Explore the woman's feelings, which may include relief, guilt, and sadness.
Do not assume that these feelings are only related to the abortion.
Let the woman express the emotions she is feeling at the time.
If the woman needs to cry or grieve, allow her to do so.
Help the woman experience her positive feelings also.

Unit 4 Working Through Spiritual and Religious Issues
Explore the woman's familial and religious beliefs about abortion.
Has she been able to discuss her abortion with her family?
Help her accept her decision and forgive herself, if appropriate.
Help her explore her relationship with G-d.
Explore ways in which people find forgiveness in her religion, and the ways in which her family has come to forgive in the past?

Unit 5 Developing a Supportive Network
Help the woman talk about her family and see if they are a possible source of support.
Help her talk about her friends and explore if she has any friends that she considers part of her support system.
Explore the reality of how many people she can talk to.
If she doesn't have any friends she can talk to, explore possibilities for social interaction.
Suggest that she join a club with people with the same interests (e.g., bicycle group, exercise group, or a book club) or that she get involved with another activity that gets her out of the house, something engaging that she is interested in and can share with others.
If the woman is, for example, shy and isolated, she should be encouraged to talk to one person per day. She should be encouraged to say hello to someone on the telephone and then perhaps meet the person for coffee or a drink, and then after some time, ask the person to join her in an activity.

(continued)

Unit 6 Emotional Resolution
Help the woman give herself permission to let go and feel better.
Help the woman forgive herself if she is blaming herself in any way.
Help the woman understand what is keeping her feeling the way she is and that she has a choice.
Help the woman to step outside of herself. Ask her: "If this was your best friend and she had made this choice and was struggling with it, what would you say to her?"

Understanding Women's Cognitive Skills

If a woman reports that she has had some issue (whether it be sadness, anxiety, guilt, or other feelings) following an abortion procedure, the therapist should first explore the woman's decision making that accompanied having an abortion. This exploration involves understanding how the decision to have an abortion was made. In other words, did the woman think about her decision for 1 second, 1 minute, 1 hour, or 1 month? Did she go over the advantages and disadvantages of each option? How exactly did this woman come to the decision that abortion was the best option for her at the time? Obviously, during pre-abortion counseling, she may still change her decision. However, during post-abortion counseling, even if her decision was not made using good cognitive skills, she can learn from her mistakes. It is probable that she makes other major decisions in a similar way so if she doesn't use good cognitive skills to come to her choice about the abortion, it is probable that she doesn't use good cognitive skills at other high-stress times, either. Learning what that means for her and how she can focus on the important content without letting feelings overwhelm her will be an area to explore outside of the abortion itself. In Survivor Therapy, this is called building a cognitive grid to contain emotions (Walker, 1994). However, the timing is an important part of clinical judgment, as the woman may not be able to cope with too much self-blame at a time.

Another cognitive skill area that is important to explore is the information the woman had before the abortion. Was she told that abortion is wrong or that it is murder; that the pregnancy was not developed at all or that the pregnancy was fully developed; that she would get cancer if she had an abortion; that she would not be able to become pregnant again; or other inaccurate information. Does she come from a culture that has many negative attributions about aborting a pregnancy? Do you have adequate information about her culture? Remember the earlier discussion in Chapter 1 and Chapter 2 about the inaccurate information that is being provided by various CPCs. Once the woman begins to understand that she was not given accurate information and therefore her attribution that her emotional difficulties were all caused by the abortion, it will be possible to share more accurate information with her. This information can be found in Chapter 4, in some of the Web sites we mention, or in other literature.

It may take women a while to be able to read and understand the accurate information due to their anxiety each time they attempt to access it. High-functioning women often hide their confusion out of embarrassment that they cannot understand things that they think they should understand because they believe that others may find these things simple. Sometimes it is helpful for the therapist to go over specific areas directly with the client in the therapy session and then give her some written material to take home. Again, it is important to keep the type of information and amount of it to each woman's pace. Remember, using cognitive skills to make good decisions is not about intelligence but about clarifying how much interference from emotions prevent thinking through issues slowly and carefully.

If the woman has a diagnosable cognitive disorder such as a psychotic disorder, then it is important to assess how much rational understanding she will have to make an appropriate decision. Most women, even those who are disorganized with schizophrenic thinking patterns, still can understand whether or not they can raise a child. Sometimes the seriously and persistently mentally disordered woman will need medication to better organize her thoughts before she can participate in a discussion about cognitive decision-making skills. Even so, dealing with her feelings as we describe subsequently can be helpful.

Neuropsychological disorders may also make it difficult for a woman to participate in looking at her own cognitive skills in decision making. For example, a woman with a frontal lobe problem may not be able to focus on cognitive issues, whereas others with the same diagnosis who do not have attention problems may have an inability to organize complex data. In each case, it is important to go slowly and try to unravel the complexities together with the woman.

Those women who have developmental disorders with limited intellectual resources will probably need detailed counseling about pregnancy prevention in the future. Depending on their cognitive limitations, the amount of repetition of simple instructions will serve them well. In some cases parents or guardians may want to have the woman sterilized so she does not have another unintended pregnancy. This is often a difficult decision for the woman to make, and it is important to encourage her to take her time before taking such irreversible steps.

Achieving Emotional Stability

Exploring the woman's feelings is a critical part of treatment. It is important not to assume that these feelings are only related to the abortion.
Allow the woman to express the emotions she is currently feeling, which
may include allowing the woman to cry or grieve if she needs to. While
exploring the woman's feelings, the therapist should also help the woman
experience her positive feelings. These might be positive feelings regarding her abortion decision or other sources of positive feelings in her life.

Of course, it is important for the therapist to encourage the woman
to express all of her feelings related to the abortion especially if this is
why she has come into counseling. However, the therapist should also
be cautioned not to allow the woman to focus solely on the abortion to
the effect that she is denying or ignoring the roots of the problem. Gentle
confrontation using suggestions to get the woman to think about other
situations in which she has had similar feelings is important for several
reasons. First, the woman can be encouraged that if she has gotten past
these confusing or negative feelings in one situation, it will be possible to
do so again. This is an example of working with the woman's strengths,
an important technique that is routinely used in trauma treatment including survivor therapy (Walker, 1994). Second, it is a good way to establish
and maintain rapport with the woman so that she knows you are connecting with her feelings. Third, it may be a good technique to help the
woman clarify her feelings so that they do not seem so overwhelming.

If the woman has a diagnosable mood disorder, whether she is
depressed all the time or her feelings are labile, moving among feeling
happy, sad, angry, anxious, and depressed, it is important to help her gain
some mastery over her feelings. There are several ways that this can be
done: using structured treatment modalities such as cognitive behavioral
therapy or dialectical behavior therapy (DBT) or simply providing supportive treatment. Teaching women to label their feelings and thoughts
accurately and to better understand how their feelings, thoughts, and
behavior all interact together is a good initial step when working with
women who seem to have little control over letting their emotions control their behavior. We described the impact of mood stabilizers and
antidepressant medication on developing fetuses in Chapter 5. Pregnancy
causes hormonal changes that in turn affect women's mood fluctuations
so it is important for the therapist to understand how these normal mood
fluctuations differ from a diagnosable mood disorder such as major
depression or bipolar disorder.

Many women describe feeling anxious when making the choice to
have an abortion. These feelings are quite normal before any medical
procedure. However, women do not always manage their anxiety well,

sometimes letting it cause them to make impulsive decisions and other times causing them to be uncertain about any decision they need to make. We discussed these disorders more fully in Chapter 5. Women may use street drugs and alcohol to help control these feelings. It is important to clarify their use of street drugs before prescribing benzodiazepines even though they may be helpful for women who have general anxiety disorder (GAD) with or without panic attacks. It is not unusual for women who were victims of sexual abuse as children to develop anxiety disorders, including panic attacks and posttraumatic stress disorder (PTSD). Here the politics of working within the movement to stop the violence against women may interact with the politics of counseling women who choose to terminate an unwanted pregnancy with an abortion and may make for interesting times (Walker, 2001). Some women have learned how to dissociate, which appears as if they are disconnected from their bodies. However, they often feel pain in various areas of the body when they are not in crisis. This is also true for women with battered woman syndrome (BWS). Survivor therapy, a combination of feminist therapy with goals of empowerment (Lerman & Porter, 1990; Rosewater & Walker, 1985) and trauma treatment to deal with the PTSD symptoms (Cling, 2004; Walker, 1994, 2006), may be of assistance in working with these women.

For those with complex PTSD, which is often confused with borderline personality disorder, a treatment approach such as DBT (Linehan, 1993a, 1993b) is also helpful. The technique of mindfulness will teach the woman to stay in the present, work through the anxiety, and deal with her issues. Learning to control the intrusive memories of trauma once they begin to break through during treatment is always a difficult part of treatment with abuse survivors who begin to flood with memories that have been controlled with dissociation, denial, and other unconscious defense mechanisms. These women may use sexual contact with men as a way to make emotional connections that they can control. Part of treatment is to help them learn to draw their own boundaries so they can have relationships with others without fearing they will be emotionally engulfed. For some of these women, a baby or child will demand a more emotional connection than they can give without feeling as if they are emotionally engulfed so this type of treatment may be helpful should they ever want to have a child at another time.

Obviously, the previous discussion is only a beginning to assist therapists and counselors in dealing with the deeper issues that women who have had an abortion and then seek counseling may be experiencing. There may be other issues that are not mentioned here. It is important for the therapist or counselor to listen carefully to the woman while remembering that the real issues may be uncovered slowly, much like unpeeling an onion, layer by layer.

Working Through Spiritual and Religious Issues

Feelings regarding abortion are often influenced by a woman's family, her religious beliefs, or both. Often women become pregnant and are faced with a decision that they never thought they would have to make. Their decision is influenced by their values and beliefs (both familial and religious). However, when the woman knows that she is unable to support a child, would have to drop out of school, or would be looked negatively upon for having intercourse, which led to her becoming pregnant, she may choose to exercise her constitutional right to have an abortion. Even when a woman knows this is the best option for her at the time, she may still be haunted by what she has been told by her family about abortion, or how her religion views abortion. Therefore, it is important to explore the woman's familial, cultural, and religious beliefs around abortion. Having a support system is important in life especially when faced with a difficult decision. The therapist should ask the woman if she has been able to discuss her abortion with her family.

If the woman is having difficulty accepting her decision and is feeling guilty, the therapist's role is to help her accept her decision and forgive herself, if appropriate. Additionally, some women report feeling guilty about having an abortion because they have internalized messages about abortion, which may be a result of teachings of their religion. Some of these women get further messages from CPCs if they have sought them out. Women often make comments like "G-d hates me now" or "G-d will never forgive me." It would be helpful if the therapist or counselor can help the woman explore her relationship with G-d. Other women who believe in a different type of spiritual being should be encouraged to find the ways they can seek atonement if that seems appropriate to them. Exploring ways in which people find forgiveness in their religion or culture and how their family has come to forgive in the past may prove beneficial as well.

Developing a Supportive Network

Developing a supportive network with whom the woman feels comfortable, to whom she can talk, and on whom she can rely is extremely important. In a group setting, the other group members can serve as a wonderful support system. Battered women may be isolated by their abusive partners and not know to whom they can turn for help. If they have been estranged from family and friends, it may be useful to refer them to the local battered woman task force or shelter for simultaneous out-client interventions. Working with other battered women helps them to normalize their experiences and empower them to try to find some physical and emotional safety. If they have other children, it will be important to help them protect them without creating a situation that could cost them custody and access to the children. It is important for counselors and therapists to understand that most battered women are not responsible for the abuse and have tried to protect themselves and their children to the best of their ability. Even asking them about what they may have done to trigger the men's anger can be interpreted as a victim-blaming statement and cause them to drop out of treatment. Worse yet, family therapy at this time might be very dangerous, as the highest risk of more serious injury or death from the batterer is at the point where he fears the woman will leave the relationship. It is important to remember that leaving the relationship does not automatically stop the violence and that it must be done very carefully (Bancroft & Silverman, 2002; Walker, 2000).

Emotional Resolution

The therapist should aid the woman in accepting and eventually letting go of her negative emotions so that she is able to move on and feel better about herself. Sometimes this can be done by simply helping the woman give herself permission to let go and feel better. If the woman is still blaming herself in any way, then the therapist will have to help the woman to forgive herself. Some of the newer literature on positive psychology may be helpful for the therapist to consult here. Restoring optimism in one's own efficacy may be part of empowerment.

Often other things are going on in the woman's life besides the abortion that play a part in how she is feeling. Helping the woman to understand what is keeping her feeling the way she is and helping her see that she has a choice can be beneficial. For example, what are the secondary rewards, in a sense, for staying in this negative emotional state?

The fact that it has been found that women who experience negative emotions following an abortion were likely distressed prior to becoming pregnant is important for the therapist to remember. As is true in helping the woman achieve emotional stability, the therapist should help the woman explore the roots of her problems. Without doing so, the woman will have more difficulty resolving not be resolved of her negative and distressing feelings for long, if at all.

Another tool that can be used by the therapist is to help the woman step outside of herself. One suggestion for doing this is to ask the woman, "If this was your best friend and she had made this choice and was struggling with it, what would you say to her?" Obviously, the woman cannot be too self-absorbed to get to this point. Remember, timing is very important in deciding when to use a particular technique when counseling clients.

SUMMARY

In some cases, therapists and other health care professionals will be able to provide emotional support both before and after a woman chooses to abort an unplanned pregnancy. This is the best-case scenario as it provides the woman with continuity of care if the counselor is properly trained. In other cases, the woman will come to a therapist afterward, sometimes with specific emotional problems that she noticed after the abortion; other times she will be confused or just need to talk to someone about what she has gone through. Therapists and health care professionals should spend some time going over the qualities that competent abortion counselors have been found to possess. A model program with some discussion of particular risk factors has also been provided here for those who wish to set up easily accessible services. Therapists should have a good understanding of diagnosable mental disorders that have been found to be present in women's histories prior to an abortion. Women who have been physically or sexually abused as children, raped as adults, or battered by their current and past partners may be at high risk for unplanned pregnancy and subsequent abortion. Therefore, it is important to include feminist and trauma theories in any therapy or counseling that is done with women who seek treatment before or after making a decision to have an abortion.

REFERENCES

Bancroft, L., & Silverman, J. G. (2002). *The batterer as parent: Addressing the impact of domestic violence on family dynamics.* Sage Series on Violence Against Women. Thousand Oaks, CA: Sage.

Cling, B. J. (Ed.) (2004). *Sexualized violence against women and children.* New York: The Guilford Press.

Hope Clinic. (n.d). *Professional services.* Retrieved January 11, 2007, from http://www.hopeclinic.com/ProfessionalServices.htm

Lerman, H., & Porter, N. (Eds.) (1990). *Feminist ethics in psychotherapy.* New York: Springer.

Linehan, M. M. (1993a). *Cognitive-behavioral treatment of borderline personality disorder.* New York: The Guilford Press.

Linehan, M. M. (1993b). *Skills training manual for treating borderline personality disorder.* New York: The Guilford Press.

National Abortion Federation (n.d.). http://www.prochoice.org

Rosewater, L. B., & Walker, L. E. A. (Eds.) (1985). *Handbook on feminist therapy: Psychotherapy for women.* New York: Springer Publishing.

Rubin, L., & Russo, N. F. (2004). Abortion and mental health: What therapists need to know. *Women & Therapy, 27*(3–4), 69–90.

Walker, L. E. A. (1994). *Abused women and survivor therapy: A guide for the psychotherapist.* Washington, DC: American Psychological Association.

Walker, L. E. A. (2000). *The Battered Woman Syndrome* (2nd ed.). New York: Springer Publishing.

Walker, L. E. A. (2001). Politics, psychology and battered women. *Journal of Trauma Practice, 1,* 81–102.

Walker, L. E. A. (2006). Battered Woman Syndrome: Empirical findings. In F. Denmark (Ed.), *Violence and exploitation against women and girls. Annals of New York Academy of Sciences.* New York: N.Y. Academy of Sciences.

World Health Organization. (2005). *World Health Report 2005. Chapter 3.* Retrieved February 5, 2007, from www.who.int/whr/2005/en

CHAPTER 8

Impact of the Abortion Debate on Clinic Workers

INTRODUCTION

If you have read the earlier chapters in this book, it should not be difficult to imagine that the politics surrounding abortion affect those involved in providing abortions. Practitioners, clinic workers, and volunteers are all affected by the abortion debate in one way or another. For this chapter, we interviewed clinic workers, abortion providers, and volunteers to help understand how the abortion debate and threat of violence affect them personally and in their work with patients. We present the interviews here in the workers' own words. We anticipate many of you reading this book will be new to providing information about abortion to your clients and patients and you should know what you may face as you work in this area.

Abortion Center Counselor #1

How Do You Think the Abortion Debate Impacts You?

I have been working at the center for 17 years now. I guess I am pretty naïve. I think to myself, this is what I do and I am proud of it. If someone doesn't like what I do, then we don't have to talk about it. There was one time within the first year that I worked at the center when I went out to

159

a bar with some friends. I began talking to someone and when I told him what I did for a living, he went off on me. So, I don't tend to talk about it with everyone anymore, just my friends.

I have a good friend who got married. She came from a religious Catholic family, and her mother has always disliked me because of my working at a center that provides abortion services. She wouldn't even allow me to be in the wedding party, which of course hurt me, but I didn't want to put my girlfriend through any drama, so I swallowed it.

I guess I try to surround myself with people who believe in what I do. I do have one close friend who is married to a hardcore Republican who is anti-abortion. But, we both respect each other as individuals and we agree to disagree. We are mature about it and we choose to talk about other topics.

How Does That Impact Affect Your Work With Clients?

From a counseling perspective there are two important things I have noticed. Because of the abortion debate, abortion is a dirty word. It's as if the women feel like they need to defend themselves for having the abortion. They are quick to state that it is clearly the right choice for them and that they want to do it, but then will comment "I don't think I should be doing this. I was told that abortion is murder. This is wrong." Then they will quickly say, "But given my circumstance, I know that this is what I need and want to do." It is almost as if the woman is scared of judgment, scared that I will judge her for making this decision to have an abortion. Or they feel they need to justify their decision to themselves. But, to me, this is offensive. It's a hot button for me. But, it is not about me, it's about the patient and what is helping the patient, so of course I have learned to hold back my feelings.

The second point I want to make has to do with the protestors. The presence of the protestors truly escalates what is sometimes a very emotional situation for some patients. Most patients come to the center completely clear on what they are doing and want to do, but especially for those who are either ambivalent or feeling guilty, the presence of the protestors really gets to them. Some patients even come in crying, in which case we of course take them straight to the back to meet with a counselor. But the protestors make our jobs, as counselors, much more difficult. The patient may have been fine before arriving at the center and then the lack of respect by the protestors (which includes screaming and chanting) makes her sob.

How Do the Protestors Impact You, if at All?

One time a few years ago I was walking into the center and one of the protestors who is notorious for being extremely obnoxious shouted at me. She said "how many babies have to die today so you can get paid?" That comment really made me mad. But, our center's policy is that we do not engage the protestors. I don't even make eye contact with them anymore. So . . . I ignored it and walked inside.

I'm not going to stop what I do. They are not going to change me or what I do. I just wish these people would find something more productive to do. There are so many people who could use some help with their children.

How Does the Threat of Violence Affect You?

I think that we are well conditioned or trained to be observant at the office. In the parking lot, for example, we all know what is supposed to be there and what is not. When we pull into the parking lot at work, that is the first thing we notice. Each of us would know if there was anything out of place at all. And if there was something out of place or suspect, we would call the police immediately and not enter the facility.

Again, I think I am naïve. When I moved into a new apartment about a year ago, someone called the police on three separate occasions saying that my dog was barking loudly. The police showed up to my house and I would tell them and show them that I don't even have a dog. It was a little annoying and scary when the policeman just showed up at my house late at night. After the third time, I went to the police station to file a complaint. When the detective found out where I worked, he started asking questions thinking that there could be a link between my work and this harassment. It was funny, because I didn't even think about that possibility until he mentioned it. That did not end up being the case, but I was surprised that I hadn't even thought of that, yet it is the first thing the detective said and really what made him take action to find out who was making these phone calls.

Abortion Center Counselor #2

Let me tell you first about how I came to work at the center. Growing up the abortion issue was never really on my radar. Abortion was something that was available. I had friends that had abortions, but I didn't really think twice about it.

I am a recovering addict and I have been sober for 8 years. I feel as if I have been given a whole new life since I became sober. I have personal experience with sexual violence and rape, and for my personal healing process I have spoken out many times at women's groups, events . . . having to do with women and sexual violence. The more open I became to my own healing process, the more I became connected to feminist issues such as abortion. I would hear women's stories and found that there was often a connection to pregnancy and abortion. I felt as if women were not getting the kind of care that they should after an abortion. This spiked my interest in the abortion issue. I became more involved and went to Washington, D.C., for the March for Women's Lives. This really opened my eyes to what existed. I began working at the abortion center soon after that. Beginning to counsel at the center, I soon realized that I did not know as much as I thought I did. I have learned over the past 2 years that that doesn't change. I can enter a counseling session with a woman thinking I know what is going on, but I truly do not. Each woman is so different, and their experiences and circumstances are so individual. With every woman who walks in, she brings her own experience with her. The only way that I can know what is going on for that woman is to listen to her and try to understand her circumstance. Counseling these women has really taught me about understanding.

When each woman tells her unique story, it is important that I do not judge or make assumptions. Working with these women has been a gift to me. I enjoy being a woman and having the ability to help other women.

How Do You Think the Abortion Debate Impacts You?

I go back and forth struggling with it. One day a woman will come in for an abortion and I will think to myself that the woman stopped a pregnancy from developing. And other days none of that matters. What matters is that the woman does not want the pregnancy for whatever reasons, and that is okay. I am here to help her.

It is easy to get caught up in the debate of "Is abortion right?" Sometimes I just have to push that out of my mind to be part of the team at the center. And it is hard for me at times. I have to say that when I became pregnant myself, while working at the center, things changed a bit for me as I began noticing the changes in my own body and thinking about development. I had something growing inside of me. But I am quick to remember that this is about choice. Terminating a pregnancy is that woman's choice. I am here to help that woman be okay with the decision she wants to make and to help her figure out what is right for herself, her family, and her life at that point in time. I am here to help empower the woman to make the best decision for her.

So, I guess that answer to your question is, that abortion debate affects my thought process at times, but it does not affect me as a counselor. The thoughts pass within a moment or two. I've become accustomed to letting the thoughts go in and out of my head quickly so that I can be there for the patient.

The key component for me is *choice*. I don't want to get into a debate about what is abortion . . . I don't think about the things I don't want to. I have a job to do and I believe in it 100%.

How Do the Protestors Impact You, if at All?

The protestors affect me, but I don't let them bother me when I am at work because I need to set the tone for the patient. If I get riled up about it, what does that say to the patient? As counselors we are cynical and joke about the protestors amongst ourselves, but we do not want the patient upset, so it ends there. At home is a different story. If I see something, a protestor, or a Choose Life license plate, it takes everything in my power to not run the person off the road. It makes me so angry and aggressive. It's become my cause so I take it extremely personal. I get mad when I see people being so callous and judgmental. I was driving home from a road trip vacation a few weeks ago and I passed a very religious part of the state. There were anti-abortion signs along the turnpike for at least an hour, one after another. I became enraged! I get mad for myself, but more importantly for my patients. I see what the protestors do to them. They become visibly more upset and angry; they suddenly become ashamed and confused. The protestors are full of lies. I am not there to say whether abortion is good or bad. I am there to help the woman. The protestors, on the other hand, are there for their free ticket to heaven (I've actually heard them discuss this) or something . . . not to help the woman. I don't truly understand it, but I know that there is nothing honest about it. The protestors judge the patients, without even knowing their individual circumstance.

How Does the Threat of Violence Affect You?

The threat of violence is scary. But I think, if I don't show up, who will do it? I care enough about the issue and the patients that I keep my fear in check. When I was on maternity leave, there was an arson at the center that I work at. With a newborn baby at home, I thought about what I should do. I now needed to be there for my son as well. But, I do believe to some extent that life is predestined. I have to trust that if anything were to happen to me, my son would be taken care of. I need to do my job. It is to important. Everything will be okay.

I do get freaked out sometimes. I am probably more hypervigilant now, but I keep going. I think about my own history with violence. If I stop living and being a progressively healthy person, then they win. I'll be damned if I'm not going to live my life. I feel like I need to do it. Everything is connected for me. Again, I have to think a certain way to get through the day and help women.

Abortion Center Counselor #3

How Do You Think the Abortion Debate Impacts You?

Like most things controversial, this debate has invited me to really look at my beliefs about abortion. Through the debates, it's given me an opportunity to examine what I feel. I consider the questions asked from all sides, and I have imagined a nation without choice . . . yet when I think about this choice being taken away—I ache inside for how our lives as women would change. It's more than a reproductive issue to me—it's a social issue. I am impacted so much by this debate because it gives me a chance to consider how our lives as women could change in an instant (should the choice be taken away). How free would I be to embrace my sexuality? My career? etcetera? It's all connected, and I don't think most women think about that every time they choose to have sex. It's a freedom in a sense.

How Does That Impact Affect Your Work With Clients?

It moves me to want to understand the patients' beliefs, their circumstances, their feelings. I wonder aloud with them [for] both sides of the argument—what would it be like to keep the pregnancy versus what it would be like to have the abortion. I can examine the decision-making process with them better, as I have done so myself. Also, in being secure and understanding how I feel—I can differentiate what are my feelings versus the patients' feelings. I know myself well enough to know when I am getting in their way—I know how to create the space for them to make the decision they need—from their own life system—not mine.

How Does the Threat of Violence Affect You?

When you work in a place where you know your life could potentially be threatened, it makes you think how important is this issue really? Is it as important as my life? Sometimes this affects me. I cry sometimes. A few months ago I asked my boyfriend, "How would you feel if I lost my life to this?"

Is this issue meaningful enough? I start thinking about existential issues. You have to talk about it with the people close to you. It really forces you to think about what's important to you. It is important enough to me to offer this opportunity to these women. I want to put my community first. Giving these rights to others makes it feel worth it to me.

When there are bomb threats at the center, my first reaction is how can I make sure the patients are okay? I don't think about myself, but rather about the patients. I feel the need to take care of them.

I suppose in order to work in this field, one has to get to be okay with one's beliefs about death, and to have a real commitment to serving others—to offering a choice.

How Do the Protestors Impact You, if at All?

As a counselor, one must ask oneself, "How defensive am I?" The protestors set a tone and the counselor may have a defensive reaction. When patients make a comment about abortion being wrong . . . I have some countertransference. It's like, I'm putting my life on the line to give you this right and you say that?

It requires a lot of empathy and cultural sensitivity to work with people making a hard decision. You have to think about what's influencing their beliefs. It invites me to tune in to what their beliefs are. Why does this feel wrong or right? What kind of beliefs does this patient have that might affect their choice today?

Abortion Center Nurse #1

How Do You Think the Abortion Debate Impacts You?

Not at all. I believe in abortion and that's it! The debate is in the way, because at any moment (because of the debate) we can lose the right to choose abortion. But, it doesn't impact the way that I think.

How Does That Impact Affect Your Work With Clients?

It can impact my work with clients if they lose their right! At times, patients will ask what I think. It actually comes up a lot when we talk about their decision. In this sense, it impacts the way I practice because it is important to me that they don't feel ashamed for having an abortion. More people believe in abortion than we think. In most cases, they may feel that everyone is against abortion and therefore they feel shame associated with having had an abortion. I see the patients again after the abortion procedure. I go over an aftercare questionnaire with them. I ask them, again, about their decision at that time.

Also, before I insert laminaria, I tell the patient what I am going to do, but before I do anything, I say to the patient, "This procedure is going to impact you for the rest of your life, so you have to be sure that this is what you want to do." Even though the counselors have already gone over the decision with the patient, I do this to be sure. As a nurse, I am used to people telling each health care professional they come in to contact with, something different. For example, at the hospital, a patient might tell the receptionist one thing, the triage nurse another, and then ultimately the doctor something completely different. So, I like to hear for myself what the patient says/would like to do. So, especially with laminaria, I talk to the patients about their decision. If I feel that they are not ready and not certain about their decision, then I will not put the laminaria in. I will have them leave and come back when they are certain about their decision. Some do return, and others do not.

Again at the 2-week follow-up appointment, we (at the center) always ask, "How do you feel about your decision?" or "Was this the best decision for you at this point in your life?" If we feel like the patient is struggling with the choice she made, which we do not hear often, we will give her referrals to a mental health clinician.

How Do the Protestors Impact You, if at All?

Not at all! I go to a Catholic church every week and practice Catholicism. My kids go to a Catholic school. Many of the protestors at the center are from my church, but they don't know who I am. The past principal of my son's school knew where I worked, and maybe the pastor does, but I don't know. My only fear is that they would hurt my children. I am not concerned for myself, but rather for my family. If they hurt my family, I don't know what I would do. I have several other jobs, so if anyone asks, I tell them about one of the others.

How Does the Threat of Violence Affect You?

I never thought about the threat of violence until the last [National Abortion Federation] NAF conference I attended where there was a workshop devoted to talking about how the violence has affected others both physically and emotionally. It was so helpful and moving to hear some of the people's stories. That is what has most influenced my practice, in that I have become more cautious of who I allow back in the center with the patient. I used to allow any significant other or family member to come to the back with the patient, but now I am much more careful.

Abortion Center Nurse #2

How Do You Think the Abortion Debate Impacts You?

It's upsetting. When you are going for other medical procedures, there's no issue. Abortion is somewhat plucked from being a medical procedure to it being a personal issue. Abortion is one of the safest medical procedures. So, it's upsetting, disturbing, and scary to me that it is a debate at all. There are constantly more and more obstacles being put into place that make access to abortion services more difficult. That's what all of these laws are designed for. They are not designed to ensure better patient care, they are specifically designed to restrict access to abortion services.

How Does That Impact Affect Your Work With Clients?

One of the most commonly asked questions that I am asked when a patient returns for her follow-up visit is, "Will my gynecologist know that I had an abortion?" This upsets me because I can see that the woman is sometimes embarrassed about having had an abortion. Many women talk about thinking that their physician will judge her and look at her differently if he or she knew that the woman had had an abortion. A woman might also say to me, "I know my gynecologist is not pro-choice. He expects me to come back to his office for a check-up and still be pregnant. I don't know what to tell him." I become upset because the woman should not have to lie to her gynecologist about having an abortion, even if her gynecologist is a family friend. It's unfortunate that patient confidentiality is not always respected if the physician is a friend of the family.

How Do the Protestors Impact You, if at All?

I, personally, don't have a problem with the protestors. I avoid them. I park in the back of the center on days when the protestors are there and so I do not usually see them. I make a conscious effort to not have any contact with the protestors because it is disturbing. Sometimes when I walk a patient out to the parking lot to meet the person driving her, I do hear the protestors. It's hard to separate the two, because I have to go back inside and help the patients. Their voices can stay in your mind sometimes, in which case they do play a factor by distracting me. So, I make a conscious effort to let it go. I remind myself that if I get upset and let them underneath my skin, they win.

I never question what it is I do. The protestors just anger me at times. It's difficult to provide adequate care to the patients and be angry at the same time. So, I avoid the protestors as best as I can, and when I do come into contact with them, I tune them out.

How Does the Threat of Violence Affect You?

To be honest with you, I feel more safe at the center than I do at any grocery store, mall, gas station. . . . A lot of that has to do with the security measures that are in place at the center. We are trained in what to do if something were to happen. When I first began working at the center 13 years ago, I did keep my guard up, but now I am just more aware of my surroundings everywhere.

Physician Who Performs Abortions

How Do You Think the Abortion Debate Impacts You?

That's a hard question to answer. I was at the grocery store yesterday and a van pulled up with a lot of anti-abortion paraphernalia all over it. And it just made me annoyed and angry. It made me think that the rest of the world just doesn't know. On a personal level, they haven't thought about it and on an experiential level, they haven't been there. It's frustrating. People are ignorant in a sense. They think they know everything, but it is really ignorance. People get their information from their buddies and trust it, never questioning it in any depth. They believe what someone who they respect tells them. They consider their friends or family members as the authority, although they don't have any credentials. But this is democracy carried to the ultimate; everyone is completely equal. In reality, that is not the case. This is perverted to mean that we are all just as good as the next person. But, in reality, some of us know things that others don't. For example, an economics professor knows more about economics than I do. Along the same lines, an abortion provider knows more about needs than does a religious churchgoer who listens to their preacher (who likely has less education than the abortion provider) telling them what life should be like with no basis.

How Does That Impact Affect Your Work With Clients?

It doesn't really. In a sense, they have selected me to take care of them. On the other hand, I have lost gynecology patients over the years because I am a known abortion provider.

How Do the Protestors Impact You, if at All?

The protestors offend me. I am disturbed by their ignorance. I would say their ignorance and hypocrisy bothers me the most.

Can You Explain More About What You Mean When You Say Hypocrisy?

The fact that they are spouting words and beliefs that aren't really theirs, when push comes to shove. They don't practice what they preach.

My wife was volunteering at a hospital, raising funds for children's health care. She walked outside and asked the protestors if they wanted to be involved or help in any way. They did not know who she was, or what her husband did. But they said, we don't do those things, we are just out here to protest.

The protestors are only concerned with the unborn. Once you are born, go fuck yourself. That's their philosophy. It's just hypocritical. They have proven that over and over again.

The anti-choice groups don't run to the aid of children affected by genocide or famine. Their motivation is anything but what they say it is. They are doing this to deal with their own demons, their own self-esteem, by finding fault in others.

How Does the Threat of Violence Affect You?

The threat of violence doesn't affect me at all. I am a realist. I realize that there is a risk, but it is a small enough risk so that I do not think twice. If you decide to think about it, then it interferes with your life. Then, they win!

I do carry a handgun, but that did not begin because of what I do. But it could prove useful. If something did happen, I would rather die fighting.

SUMMARY

Women and men who choose to work in the field of reproductive health care, especially in the centers who incorporate abortion services in their care, continue to face a gambit of issues relating to the threat of violence on a daily basis. They are exposed to risk factors involving the potential of physical violence to themselves or their office setting, as well as verbal harassment. Although abortion was legally defined by the U.S. Constitution as a decision between a woman and her doctor, it has become an act open to moral value judgments by various religious groups and politicians who feel that they should legislate their own presumed interest in the morality of others (this of course affects the women who seek abortion services as well).

One can only begin to imagine what a typical day might be like for those who are part of the care delivery system in reproductive health. What has been obvious is the level of commitment, dedication, sensitivity, and understanding that these professionals feel toward their work. Although their centers incorporate safety, security factors of preparedness to include training by national facilitators, and handbooks and drills to insure full awareness, there is little that can fully prepare one for the great lengths which the anti-abortion community will go to in their often unsavory attempts to restrict access to abortion care. Whether a health care center closes because of these tactics or loses employees that give so much to their patients, it remains an unfortunate reality in the provision of abortion care today.

Many have been unable to continue their work due to the pressure and stress that the anti-abortion community has created with their extreme tactics. These have included verbal harassment, using bull horns to scream messages of shame and distorted information. They have stalked these professionals by following them home, taking their pictures, going to the schools their children attend, and in many rural communities where there are few providers; they have demonstrated outside their homes—their neighborhoods. There have been many professionals who just couldn't handle this stress anymore—especially when the tactics crossed the line and impacted their personal domain. The skills to balance the work one loves and believes in so deeply becomes difficult when you feel your family is exposed to these risks as well.

The toll this can take cannot be denied. Those who are able to continue forward in their work often become more determined to provide this needed care. They are of course conscious of the physical surroundings that often make their workplace secure—the fences, walls, elaborate security systems, the presence of security guards, and law enforcement becomes a part of the daily routine. The training and drills of being prepared for bomb threats, invasions, butyric acid attacks, arson, and even anthrax exposure becomes part of the normal routine. Many of the administrative personnel carry the phone numbers of the FBI, the Bureau of Alcohol, Tobacco, Firearms, and Explosives (ATF), and local law enforcement in their cell phones on speed dial. This has become their normalcy—their standard routine.

The staff in these health care centers are often very close and their team is very cohesive in their commitment to their work—mainly the women they care for. They are determined to provide a dignified environment of support, warmth, understanding, and respect. They achieve this every day and express deep fulfillment and meaning in their work. Often the comments from their patients are those of sincere appreciation and gratitude for receiving care they have never experienced in any other medical setting. It is this sense of making a difference that recommits those professionals over and over again into continuing with their work.

Those that work in this field have to also find their own comfort level in addressing issues relating to work and careers in a personal and social setting. The answer to the typical question that might be asked as part of getting to know someone new, such as, "What do you do?" or "Where do you work?" is often initially vague due to uncertainty of how the person who asked the question might feel about the issue of abortion. There is also an impulse to establish privacy and boundaries. Those who continue their work in the provision of abortion care are often guarded and careful in how they discuss the work they do. The issues of security and safety transcend to all aspects of the person's life.

For many who choose to work in this field, the devotion and strength is almost heroic. They have successfully formed their own sense of personal balance to continue forward with their belief and involvement in this important work. The layers of harassment and interference by those who oppose abortion add a set of factors that is almost nonexistent in other professions. But these issues are an integral part of the preparation of their mission, and many see their work as an issue relating to social justice. They refuse to feel shame—only pride in providing the levels of respect and dignity deserved for all women who make important decisions for themselves. The work amid the climate of threats of restricting access to services utilized by over 1.3 million women in the United States demands that we understand and value the work that must continue.

CHAPTER 9

Summary and Conclusions

Studies indicate that approximately one-half of the 6 million pregnancies each year in the United States are unplanned and approximately one-half of those will end in an abortion. This means that 1.5 million American women will undergo similar procedures to what we have outlined in this book. We do not have any statistics for women in other parts of the world, but there is no reason to believe that they are different from American women, although many live in countries where they do not have the same choices as do Americans. For some, they live in countries where, due to government mandates, they are only permitted one child per family. Others live in countries regulated by religious ideals, where citizens are told that they must have all the children that God sends them. The major worldwide organizations discussed in Chapter 4, like the United Nations and the World Health Organization, have stated that women deserve the best counseling available in order to obtain access to the best reproductive health care.

We have written this book to encourage all health professionals including counselors and therapists to provide these counseling services to women. There is no scientific evidence showing that there is a syndrome that occurs for women following an abortion procedure. Few women experience negative emotions following an abortion procedure. Those few who do develop psychological symptoms afterward often can be identified before the procedure, and with good counseling, they can be treated to avoid a worsening of their emotional problems. Many of these women had psychological risk factors that would have made even carrying the pregnancy to term a trigger to negative emotions. Some women may develop emotional problems due to the biased and erroneous information provided by Centers for Pregnancy Counseling (CPCs) that are unwilling to permit women to make their own, fully informed, choices.

The majority of women who come to an abortion center have made up their minds about wanting to have the procedure. Most facilities that provide abortion services include counseling as part of the woman's visit. The counseling session typically includes a discussion of the woman's decision to have an abortion and her comfort with that decision. During this process the counselor will listen and ask questions to make sure that this is the woman's decision and that her decision is free from coercion or pressure from others.

Most women do not experience negative emotions following having an abortion. Many of the women who do experience some fluctuations in mood following an abortion only do so for a few days after the procedure. For those women who are experiencing negative emotions for more than a few days following an abortion, they may choose to speak to a therapist or call the center where they had the abortion procedure. Women can receive therapist referrals from the centers where they had the abortion procedure. Therapists might want to contact local abortion providers and make themselves known as a source for referrals. As shown in Chapter 6, no psychological sequelae have been scientifically validated as caused by having an abortion. In fact, the American Psychological Association comments that "severe negative reactions are rare, and they parallel those following other normal life stresses" (Adler et al., 1992).

Up until now, abortion counseling has been divided into pre-abortion counseling, which involves the decision to have an abortion, and post-abortion counseling, which includes the emotions that sometimes follow an abortion. In this book we aimed to bring together these two groups. Our goal was to give therapists and health care professionals the tools and information to handle both pre-abortion and post-abortion counseling. These tools include understanding the way people think about making decisions (cognition) and the emotions associated with making decisions (emotional regulation). In addition, it is important to know what is typically associated with termination of a pregnancy. This includes factual issues about women's reproductive health, such as the typical types of abortion procedures used today and the steps that women will most probably experience when going to a National Abortion Federation–affiliated abortion center. It is also important to recognize the misinformation and biased counseling that some women have experienced at CPCs, as described in Chapter 1.

Moreover, it is impossible to separate the counseling from the politics surrounding the abortion issue. It is important that all health professionals, especially mental health professionals, give and are aware of the accurate information. As we described in this book, it is not uncommon for women to be given inaccurate information regarding consequences of having an abortion. The scientific research is still quite clear that there is no such thing as a post-abortion syndrome (PAS) although a very small minority of women who have had an abortion may also have some emotional upset that they may attribute to the abortion. The research suggests, however, it may be more likely due to emotional issues that the woman had before the abortion. This book helps to ensure that people counseling women have accurate information and know how to recognize normal and not-so-normal emotional patterns in women.

ABORTION LEGISLATION

We begin this book by discussing the abundance of anti-choice legislation and regulations restricting access to safe and legal reproductive health care services that have been passed since the Supreme Court decision of *Roe v. Wade* in 1973. Legislation limiting funding for abortion was passed, namely, The Hyde Amendment, which prohibits the use of federal funds to pay for abortion services with the only exception being if continuing the pregnancy would endanger the woman's life. This amendment created an economic barrier to poor women in need of abortions. Parental notification and consent laws add burden to those women who are unable to speak to their parents about their pregnancy or abortion decision. The aforementioned CPCs often mislead women and persuade them against choosing an abortion, often by providing them with inaccurate information regarding abortion. Targeted Regulation of Abortion Providers (TRAP) laws attempt to regulate the medical practices of doctors who provide abortions by imposing burdensome requirements that are different and more stringent than regulations applied to comparable medical practices. There are many requirements that are stipulated in these laws. Some of the mandated requirements include airflow and circulation requisites, square footage minimums for hallways, recovery rooms, counseling rooms and changing rooms, specific sink designs, and lawn care standards. The term partial-birth abortion (PBA) is a political term rather than a medical one.

The most significant legislation limiting access to abortion services are limited funding for abortions, parental consent and notification, CPCs, TRAP laws, biased counseling, and mandated waiting periods. These laws all attempt to make it burdensome for a woman to obtain an abortion even though she is legally entitled to obtain one if she chooses to do so. Mandated waiting periods are said to be required for the woman's health, but no reason exists to require this delay; in some cases, it actually puts such barriers in front of the woman that she becomes unable to obtain an abortion.

THE IMPACT OF ABORTION POLITICS ON THERAPISTS

Due to the high controversy surrounding the abortion issue, it is important that therapists and counselors recognize and confront their own values and biases in this emotionally charged area. Suggestions about how to do so are discussed in Chapter 2. It is important to remember that research studies indicate that the appraisal of an event may be even more important than the event itself in the person's emotional response. If counselors believe that an abortion will not have any deleterious impact on the woman, then the chances are great that it won't. However, the opposite is also true. If the counselor believes that the woman will develop emotional issues from an abortion, then the woman most probably will. Counselors working in CPCs may well be iatrogenically causing any emotional distress experienced by the women simply because they tell them that they will experience PAS. Even so, very few women develop any emotional reaction that lasts beyond a few days post-abortion, and those that do usually admit to having had some emotional issues before the abortion.

COMPETENCY AND DECISION-MAKING SKILLS

Assessment of the woman's competency to make the decision to have an abortion is an important part of the pre-abortion counseling. In Chapter 3 we explored the development of moral values and its impact on women's decision-making skills. We explained the two competing theories, Kohlberg's and Gilligan's, and the ways they may affect a woman's decision to obtain an abortion, and we also described some of the latest theories on cognitive decision-making using a stage development or domain development theory. We analyzed the impact of legislating adolescents to obtain parental notification or consent from the point of view of the psychological literature, and we find that there does not seem to be any benefit to teens or families to force this step on them. Most teens tell their families, and when they don't, they usually have good reasons.

FACTUAL ISSUES ABOUT WOMEN'S REPRODUCTIVE HEALTH CARE

The world's primary health organizations have made it clear that all women are entitled to obtain adequate health care, which includes access to a safe therapeutic abortion if they so choose. Many countries, in the past decade, have begun to legalize abortion. In Chapter 4, we described the typical procedures, both before, during, and after, used in abortion centers around the world. We also discussed options for women who do not choose to abort but still are unable to care for a child, and note the growing numbers of women who kill or abandon their babies at birth. Most of these babies die, and yet their abandonment could be preventable with some proper counseling. In Chapter 4 we also discussed what entails a healthy environment for a pregnant woman. We examined prepregnancy issues about selecting the gender of the baby, as well as maternal–fetal conflicts. We also examined briefly some disputes regarding frozen embryos, especially those that occur during divorce or family violence conflicts.

Emotional Regulation and Its Impact on Competency to Make Decisions

Emotions are regulated by the brain and nervous system and its array of biochemical neurotransmitters that carry messages from one place to another. We explain the role of the autonomic nervous system and the potential toxicity of various medications used for health conditions. Fetal exposure to alcohol and other illicit drugs that can cause fetal alcohol syndrome and other serious disorders makes it clear that these drugs should not be used when pregnant. The use of these drugs may influence the choice to abort.

Recognizing stable or unstable emotions in a woman seeking abortion, or post-abortion, is part of the therapist's or counselor's role. Understanding how emotions influence choice can be best observed when understanding self-esteem, self-confidence, and self-efficacy. When stressors get too high women need to utilize coping strategies. We also review studies of culture and other factors that influence the development of these coping strategies, such as factors that influence feelings of ambivalence or other reasons for multiple feelings of strong emotions about the legitimizing of feelings of ambivalence when seeking an abortion.

Post-Abortion Syndrome

Perhaps the most frequently asked question is one that implicates certain kinds of emotional distress that allegedly come from having an abortion. We believe that it is easier to accept scientific evidence that the physical procedures used in terminating pregnancies are safe but it is more difficult to assess if there are lasting emotional aftereffects. Maybe it is the ambivalence that so many women feel about terminating a pregnancy that keeps the question of emotional harm from being resolved. Women demand that all women should have the choice of whether or not to become pregnant, which requires access to safe birth control methods and, if an unwanted pregnancy should occur, the choice of whether or not to carry the pregnancy. Over half of the pregnancies in the United States are unplanned, and over half of those are terminated since women have had the legal right to make these choices. Women have the right to control their bodies and their lives, as child-raising still falls mostly to women, despite many men taking more responsibility than they used to do. Although it may seem counterintuitive, no studies have found a distinct PAS. In some cases, negative emotions linger, but most of them occurred even before the abortion or are due to complex reasons apart from the abortion. In other cases, particularly those being touted by the faith-based groups springing up around the country looking for women who had abortions earlier and now have emotional difficulties, the attribution of the abortion is but one of many difficulties in these women's lives. The *New York Times Magazine* article written by Emily Bazelon (2007, January 21), which was further described in Chapter 6, presented interviews with women who had abortions earlier in their lives and were now serving prison sentences for a variety of criminal convictions. Prison is clearly a negative environment for most women, especially those who have experienced other kinds of legal difficulties that have nothing to do with their abortions. It may well be an unfortunate misattribution that these women believe their emotional problems are due to an abortion rather than the result of their other life circumstances, such as exposure to abuse, poverty, and crime in their communities.

Abortion Counseling

Nonetheless, women who do have emotional issues post-abortion deserve good interventions from trained therapists and health professionals. Hopefully, the information we provide in this book will help counselors and therapists to provide nonbiased treatment.

Therefore, we have provided some ideas for individual as well as group counseling programs when working with pre- or post-abortion women. We also provided some stories about professionals who have been providing counseling, mostly to pre-abortion women, and the impact the disruption to the abortion centers by protestors has had on their lives and work. In the Appendices are assessment forms and scripts that can be used in the counseling process.

Finally, in conclusion, it is clear that the women and men who have been working in the abortion centers for the past 30 years, since *Roe v. Wade* became the law, have been brave and courageous souls, many of whom have devoted their entire lives to keep the choice for women. It is time for all of us who are trained counselors and therapists to join this group so that every woman has the right to make the choice about whether and when she wants to become pregnant and raise a child. If each of us does a little, it will be less of a burden, and our contributions will bring us closer to a reality of necessary rights for all.

REFERENCES

Adler, N. E., David, H., Major, P., Roth, B. N., Russo, N. F., & Wyatt, G. (1992). Psychological factors in abortion: A review. *American Psychologist, 47*(10), 1194–1204.

Bazelon, E. (2007, January 21). Is there a post-abortion syndrome? *New York Times Magazine, 41.*

Appendix 1
Pre-Abortion Needs Assessment

Patient's Name _____ Date _____

To participate with you in an abortion, we want to know if the following statements are True or False for you? Please answer the questions *in all honesty* in a spirit of cooperation with your emotional and physical care.

Check the box that best describes you, so we'll know how to better serve you today.

Your Decision	True	Kind of	False
I am SURE of my decision to have an abortion.	☐	☐	☐
I'm here for an abortion **because** someone else wants me to.	☐	☐	☐

Who is pushing you to have the abortion? (**circle all that are true**)

my Mom	Boyfriend	Husband	the partner in the pregnancy
my Dad	Grandmother	Aunt	"Everybody"
Other_____			

	True	Kind of	False
I want to have the baby instead of abortion.	☐	☐	☐
I want to put the baby up for adoption instead of an abortion.	☐	☐	☐

Generally, after I make a decision,
I keep thinking about it and
doubting myself.   ☐   ☐   ☐

How you're feeling today: (Check off as many as are true for you)

Very scared ☐   A little nervous ☐   Pretty calm ☐
Confident ☐   Relieved ☐   Angry ☐   Very sick ☐
A little guilty ☐   Very guilty ☐   Ashamed ☐   Very sad ☐
A little sad ☐   Other_____

How do you view abortion?

At my stage of pregnancy, I think it's the same as killing a baby that's already born.

True   Kind of   False
☐   ☐   ☐

Abortion is a better choice for me at this time than having the baby

True   Kind of   False
☐   ☐   ☐

Any Comment?_____

This **pregnancy is a result of being forced to have sex (rape).**

True ☐   False ☐

I have *or* **have had:** (check all that are true)

Depression ☐   Anxiety ☐   Panic attacks ☐   BiPolar ☐
A.D.D. ☐   Schizophrenia ☐   Borderline Personality Disorder ☐
Eating Disorder ☐

For confidentiality's sake, who are the ONLY people who know you're having an abortion? (please check off all that are true for you)

Who knows? Is this person supportive to you in what you want to do?

☐ Boyfriend	Yes ☐	Not much ☐	No ☐
☐ Ex-boyfriend	Yes ☐	Not much ☐	No ☐

☐ Husband	Yes ☐	Not much ☐	No ☐
☐ Ex-husband	Yes ☐	Not much ☐	No ☐
☐ The father	Yes ☐	Not much ☐	No ☐
☐ Friend	Yes ☐	Not much ☐	No ☐
☐ My mom	Yes ☐	Not much ☐	No ☐
☐ My dad	Yes ☐	Not much ☐	No ☐
☐ My cousin	Yes ☐	Not much ☐	No ☐
☐ My sister	Yes ☐	Not much ☐	No ☐

Is there anyone else you told? (Who?)_____

If you've had one or more abortions in the past, then answer (a) and (b) please.

If not, go on to #12 and answer questions about spiritual concerns.

	True	Kind of	False
(a) I did well emotionally afterward.	☐	☐	☐
(b) I had a very hard time dealing with it afterward.	☐	☐	☐

If you have any belief in God (or a Higher Power), please answer these questions.

	True	Kind of	False
I have some spiritual concerns about abortion.	☐	☐	☐
I'm afraid God won't forgive me.	☐	☐	☐
Spiritually, I'm at peace with this decision.	☐	☐	☐

Comments_____

Coping Emotionally After the Abortion

Women report feelings afterward that can range from relieved and confident to sad, guilty, or angry and regretful. Some women cope well no matter what feelings come up, and others have a hard time.

How do you think you may feel after having this abortion? (Circle all that apply)

Confident in the decision ☐   Relieved ☐   Happy ☐
A little guilty ☐   A little sad ☐   Very guilty ☐   Very Sad ☐
Ashamed ☐   Angry ☐   I'll wish I never went through with the abortion ☐   Other_____

How do you think you'll deal with the feelings you checked?

☐ I'll deal with my feelings fine afterward.

☐ It might be a little hard at first, but then I'll be fine and won't regret my decision.

☐ It will probably be VERY hard for me afterward.

☐ I'll wish I never went through with the abortion, but had the baby instead.

☐ I believe I will be able to cope with this decision better than parenting or adoption at this time.

I have answered this form truthfully, in the spirit of cooperation with my care.

_____

    Signature of Patient   **Date**

Appendix 2

Legislative Summaries
for the United States

ALABAMA (AL)

"Partial-Birth Abortion" Bans	Permanently Enjoined; law not in effect
Contraceptive Equity	No
Emergency Contraception for Sexual Assault Survivors in the Emergency Room	No
Pharmacy Access to Emergency Contraception	No
Must be performed by a licensed physician	Yes
Must be performed in a hospital if at:	Viability
Second physician must participate if at:	Viability
Prohibited except in cases of life or health endangerment if at:	Viability; except in case of threat to woman's physical health.
Public funding of abortion	
Funds all or most medically necessary abortions	No
Funds limited to life endangerment, rape, and incest	Yes
Private insurance coverage limited to life endangerment	No
Providers may refuse to participate	
Individual	No
Institution	No

(continued)

ALABAMA (AL)   Continued

"Partial-Birth Abortion" Bans	Permanently Enjoined; law not in effect
Mandate counseling includes	No
Breast cancer	No
Fetal pain	No
Serious psychological effects	No
Abortion alternatives and support services	Yes
Waiting period (in hours) after counseling	24 Hours
Parental involvement required for minors	Consent of one parent required. Judicial bypass option available.

ALASKA (AK)

"Partial-Birth Abortion" Bans	Permanently enjoined; law not in effect
Contraceptive Equity	Requires equal coverage of FDA-approved contraceptive drugs and devices, excluding emergency contraceptives. Religious exemption.
Emergency Contraception for Sexual Assault Survivors in the Emergency Room	No
Pharmacy Access to Emergency Contraception	Yes
Must be performed by a licensed physician	Yes
Must be performed in a hospital if at:	No
Second physician must participate if at:	No
Prohibited except in cases of life or health endangerment if at:	No
Public funding of abortion	
Funds all or most medically necessary abortions	Yes. Ordered by court to provide Medicaid coverage for all medically necessary abortions. (Contrary statute enacted 7/1/03 but not yet enforced.)
Funds limited to life endangerment, rape, and incest	No
Private insurance coverage limited to life endangerment	No
Providers may refuse to participate	
Individual	No
Institution	Private
Mandate counseling includes	
Breast cancer	No
Fetal pain	No
Serious psychological effects	No
Abortion alternatives and support services	Yes
Waiting period (in hours) after counseling	No delay. Law requires woman to receive information from health care provider.
Parental involvement required for minors	Permanently enjoined, law not in effect.

ARIZONA (AZ)

"Partial-Birth Abortion" Bans	Permanently enjoined; law not in effect
Contraceptive Equity	Requires equal coverage of FDA-approved contraceptive drugs and devices. Religious exemption.
Emergency Contraception for Sexual Assault Survivors in the Emergency Room	No
Pharmacy Access to Emergency Contraception	No
Must be performed by a licensed physician	Yes
Must be performed in a hospital if at:	No
Second physician must participate if at:	Viability
Prohibited except in cases of life or health endangerment if at:	Viability
Public funding of abortion	
Funds all or most medically necessary abortions	Yes. Ordered by court to provide Medicaid coverage for all medically necessary abortions.
Funds limited to life endangerment, rape, and incest	No
Private insurance coverage limited to life endangerment	No
Providers may refuse to participate	
Individual	Yes
Institution	Yes
Mandate counseling includes	
Breast cancer	No
Fetal pain	No
Serious psychological effects	No
Abortion alternatives and support services	No
Waiting period (in hours) after counseling	No
Parental involvement required for minors	Consent of one parent required. Judicial bypass option available.

ARKANSAS (AR)

"Partial-Birth Abortion" Bans	Permanently enjoined; law not in effect
Contraceptive Equity	Requires equal coverage of FDA-approved drugs and devices. Religious exemption.
Emergency Contraception for Sexual Assault Survivors in the Emergency Room	No
Pharmacy Access to Emergency Contraception	No
Must be performed by a licensed physician	Yes
Must be performed in a hospital if at:	No
Second physician must participate if at:	Viability
Prohibited except in cases of life or health endangerment if at:	Viability; except in case of rape or incest.
Public funding of abortion	
Funds all or most medically necessary abortions	No
Funds limited to life endangerment, rape, and incest	Yes
Private insurance coverage limited to life endangerment	No
Providers may refuse to participate	
Individual	Yes
Institution	Yes
Mandate counseling includes	
Breast cancer	No
Fetal pain	Fetal pain information given to women who are at least 20 weeks gestation.
Serious psychological effects	Yes
Abortion alternatives and support services	Yes
Waiting period (in hours) after counseling	Day before abortion. "Prior to and in no event on the same day as the abortion."
Parental involvement required for minors	Consent of one parent required. Physician can waive if child abuse verified. Judicial bypass option available.

CALIFORNIA (CA)

"Partial-Birth Abortion" Bans	No
Contraceptive Equity	Requires equal coverage of FDA-approved contraceptive drugs and devices. Religious exemption.
Emergency Contraception for Sexual Assault Survivors in the Emergency Room	ERs are mandated to provide information about EC and dispense EC upon request.
Pharmacy Access to Emergency Contraception	EC is available directly from the pharmacist.
Must be performed by a licensed physician	Yes
Must be performed in a hospital if at:	No
Second physician must participate if at:	No
Prohibited except in cases of life or health endangerment if at:	Viability
Public funding of abortion	
Funds all or most medically necessary abortions	Yes. Ordered by court to provide Medicaid coverage for all medically necessary abortions.
Funds limited to life endangerment, rape, and incest	No
Private insurance coverage limited to life endangerment	No
Providers may refuse to participate	
Individual	Yes
Institution	Religious
Mandate counseling includes	
Breast cancer	No
Fetal pain	No
Serious psychological effects	No
Abortion alternatives and support services	No
Waiting period (in hours) after counseling	No
Parental involvement required for minors	Permanently enjoined; law not in effect.

COLORADO (CO)

"Partial-Birth Abortion" Bans	No
Contraceptive Equity	No
Emergency Contraception for Sexual Assault Survivors in the Emergency Room	No
Pharmacy Access to Emergency Contraception	No
Must be performed by a licensed physician	Yes
Must be performed in a hospital if at:	No
Second physician must participate if at:	No
Prohibited except in cases of life or health endangerment if at:	No
Public funding of abortion	
Funds all or most medically necessary abortions	No
Funds limited to life endangerment, rape, and incest	Yes
Private insurance coverage limited to life endangerment	No
Providers may refuse to participate	
Individual	Yes
Institution	Yes
Mandate counseling includes	
Breast cancer	No
Fetal pain	No
Serious psychological effects	No
Abortion alternatives and support services	No
Waiting period (in hours) after counseling	No
Parental involvement required for minors	Notice to two parents required unless minor declares that she is abused or neglected and the physician reports such abuse or neglect. Judicial bypass option available.

CONNECTICUT (CT)

"Partial-Birth Abortion" Bans	No
Contraceptive Equity	Requires equal coverage of FDA-approved contraceptive drugs and devices. Religious exemption.
Emergency Contraception for Sexual Assault Survivors in the Emergency Room	No
Pharmacy Access to Emergency Contraception	No
Must be performed by a licensed physician	Yes
Must be performed in a hospital if at:	Viability
Second physician must participate if at:	No
Prohibited except in cases of life or health endangerment if at:	Viability
Public funding of abortion	
Funds all or most medically necessary abortions	Yes. Ordered by court to provide Medicaid coverage for all medically necessary abortions.
Funds limited to life endangerment, rape, and incest	No
Private insurance coverage limited to life endangerment	No
Providers may refuse to participate	
Individual	Yes
Institution	No
Mandate counseling includes	
Breast cancer	No
Fetal pain	No
Serious psychological effects	No
Abortion alternatives and support services	No
Waiting period (in hours) after counseling	No
Parental involvement required for minors	No

DELAWARE (DE)

"Partial-Birth Abortion" Bans	**No**
Contraceptive Equity	Requires equal coverage of FDA-approved contraceptive drugs and devices. Religious exemption.
Emergency Contraception for Sexual Assault Survivors in the Emergency Room	No
Pharmacy Access to Emergency Contraception	No
Must be performed by a licensed physician	No
Must be performed in a hospital if at:	No
Second physician must participate if at:	No
Prohibited except in cases of life or health endangerment if at:	Permanently enjoined; law not in effect. Exception in case of life endangerment only.
Public funding of abortion	
Funds all or most medically necessary abortions	No
Funds limited to life endangerment, rape, and incest	Yes
Private insurance coverage limited to life endangerment	No
Providers may refuse to participate	
Individual	Yes
Institution	Yes
Mandate counseling includes	
Breast cancer	No
Fetal pain	No
Serious psychological effects	No
Abortion alternatives and support services	Yes
Waiting period (in hours) after counseling	24. Enforcement stayed or enjoined by a federal court; law not in effect.
Parental involvement required for minors	Notice to one parent or grandparent. Specified health professionals may waive parental involvement in certain circumstances. Judicial bypass option available.

WASHINGTON, D.C. (DC)

"Partial-Birth Abortion" Bans	No
Contraceptive Equity	No
Emergency Contraception for Sexual Assault Survivors in the Emergency Room	No
Pharmacy Access to Emergency Contraception	No
Must be performed by a licensed physician	No
Must be performed in a hospital if at:	No
Second physician must participate if at:	No
Prohibited except in cases of life or health endangerment if at:	No
Public funding of abortion	
Funds all or most medically necessary abortions	No
Funds limited to life endangerment, rape, and incest	Yes
Private insurance coverage limited to life endangerment	No
Providers may refuse to participate	
Individual	No
Institution	No
Mandate counseling includes	
Breast cancer	No
Fetal pain	No
Serious psychological effects	No
Abortion alternatives and support services	No
Waiting period (in hours) after counseling	No
Parental involvement required for minors	No

FLORIDA (FL)

"Partial-Birth Abortion" Bans	Law permanently blocked (U.S. District Court issued permanent injunction against second abortion ban statute, 7/6/00). First statute permanently blocked (U.S. District Court, 12/2/98) in 1998; law not in effect.
Contraceptive Equity	No
Emergency Contraception for Sexual Assault Survivors in the Emergency Room	No
Pharmacy Access to Emergency Contraception	No
Must be performed by a licensed physician	Yes
Must be performed in a hospital if at:	Yes, at the 3rd trimester
Second physician must participate if at:	3rd trimester
Prohibited except in cases of life or health endangerment if at:	3rd trimester
Public funding of abortion	
Funds all or most medically necessary abortions	No
Funds limited to life endangerment, rape, and incest	Yes
Private insurance coverage limited to life endangerment	No
Providers may refuse to participate	
Individual	Yes
Institution	Yes
Mandate counseling includes	Requires woman to receive information in person from physician performing procedure or referring physician. Enforcement stayed or enjoined by a state court.
Breast cancer	No
Fetal pain	No
Serious psychological effects	No
Abortion alternatives and support services	Yes (risks and gestational age)
Waiting period (in hours) after counseling	No
Parental involvement required for minors	Notice to one parent required. Judicial bypass option available.

GEORGIA (GA)

"Partial-Birth Abortion" Bans	Law limited to postviability bans on abortion, with life and health exceptions
Contraceptive Equity	Requires equal coverage of FDA-approved contraceptive drugs and devices.
Emergency Contraception for Sexual Assault Survivors in the Emergency Room	No
Pharmacy Access to Emergency Contraception	No
Must be performed by a licensed physician	Yes
Must be performed in a hospital if at:	No
Second physician must participate if at:	3rd trimester
Prohibited except in cases of life or health endangerment if at:	3rd trimester
Public funding of abortion	
Funds all or most medically necessary abortions	No
Funds limited to life endangerment, rape, and incest	Yes
Private insurance coverage limited to life endangerment	No
Providers may refuse to participate	
Individual	Yes
Institution	Yes
Mandate counseling includes	
Breast cancer	No
Fetal pain	Yes
Serious psychological effects	No
Abortion alternatives and support services	Yes
Waiting period (in hours) after counseling	24
Parental involvement required for minors	Notice to one parent required. Judicial bypass option available.

HAWAII (HI)

"Partial-Birth Abortion" Bans	**No**

Contraceptive Equity	Requires equal coverage of FDA-approved contraceptive drugs and devices. Religious exemption.
Emergency Contraception for Sexual Assault Survivors in the Emergency Room	No
Pharmacy Access to Emergency Contraception	EC is available directly from the pharmacist.
Must be performed by a licensed physician	Yes
Must be performed in a hospital if at:	No
Second physician must participate if at:	No
Prohibited except in cases of life or health endangerment if at:	No
Public funding of abortion	
Funds all or most medically necessary abortions	Yes. Voluntarily provides coverage for all medically necessary abortions.
Funds limited to life endangerment, rape, and incest	No
Private insurance coverage limited to life endangerment	No
Providers may refuse to participate	
Individual	Yes
Institution	Yes
Mandate counseling includes	
Breast cancer	No
Fetal pain	No
Serious psychological effects	
Abortion alternatives and support services	No
Waiting period (in hours) after counseling	No
Parental involvement required for minors	No

IDAHO (ID)

	Yes. Law permanently blocked (U.S. District Court, 10/12/99).
"Partial-Birth Abortion" Bans	
Contraceptive Equity	No
Emergency Contraception for Sexual Assault Survivors in the Emergency Room	No
Pharmacy Access to Emergency Contraception	No
Must be performed by a licensed physician	Yes
Must be performed in a hospital if at:	Viability
Second physician must participate if at:	3rd trimester
Prohibited except in cases of life or health endangerment if at:	Viability. Exception in case of life endangerment only.
Public funding of abortion	
Funds all or most medically necessary abortions	No
Funds limited to life endangerment, rape, and incest	Yes
Private insurance coverage limited to life endangerment	Yes
Providers may refuse to participate	
Individual	Yes
Institution	Yes
Mandate counseling includes	
Breast cancer	No
Fetal pain	No
Serious psychological effects	No
Abortion alternatives and support services	No
Waiting period (in hours) after counseling	24
Parental involvement required for minors	Temporarily enjoined; law not in effect.

ILLINOIS (IL)

"Partial-Birth Abortion" Bans	**Law permanently blocked (U.S. Court of Appeals, Seventh Circuit affirmed district court's permanent injunction, 4/26/01); law not in effect.**
Contraceptive Equity	Requires equal coverage of FDA-approved contraceptive drugs and devices. Religious exemption under state's Health Care Right of Conscience Act. Goes into effect June 1, 2004.
Emergency Contraception for Sexual Assault Survivors in the Emergency Room	Yes—ERs are mandated to provide information about EC.
Pharmacy Access to Emergency Contraception	No
Must be performed by a licensed physician	Yes
Must be performed in a hospital if at:	No
Second physician must participate if at:	Viability
Prohibited except in cases of life or health endangerment if at:	Viability
Public funding of abortion	
Funds all or most medically necessary abortions	Yes. Ordered by court to provide Medicaid coverage for all medically necessary abortions.
Funds limited to life endangerment, rape, and incest	No
Private insurance coverage limited to life endangerment	No
Providers may refuse to participate	
Individual	Yes
Institution	Private
Mandate counseling includes	
Breast cancer	No
Fetal pain	Yes
Serious psychological effects	No
Abortion alternatives and support services	No
Waiting period (in hours) after counseling	No
Parental involvement required for minors	Permanently enjoined; law not in effect.

INDIANA (IN)

	Unchallenged in court although this policy is presumably unenforceable under the terms set out in *Stenberg v. Carhart.*
"Partial-Birth Abortion" Bans	
Contraceptive Equity	No
Emergency Contraception for Sexual Assault Survivors in the Emergency Room	No
Pharmacy Access to Emergency Contraception	No
Must be performed by a licensed physician	Yes
Must be performed in a hospital if at:	2nd trimester
Second physician must participate if at:	Viability
Prohibited except in cases of life or health endangerment if at:	Viability. Exception in case of threat to the woman's physical health.
Public funding of abortion	
Funds all or most medically necessary abortions	No
Funds limited to life endangerment, rape, and incest	Yes. Exception in case of threat to the woman's physical health.
Private insurance coverage limited to life endangerment	No
Providers may refuse to participate	
Individual	Yes
Institution	Private
Mandate counseling includes	
Breast cancer	No
Fetal pain	No
Serious psychological effects	No
Abortion alternatives and support services	Yes
Waiting period (in hours) after counseling	18. Requires woman to receive state-mandated biased information in person from a health care provider.
Parental involvement required for minors	Consent of one parent required. Judicial bypass option available.

IOWA (IA)

"Partial-Birth Abortion" Bans	Law permanently blocked (U.S. Court of Appeals, Eighth Circuit affirmed district court's permanent injunction, 7/1/99); law not in effect.
Contraceptive Equity	Requires equal coverage of FDA-approved contraceptive drugs and devices.
Emergency Contraception for Sexual Assault Survivors in the Emergency Room	No
Pharmacy Access to Emergency Contraception	No
Must be performed by a licensed physician	Yes
Must be performed in a hospital if at:	No
Second physician must participate if at:	No
Prohibited except in cases of life or health endangerment if at:	3rd trimester
Public funding of abortion	
Funds all or most medically necessary abortions	No
Funds limited to life endangerment, rape, and incest	Yes. Exception in case of fetal abnormality.
Private insurance coverage limited to life endangerment	No
Providers may refuse to participate	
Individual	Yes
Institution	Private
Mandate counseling includes	
Breast cancer	No
Fetal pain	No
Serious psychological effects	No
Abortion alternatives and support services	No
Waiting period (in hours) after counseling	No
Parental involvement required for minors	Notice to one parent, or to grandparent if reason given to physician, required. Judicial bypass option available.

KANSAS (KS)

"Partial-Birth Abortion" Bans	Law limited to postviability bans on abortion, with life and health exceptions.
Contraceptive Equity	No
Emergency Contraception for Sexual Assault Survivors in the Emergency Room	No
Pharmacy Access to Emergency Contraception	No
Must be performed by a licensed physician	No
Must be performed in a hospital if at:	No
Second physician must participate if at:	Viability
Prohibited except in cases of life or health endangerment if at:	Viability
Public funding of abortion	
Funds all or most medically necessary abortions	No
Funds limited to life endangerment, rape, and incest	Yes
Private insurance coverage limited to life endangerment	No
Providers may refuse to participate	
Individual	Yes
Institution	Yes
Mandate counseling includes	
Breast cancer	No
Fetal pain	No
Serious psychological effects	No
Abortion alternatives and support services	Yes
Waiting period (in hours) after counseling	24
Parental involvement required for minors	Notice to one parent required. Judicial bypass option available.

KENTUCKY (KY)

"Partial-Birth Abortion" Bans	Law permanently blocked (U.S. Court of Appeals, Sixth Circuit affirmed district court's permanent injunction, 7/31/00); law not in effect.
Contraceptive Equity	No
Emergency Contraception for Sexual Assault Survivors in the Emergency Room	No
Pharmacy Access to Emergency Contraception	No
Must be performed by a licensed physician	No
Must be performed in a hospital if at:	2nd trimester
Second physician must participate if at:	No
Prohibited except in cases of life or health endangerment if at:	Viability
Public funding of abortion	
Funds all or most medically necessary abortions	No
Funds limited to life endangerment, rape, and incest	Yes
Private insurance coverage limited to life endangerment	Yes
Providers may refuse to participate	
Individual	Yes
Institution	Yes
Mandate counseling includes	
Breast cancer	No
Fetal pain	No
Serious psychological effects	No
Abortion alternatives and support services	Yes
Waiting period (in hours) after counseling	24
Parental involvement required for minors	Consent of one parent required. Judicial bypass option available.

LOUISIANA (LA)

"Partial-Birth Abortion" Bans	Law permanently blocked (U.S. Court of Appeals, Fifth Circuit affirmed district court judgment declaring "partial-Birth Abortion" ban unconstitutional, 8/17/00); law not in effect.
Contraceptive Equity	No
Emergency Contraception for Sexual Assault Survivors in the Emergency Room	No
Pharmacy Access to Emergency Contraception	No
Must be performed by a licensed physician	Yes
Must be performed in a hospital if at:	No
Second physician must participate if at:	Viability
Prohibited except in cases of life or health endangerment if at:	Viability
Public funding of abortion	
Funds all or most medically necessary abortions	No
Funds limited to life endangerment, rape, and incest	Yes
Private insurance coverage limited to life endangerment	No
Providers may refuse to participate	
Individual	Yes
Institution	Yes
Mandate counseling includes	Requires woman to receive state-mandated biased information in person from a health care provider.
Breast cancer	No
Fetal pain	No
Serious psychological effects	No
Abortion alternatives and support services	Yes
Waiting period (in hours) after counseling	24
Parental involvement required for minors	Consent of one parent required. Judicial bypass option available.

MAINE (ME)

"Partial-Birth Abortion" Bans	No
Contraceptive Equity	Requires equal coverage of FDA-approved contraceptive drugs and devices. Religious exemption.
Emergency Contraception for Sexual Assault Survivors in the Emergency Room	No
Pharmacy Access to Emergency Contraception	No
Must be performed by a licensed physician	Yes
Must be performed in a hospital if at:	No
Second physician must participate if at:	No
Prohibited except in cases of life or health endangerment if at:	Viability
Public funding of abortion	
Funds all or most medically necessary abortions	No
Funds limited to life endangerment, rape, and incest	Yes
Private insurance coverage limited to life endangerment	No
Providers may refuse to participate	
Individual	Yes
Institution	Yes
Mandate counseling includes	
Breast cancer	No
Fetal pain	No
Serious psychological effects	No
Abortion alternatives and support services	No
Waiting period (in hours) after counseling	No
Parental involvement required for minors	Consent of one parent, or health care provider, or adult family member, required-unless minor receives specified counseling. Judicial bypass option available.

MARYLAND (MD)

"Partial-Birth Abortion" Bans	No
Contraceptive Equity	Requires equal coverage of FDA-approved contraceptive drugs and devices. Religious exemption.
Emergency Contraception for Sexual Assault Survivors in the Emergency Room	No
Pharmacy Access to Emergency Contraception	No
Must be performed by a licensed physician	Yes
Must be performed in a hospital if at:	No
Second physician must participate if at:	No
Prohibited except in cases of life or health endangerment if at:	Viability. Exception in case of fetal abnormality.
Public funding of abortion	
Funds all or most medically necessary abortions	Yes. Some Medicaid coverage, but not full Medicaid coverage for medically necessary abortions.
Funds limited to life endangerment, rape, and incest	No
Private insurance coverage limited to life endangerment	No
Providers may refuse to participate	
Individual	No
Institution	No
Mandate counseling includes	
Breast cancer	Yes
Fetal pain	Yes
Serious psychological effects	No
Abortion alternatives and support services	No
Waiting period (in hours) after counseling	No
Parental involvement required for minors	Notice to one parent required unless physician determines either: that notice may lead to physical or mental abuse, that the minor is mature and capable of giving informed consent, or that notice would not be in the minor's best interest.

MASSACHUSETTS (MA)

"Partial-Birth Abortion" Bans	No
Contraceptive Equity	Requires equal coverage of FDA-approved contraceptive drugs and devices. Religious exemption.
Emergency Contraception for Sexual Assault Survivors in the Emergency Room	No
Pharmacy Access to Emergency Contraception	No
Must be performed by a licensed physician	Yes
Must be performed in a hospital if at:	12 weeks
Second physician must participate if at:	No
Prohibited except in cases of life or health endangerment if at:	24 weeks
Public funding of abortion	
Funds all or most medically necessary abortions	Yes. Ordered by court to provide Medicaid coverage for all medically necessary abortions.
Funds limited to life endangerment, rape, and incest	No
Private insurance coverage limited to life endangerment	No
Providers may refuse to participate	
Individual	Yes
Institution	Yes
Mandate counseling includes	
Breast cancer	No
Fetal pain	No
Serious psychological effects	No
Abortion alternatives and support services	No
Waiting period (in hours) after counseling	24. Enforcement stayed or enjoined by a federal court; law not in effect.
Parental involvement required for minors	Consent of one parent required. Judicial bypass option available.

MICHIGAN (MI)

"Partial-Birth Abortion" Bans	New law, called the "Legal Birth Definition Act," permanently blocked (U.S. District Court, 9/12/05). Second law permanently blocked (U.S. District Court, 4/26/01). First statute permanently blocked (U.S. District Court, 7/31/97); law not in effect.
Contraceptive Equity	No
Emergency Contraception for Sexual Assault Survivors in the Emergency Room	No
Pharmacy Access to Emergency Contraception	No
Must be performed by a licensed physician	Yes
Must be performed in a hospital if at:	No
Second physician must participate if at:	No
Prohibited except in cases of life or health endangerment if at:	Viability. Exception in the case of life endangerment only.
Public funding of abortion	
Funds all or most medically necessary abortions	No
Funds limited to life endangerment, rape, and incest	Yes
Private insurance coverage limited to life endangerment	No
Providers may refuse to participate	
Individual	Yes
Institution	Yes
Mandate counseling includes	
Breast cancer	No
Fetal pain	No
Serious psychological effects	No
Abortion alternatives and support services	Yes
Waiting period (in hours) after counseling	24
Parental involvement required for minors	Consent of one parent required. Judicial bypass option available.

MINNESOTA (MN)

"Partial-Birth Abortion" Bans	No

Contraceptive Equity	No
Emergency Contraception for Sexual Assault Survivors in the Emergency Room	No
Pharmacy Access to Emergency Contraception	No
Must be performed by a licensed physician	Yes
Must be performed in a hospital if at:	2nd trimester
Second physician must participate if at:	Permanently enjoined; law not in effect.
Prohibited except in cases of life or health endangerment if at:	Permanently enjoined; law not in effect.
Public funding of abortion	
Funds all or most medically necessary abortions	Yes. Ordered by court to provide Medicaid coverage for medically necessary abortions
Funds limited to life endangerment, rape, and incest	No
Private insurance coverage limited to life endangerment	No
Providers may refuse to participate	
Individual	Yes
Institution	Private
Mandate counseling includes	
Breast cancer	Yes
Fetal pain	Yes. Fetal pain information is given to women who are at least 20 weeks gestation.
Serious psychological effects	No
Abortion alternatives and support services	Yes
Waiting period (in hours) after counseling	24
Parental involvement required for minors	Notice to two parents required. Judicial bypass option available.

MISSISSIPPI (MS)

"Partial-Birth Abortion" Bans	Unchallenged in court although this policy is presumably unenforceable under the terms set out in *Stenberg v. Carhart.*
Contraceptive Equity	No
Emergency Contraception for Sexual Assault Survivors in the Emergency Room	No
Pharmacy Access to Emergency Contraception	No
Must be performed by a licensed physician	Yes
Must be performed in a hospital if at:	No
Second physician must participate if at:	No
Prohibited except in cases of life or health endangerment if at:	No
Public funding of abortion	
Funds all or most medically necessary abortions	No
Funds limited to life endangerment, rape, and incest	Yes. Exception when woman's life is endangered, when result of rape/incest or in case of fetal abnormality (in violation of Hyde Amendment).
Private insurance coverage limited to life endangerment	No
Providers may refuse to participate	
Individual	Yes
Institution	Yes
Mandate counseling includes	
Breast cancer	Yes
Fetal pain	No
Serious psychological effects	No
Abortion alternatives and support services	Yes
Waiting period (in hours) after counseling	24
Parental involvement required for minors	Consent. Both parents must consent to the abortion.

MISSOURI (MO)

"Partial-Birth Abortion" Bans	**Law permanently blocked (U.S. Court of Appeals, Eight Circuit, affirmed district court's permanent injunction, 11/28/05); law not in effect.**
Contraceptive Equity	Requires equal coverage of FDA-approved contraceptive drugs and devices. Religious exemption.
Emergency Contraception for Sexual Assault Survivors in the Emergency Room	No
Pharmacy Access to Emergency Contraception	No
Must be performed by a licensed physician	Yes
Must be performed in a hospital if at:	Viability
Second physician must participate if at:	Viability
Prohibited except in cases of life or health endangerment if at:	Viability
Public funding of abortion	
Funds all or most medically necessary abortions	No
Funds limited to life endangerment, rape, and incest	Yes
Private insurance coverage limited to life endangerment	Yes
Providers may refuse to participate	
Individual	Yes
Institution	Yes
Mandate counseling includes	
Breast cancer	No
Fetal pain	No
Serious psychological effects	No
Abortion alternatives and support services	No
Waiting period (in hours) after counseling	24
Parental involvement required for minors	Consent of one parent required. Judicial bypass option available.

MONTANA (MT)

"Partial-Birth Abortion" Bans	Unchallenged in court although this policy is presumably unenforceable under the terms set out in *Stenberg v. Carhart*. Law limited to postviability bans on abortion, with life exceptions.
Contraceptive Equity	No
Emergency Contraception for Sexual Assault Survivors in the Emergency Room	No
Pharmacy Access to Emergency Contraception	No
Must be performed by a licensed physician	No
Must be performed in a hospital if at:	No
Second physician must participate if at:	Viability
Prohibited except in cases of life or health endangerment if at:	Viability. Exception in case of threat to the woman's physical health.
Public funding of abortion	
Funds all or most medically necessary abortions	Yes. Ordered by court to provide Medicaid coverage for all medically necessary abortions
Funds limited to life endangerment, rape, and incest	No
Private insurance coverage limited to life endangerment	No
Providers may refuse to participate	
Individual	Yes
Institution	Private
Mandate counseling includes	
Breast cancer	No
Fetal pain	No
Serious psychological effects	No
Abortion alternatives and support services	No
Waiting period (in hours) after counseling	24. Permanently enjoined; law not in effect.
Parental involvement required for minors	Permanently enjoined; law not in effect.

NEBRASKA (NE)

"Partial-Birth Abortion" Bans	Law permanently blocked (U.S. Supreme Court 6/28/00); law not in effect.
Contraceptive Equity	No
Emergency Contraception for Sexual Assault Survivors in the Emergency Room	No
Pharmacy Access to Emergency Contraception	No
Must be performed by a licensed physician	Yes
Must be performed in a hospital if at:	No
Second physician must participate if at:	No
Prohibited except in cases of life or health endangerment if at:	Viability
Public funding of abortion	
Funds all or most medically necessary abortions	No
Funds limited to life endangerment, rape, and incest	Yes
Private insurance coverage limited to life endangerment	No
Providers may refuse to participate	
Individual	Yes
Institution	Yes
Mandate counseling includes	
Breast cancer	No
Fetal pain	No
Serious psychological effects	No
Abortion alternatives and support services	Yes
Waiting period (in hours) after counseling	24
Parental involvement required for minors	Notice to one parent required. Judicial bypass option available.

NEVADA (NV)

"Partial-Birth Abortion" Bans	No
Contraceptive Equity	Requires equal coverage of FDA-approved contraceptive drugs and devices. Religious exemption.
Emergency Contraception for Sexual Assault Survivors in the Emergency Room	No
Pharmacy Access to Emergency Contraception	No
Must be performed by a licensed physician	Yes
Must be performed in a hospital if at:	24 weeks
Second physician must participate if at:	No
Prohibited except in cases of life or health endangerment if at:	24 weeks
Public funding of abortion	
Funds all or most medically necessary abortions	No
Funds limited to life endangerment, rape, and incest	Yes
Private insurance coverage limited to life endangerment	No
Providers may refuse to participate	
Individual	Yes
Institution	Private
Mandate counseling includes	
Breast cancer	No
Fetal pain	No
Serious psychological effects	Yes
Abortion alternatives and support services	No
Waiting period (in hours) after counseling	No
Parental involvement required for minors	Permanently enjoined; law not in effect.

NEW HAMPSHIRE (NH)

"Partial-Birth Abortion" Bans	No
Contraceptive Equity	Requires equal coverage of FDA-approved contraceptive drugs and devices.
Emergency Contraception for Sexual Assault Survivors in the Emergency Room	No
Pharmacy Access to Emergency Contraception	No
Must be performed by a licensed physician	No
Must be performed in a hospital if at:	No
Second physician must participate if at:	No
Prohibited except in cases of life or health endangerment if at:	No
Public funding of abortion	
Funds all or most medically necessary abortions	No
Funds limited to life endangerment, rape, and incest	Yes
Private insurance coverage limited to life endangerment	No
Providers may refuse to participate	
Individual	No
Institution	No
Mandate counseling includes	
Breast cancer	No
Fetal pain	No
Serious psychological effects	No
Abortion alternatives and support services	No
Waiting period (in hours) after counseling	No
Parental involvement required for minors	Parental notification law enjoined or not enforced. Constitutionality of the statute currently being challenged.

NEW JERSEY (NJ)

"Partial-Birth Abortion" Bans	Law permanently blocked (U.S. Court of Appeals, Third Circuit affirmed district court's permanent injunction, 7/26/00); law not in effect.
Contraceptive Equity	No
Emergency Contraception for Sexual Assault Survivors in the Emergency Room	No
Pharmacy Access to Emergency Contraception	No
Must be performed by a licensed physician	Yes
Must be performed in a hospital if at:	14 weeks
Second physician must participate if at:	No
Prohibited except in cases of life or health endangerment if at:	No
Public funding of abortion	
Funds all or most medically necessary abortions	Yes. Ordered by court to provide Medicaid coverage for all medically necessary abortions
Funds limited to life endangerment, rape, and incest	No
Private insurance coverage limited to life endangerment	No
Providers may refuse to participate	
Individual	Yes
Institution	Private
Mandate counseling includes	
Breast cancer	No
Fetal pain	No
Serious psychological effects	No
Abortion alternatives and support services	No
Waiting period (in hours) after counseling	No
Parental involvement required for minors	Permanently enjoined; law not in effect.

NEW MEXICO (NM)

"Partial-Birth Abortion" Bans	Law limited to postviability bans on abortion, with life and health exceptions.
Contraceptive Equity	Requires equal coverage of FDA-approved contraceptive drugs and devices. Religious exemption.
Emergency Contraception for Sexual Assault Survivors in the Emergency Room	ERs are mandated to provide information about EC and dispense EC upon request.
Pharmacy Access to Emergency Contraception	EC is available directly from the pharmacist.
Must be performed by a licensed physician	No
Must be performed in a hospital if at:	No
Second physician must participate if at:	No
Prohibited except in cases of life or health endangerment if at:	No
Public funding of abortion	
Funds all or most medically necessary abortions	Yes. Ordered by court to provide Medicaid coverage for all medically necessary abortions
Funds limited to life endangerment, rape, and incest	No
Private insurance coverage limited to life endangerment	No
Providers may refuse to participate	
Individual	Yes
Institution	Yes
Mandate counseling includes	
Breast cancer	No
Fetal pain	No
Serious psychological effects	No
Abortion alternatives and support services	No
Waiting period (in hours) after counseling	No
Parental involvement required for minors	Permanently enjoined; law not in effect.

NEW YORK (NY)

"Partial-Birth Abortion" Bans	No
Contraceptive Equity	Requires equal coverage of FDA-approved contraceptive drugs and devices. Religious exemption.
Emergency Contraception for Sexual Assault Survivors in the Emergency Room	ERs are mandated to provide information about EC and dispense EC upon request (effective January 28, 2004).
Pharmacy Access to Emergency Contraception	No
Must be performed by a licensed physician	No
Must be performed in a hospital if at:	No
Second physician must participate if at:	24 weeks
Prohibited except in cases of life or health endangerment if at:	24 weeks. Exception in the case of life endangerment only.
Public funding of abortion	
Funds all or most medically necessary abortions	Yes. Voluntarily provides coverage for all medically necessary abortions.
Funds limited to life endangerment, rape, and incest	No
Private insurance coverage limited to life endangerment	No
Providers may refuse to participate	
Individual	Yes
Institution	No
Mandate counseling includes	
Breast cancer	No
Fetal pain	No
Serious psychological effects	No
Abortion alternatives and support services	No
Waiting period (in hours) after counseling	No
Parental involvement required for minors	No

NORTH CAROLINA (NC)

"Partial-Birth Abortion" Bans	No
Contraceptive Equity	Requires equal coverage of FDA-approved contraceptive drugs and devices. Religious exemption.
Emergency Contraception for Sexual Assault Survivors in the Emergency Room	No
Pharmacy Access to Emergency Contraception	No
Must be performed by a licensed physician	Yes
Must be performed in a hospital if at:	20 weeks
Second physician must participate if at:	No
Prohibited except in cases of life or health endangerment if at:	20 weeks
Public funding of abortion	
Funds all or most medically necessary abortions	No
Funds limited to life endangerment, rape, and incest	Yes
Private insurance coverage limited to life endangerment	No
Providers may refuse to participate	
Individual	Yes
Institution	Yes
Mandate counseling includes	
Breast cancer	No
Fetal pain	No
Serious psychological effects	No
Abortion alternatives and support services	No
Waiting period (in hours) after counseling	No
Parental involvement required for minors	Consent of one parent, or a grandparent with whom the minor has lived for 6 months, required. Judicial bypass option available.

NORTH DAKOTA (ND)

"Partial-Birth Abortion" Bans	Unchallenged in court although this policy is presumably unenforceable under the terms set out in *Stenberg v. Carhart.*
Contraceptive Equity	No
Emergency Contraception for Sexual Assault Survivors in the Emergency Room	No
Pharmacy Access to Emergency Contraception	No
Must be performed by a licensed physician	Yes
Must be performed in a hospital if at:	12 weeks
Second physician must participate if at:	12 weeks
Prohibited except in cases of life or health endangerment if at:	Viability
Public funding of abortion	
Funds all or most medically necessary abortions	No
Funds limited to life endangerment, rape, and incest	Yes
Private insurance coverage limited to life endangerment	Yes
Providers may refuse to participate	
Individual	Yes
Institution	Yes
Mandate counseling includes	
Breast cancer	No
Fetal pain	No
Serious psychological effects	No
Abortion alternatives and support services	Yes
Waiting period (in hours) after counseling	24
Parental involvement required for minors	Consent of two parents required. Judicial bypass option available.

OHIO (OH)

"Partial-Birth Abortion" Bans	Entire Pregnancy. Law upheld (U.S. Court of Appeals, Sixth Circuit reversed judgment and vacated district court's permanent injunction, 12/17/03). First statute permanently blocked (U.S. Court of Appeals, Sixth Circuit affirmed district court's permanent injunction, 11/18/97).
Contraceptive Equity	No
Emergency Contraception for Sexual Assault Survivors in the Emergency Room	No
Pharmacy Access to Emergency Contraception	No
Must be performed by a licensed physician	Yes
Must be performed in a hospital if at:	No
Second physician must participate if at:	Permanently enjoined; law not in effect.
Prohibited except in cases of life or health endangerment if at:	Permanently enjoined; law not in effect.
Public funding of abortion	
Funds all or most medically necessary abortions	No
Funds limited to life endangerment, rape, and incest	Yes
Private insurance coverage limited to life endangerment	No
Providers may refuse to participate	
Individual	Yes
Institution	Yes
Mandate counseling includes	Requires women to receive state-mandated biased information in person from a health care provider.
Breast cancer	No
Fetal pain	No
Serious psychological effects	No
Abortion alternatives and support services	Yes
Waiting period (in hours) after counseling	24
Parental involvement required for minors	Consent of one parent required. Judicial bypass option available.

OKLAHOMA (OK)

"Partial-Birth Abortion" Bans	Unchallenged in court although this policy is presumably unenforceable under the terms set out in *Stenberg v. Carhart.*
Contraceptive Equity	No
Emergency Contraception for Sexual Assault Survivors in the Emergency Room	No
Pharmacy Access to Emergency Contraception	No
Must be performed by a licensed physician	Yes
Must be performed in a hospital if at:	2nd trimester
Second physician must participate if at:	Viability
Prohibited except in cases of life or health endangerment if at:	Viability
Public funding of abortion	
Funds all or most medically necessary abortions	No
Funds limited to life endangerment, rape, and incest	Yes
Private insurance coverage limited to life endangerment	No
Providers may refuse to participate	
Individual	Yes
Institution	Private
Mandate counseling includes	
Breast cancer	No
Fetal pain	No
Serious psychological effects	No
Abortion alternatives and support services	Yes
Waiting period (in hours) after counseling	24-hour delay requirement enacted but not yet enforced.
Parental involvement required for minors	Notice to one parent required. Judicial bypass option available. Constitutionality of statute currently being challenged.

OREGON (OR)

"Partial-Birth Abortion" Bans	No
Contraceptive Equity	No
Emergency Contraception for Sexual Assault Survivors in the Emergency Room	No
Pharmacy Access to Emergency Contraception	No
Must be performed by a licensed physician	No
Must be performed in a hospital if at:	No
Second physician must participate if at:	No
Prohibited except in cases of life or health endangerment if at:	No
Public funding of abortion	
Funds all or most medically necessary abortions	Yes. Ordered by court to provide Medicaid coverage for all medically necessary abortions.
Funds limited to life endangerment, rape, and incest	No
Private insurance coverage limited to life endangerment	No
Providers may refuse to participate	
Individual	Yes
Institution	Private
Mandate counseling includes	
Breast cancer	No
Fetal pain	No
Serious psychological effects	No
Abortion alternatives and support services	No
Waiting period (in hours) after counseling	No
Parental involvement required for minors	No

PENNSYLVANIA (PA)

"Partial-Birth Abortion" Bans	No
Contraceptive Equity	No
Emergency Contraception for Sexual Assault Survivors in the Emergency Room	No
Pharmacy Access to Emergency Contraception	No
Must be performed by a licensed physician	Yes
Must be performed in a hospital if at:	Viability
Second physician must participate if at:	Viability
Prohibited except in cases of life or health endangerment if at:	24 weeks. Exception in case of threat to the woman's physical health.
Public funding of abortion	
Funds all or most medically necessary abortions	No
Funds limited to life endangerment, rape, and incest	Yes
Private insurance coverage limited to life endangerment	No
Providers may refuse to participate	
Individual	Yes
Institution	Private
Mandate counseling includes	
Breast cancer	No
Fetal pain	No
Serious psychological effects	No
Abortion alternatives and support services	Yes
Waiting period (in hours) after counseling	24
Parental involvement required for minors	Consent of one parent required. Judicial bypass option available.

RHODE ISLAND (RI)

	Law permanently blocked (U.S. Court of Appeals, First Circuit affirmed district court's permanent injunction, 2/13/01); law not in effect.
"Partial-Birth Abortion" Bans	
Contraceptive Equity	Requires equal coverage of FDA-approved contraceptive drugs and devices. Religious exemption.
Emergency Contraception for Sexual Assault Survivors in the Emergency Room	No
Pharmacy Access to Emergency Contraception	No
Must be performed by a licensed physician	Yes
Must be performed in a hospital if at:	14 weeks
Second physician must participate if at:	No
Prohibited except in cases of life or health endangerment if at:	24 weeks. Exception in case of life endangerment only.
Public funding of abortion	
Funds all or most medically necessary abortions	No
Funds limited to life endangerment, rape, and incest	Yes
Private insurance coverage limited to life endangerment	Permanently enjoined; law not in effect.
Providers may refuse to participate	
Individual	Yes
Institution	No
Mandate counseling includes	
Breast cancer	No
Fetal pain	No
Serious psychological effects	No
Abortion alternatives and support services	Yes
Waiting period (in hours) after counseling	No
Parental involvement required for minors	Consent of one parent required. Judicial bypass option available.

SOUTH CAROLINA (SC)

	Unchallenged in court although this policy is presumably unenforceable under the terms set out in *Stenberg v. Carhart.*
"Partial-Birth Abortion" Bans	
Contraceptive Equity	No
Emergency Contraception for Sexual Assault Survivors in the Emergency Room	No
Pharmacy Access to Emergency Contraception	No
Must be performed by a licensed physician	Yes
Must be performed in a hospital if at:	3rd trimester
Second physician must participate if at:	3rd trimester
Prohibited except in cases of life or health endangerment if at:	3rd trimester
Public funding of abortion	
Funds all or most medically necessary abortions	No
Funds limited to life endangerment, rape, and incest	Yes
Private insurance coverage limited to life endangerment	No
Providers may refuse to participate	
Individual	Yes
Institution	Private
Mandate counseling includes	
Breast cancer	No
Fetal pain	No
Serious psychological effects	No
Abortion alternatives and support services	Yes
Waiting period (in hours) after counseling	1
Parental involvement required for minors	Consent of one parent or grandparent required. Judical bypass option available. Applies to minors under 17.

SOUTH DAKOTA (SD)

Ban on all abortion procedures	Exception for woman's life. Struck down by voter referendum 11/7/06.
"Partial-Birth Abortion" Bans	Unchallenged in court although this policy is presumably unenforceable under the terms set out in *Stenberg v. Carhart.*
Contraceptive Equity	No
Emergency Contraception for Sexual Assault Survivors in the Emergency Room	No
Pharmacy Access to Emergency Contraception	No
Must be performed by a licensed physician	Yes
Must be performed in a hospital if at:	24 weeks
Second physician must participate if at:	No
Prohibited except in cases of life or health endangerment if at:	24 weeks
Public funding of abortion	
Funds all or most medically necessary abortions	No
Funds limited to life endangerment, rape, and incest	Coverage only when woman's life is endangered (in violation of Hyde Amendment).
Private insurance coverage limited to life endangerment	No
Providers may refuse to participate	
Individual	Yes
Institution	Yes
Mandate counseling includes	
Breast cancer	No
Fetal pain	No
Serious psychological effects	Permanently enjoined; law not in effect.
Abortion alternatives and support services	Yes
Waiting period (in hours) after counseling	24
Parental involvement required for minors	Notice of one parent required. Judicial bypass option available.

TENNESSEE (TN)

"Partial-Birth Abortion" Bans	Unchallenged in court although this policy is presumably unenforceable under the terms set out in *Stenberg v. Carhart.*
Contraceptive Equity	No
Emergency Contraception for Sexual Assault Survivors in the Emergency Room	No
Pharmacy Access to Emergency Contraception	No
Must be performed by a licensed physician	Yes
Must be performed in a hospital if at:	No
Second physician must participate if at:	No
Prohibited except in cases of life or health endangerment if at:	Viability
Public funding of abortion	
Funds all or most medically necessary abortions	No
Funds limited to life endangerment, rape, and incest	Yes
Private insurance coverage limited to life endangerment	No
Providers may refuse to participate	
Individual	Yes
Institution	Yes
Mandate counseling includes	
Breast cancer	No
Fetal pain	No
Serious psychological effects	No
Abortion alternatives and support services	Yes
Waiting period (in hours) after counseling	2-day delay (excluding the day on which information is given and day of procedure). Enforcement stayed or enjoined by a state court; law not in effect.
Parental involvement required for minors	Consent of one parent required. Judicial bypass option available.

TEXAS (TX)

"Partial-Birth Abortion" Bans	No
Contraceptive Equity	Requires equal coverage of FDA-approved contraceptive drugs and devices. Religious exemption.
Emergency Contraception for Sexual Assault Survivors in the Emergency Room	No
Pharmacy Access to Emergency Contraception	No
Must be performed by a licensed physician	Yes
Must be performed in a hospital if at:	No
Second physician must participate if at:	No
Prohibited except in cases of life or health endangerment if at:	3rd trimester
Public funding of abortion	
Funds all or most medically necessary abortions	No
Funds limited to life endangerment, rape, and incest	Yes
Private insurance coverage limited to life endangerment	No
Providers may refuse to participate	
Individual	Yes
Institution	Private
Mandate counseling includes	
Breast cancer	Yes
Fetal pain	No
Serious psychological effects	No
Abortion alternatives and support services	Yes
Waiting period (in hours) after counseling	24
Parental involvement required for minors	Consent of one parent required. Judicial bypass option available.

UTAH (UT)

"Partial-Birth Abortion" Bans	Amended law blocked by temporary restraining order (U.S. District Court 5/4/04); law not in effect.
Contraceptive Equity	No
Emergency Contraception for Sexual Assault Survivors in the Emergency Room	No
Pharmacy Access to Emergency Contraception	No
Must be performed by a licensed physician	Yes
Must be performed in a hospital if at:	90 days
Second physician must participate if at:	No
Prohibited except in cases of life or health endangerment if at:	Permanently enjoined; law not in effect. Exception in the case of threat to the woman's physical health.
Public funding of abortion	
Funds all or most medically necessary abortions	No
Funds limited to life endangerment, rape, and incest	Yes. Exception in the case of threat to the woman's physical health. Exception in the case of fetal abnormality.
Private insurance coverage limited to life endangerment	No
Providers may refuse to participate	
Individual	Yes
Institution	Private
Mandate counseling includes	Requires woman to receive state-mandated biased information in person from a health care provider.
Breast cancer	No
Fetal pain	No
Serious psychological effects	No
Abortion alternatives and support services	Yes
Waiting period (in hours) after counseling	24. The waiting period is waived if the pregnancy is the result of rape or incest, the fetus has grave defects or

(continued)

UTAH (UT)   Continued

"Partial-Birth Abortion" Bans	Amended law blocked by temporary restraining order (U.S. District Court 5/4/04); law not in effect.
Parental involvement required for minors	the patient is younger than 15. If possible, notice to two parents is required. No judicial bypass option available. ****** Consent and Notice.

VERMONT (VT)

"Partial-Birth Abortion" Bans	No
Contraceptive Equity	Requires equal coverage of FDA-approved contraceptive drugs and devices.
Emergency Contraception for Sexual Assault Survivors in the Emergency Room	No
Pharmacy Access to Emergency Contraception	No
Must be performed by a licensed physician	No
Must be performed in a hospital if at:	No
Second physician must participate if at:	No
Prohibited except in cases of life or health endangerment if at:	No
Public funding of abortion	
Funds all or most medically necessary abortions	Yes. Ordered by court to provide Medicaid coverage for all medically necessary abortions.
Funds limited to life endangerment, rape, and incest	No
Private insurance coverage limited to life endangerment	No
Providers may refuse to participate	
Individual	No
Institution	No
Mandate counseling includes	
Breast cancer	No
Fetal pain	No
Serious psychological effects	No
Abortion alternatives and support services	No
Waiting period (in hours) after counseling	No
Parental involvement required for minors	No

VIRGINIA (VA)

"Partial-Birth Abortion" Bans	Law permanently blocked (U.S. Court of Appeals, Fourth Circuit affirmed district court's permanent injunction, 6/3/05). First statute permanently enjoined (U.S. Court of Appeals, Fourth Circuit affirmed district court's permanent injunction, 8/9/00); law not in effect.
Contraceptive Equity	No
Emergency Contraception for Sexual Assault Survivors in the Emergency Room	No
Pharmacy Access to Emergency Contraception	No
Must be performed by a licensed physician	Yes
Must be performed in a hospital if at:	2nd trimester
Second physician must participate if at:	Viability
Prohibited except in cases of life or health endangerment if at:	3rd trimester
Public funding of abortion	
Funds all or most medically necessary abortions	No. Some Medicaid coverage, but not full Medicaid coverage for medically necessary abortions.
Funds limited to life endangerment, rape, and incest	Yes. Exception in the case of fetal abnormality.
Private insurance coverage limited to life endangerment	No
Providers may refuse to participate	
Individual	Yes
Institution	Yes
Mandate counseling includes	
Breast cancer	No
Fetal pain	No
Serious psychological effects	No
Abortion alternatives and support services	Yes
Waiting period (in hours) after counseling	24

(continued)

VIRGINIA (VA)   Continued

"Partial-Birth Abortion" Bans	Law permanently blocked (U.S. Court of Appeals, Fourth Circuit affirmed district court's permanent injunction, 6/3/05). First statute permanently enjoined (U.S. Court of Appeals, Fourth Circuit affirmed district court's permanent injunction, 8/9/00); law not in effect.
Parental involvement required for minors	Consent of one parent required unless minor declares that she is abused or neglected and the physician reports such abuse or neglect. Judicial bypass option available.

WASHINGTON (WA)

"Partial-Birth Abortion" Bans	**No**
Contraceptive Equity	By regulation, requires equal coverage of FDA-approved contraceptive drugs and devices.
Emergency Contraception for Sexual Assault Survivors in the Emergency Room	ERs are mandated to provide information about EC and dispense EC upon request.
Pharmacy Access to Emergency Contraception	EC is available directly from the pharmacist.
Must be performed by a licensed physician	No
Must be performed in a hospital if at:	No
Second physician must participate if at:	No
Prohibited except in cases of life or health endangerment if at:	Viability
Public funding of abortion	
Funds all or most medically necessary abortions	Yes. Voluntarily provides coverage for all medically necessary abortions.
Funds limited to life endangerment, rape, and incest	No
Private insurance coverage limited to life endangerment	No
Providers may refuse to participate	
Individual	Yes
Institution	Yes
Mandate counseling includes	
Breast cancer	No
Fetal pain	No
Serious psychological effects	No
Abortion alternatives and support services	No
Waiting period (in hours) after counseling	No
Parental involvement required for minors	No

WEST VIRGINIA (WV)

"Partial-Birth Abortion" Bans	Law permanently blocked (U.S. District Court, 7/7/00); law not in effect.
Contraceptive Equity	Requires equal coverage of FDA-approved drugs and devices. Religious exemption.
Emergency Contraception for Sexual Assault Survivors in the Emergency Room	No
Pharmacy Access to Emergency Contraception	No
Must be performed by a licensed physician	No
Must be performed in a hospital if at:	No
Second physician must participate if at:	No
Prohibited except in cases of life or health endangerment if at:	No
Public funding of abortion	
Funds all or most medically necessary abortions	Yes. Ordered by court to provide Medicaid coverage for all medically necessary abortions.
Funds limited to life endangerment, rape, and incest	No
Private insurance coverage limited to life endangerment	No
Providers may refuse to participate	
Individual	No
Institution	No
Mandate counseling includes	
Breast cancer	No
Fetal pain	No
Serious psychological effects	No
Abortion alternatives and support services	Yes
Waiting period (in hours) after counseling	24
Parental involvement required for minors	Notice. Notice to one parent or physician required. Judicial bypass option available. Specified health professionals may waive parental involvement in certain circumstances.

WISCONSIN (WI)

"Partial-Birth Abortion" Bans	**Law permanently blocked (U.S. Court of Appeals, Seventh Circuit reversed district court's denial of permanent injunction, 4/26/01); law not in effect.**
Contraceptive Equity	Although a contraceptive equity law has not been enacted, an Attorney General opinion interpreted state law to prohibit employers from excluding prescription contraceptives from benefit plans that provide prescription drug coverage.
Emergency Contraception for Sexual Assault Survivors in the Emergency Room	No
Pharmacy Access to Emergency Contraception	No
Must be performed by a licensed physician	Yes
Must be performed in a hospital if at:	12 weeks
Second physician must participate if at:	No
Prohibited except in cases of life or health endangerment if at:	Viability
Public funding of abortion	
Funds all or most medically necessary abortions	No
Funds limited to life endangerment, rape, and incest	Yes. Some Medicaid coverage, but not full Medicaid coverage for medically necessary abortions. Exception in case of threat to the woman's physical health.
Private insurance coverage limited to life endangerment	No
Providers may refuse to participate	
Individual	Yes
Institution	Yes
Mandate counseling includes	Requires woman to receive state-mandated biased information in person from a health care provider.

(continued)

WISCONSIN (WI)   Continued

"Partial-Birth Abortion" Bans	Law permanently blocked (U.S. Court of Appeals, Seventh Circuit reversed district court's denial of permanent injunction, 4/26/01); law not in effect.

Breast cancer	No
Fetal pain	No
Serious psychological effects	Yes
Abortion alternatives and support services	Yes
Waiting period (in hours) after counseling	24
Parental involvement required for minors	Consent of one parent required. Adult family member or psychologist/psychiatrist can waive if threat of suicide. Judicial bypass option available.

WYOMING (WY)

"Partial-Birth Abortion" Bans	No
Contraceptive Equity	No
Emergency Contraception for Sexual Assault Survivors in the Emergency Room	No
Pharmacy Access to Emergency Contraception	No
Must be performed by a licensed physician	Yes
Must be performed in a hospital if at:	No
Second physician must participate if at:	No
Prohibited except in cases of life or health endangerment if at:	Viability
Public funding of abortion	
Funds all or most medically necessary abortions	No
Funds limited to life endangerment, rape, and incest	Yes
Private insurance coverage limited to life endangerment	No
Providers may refuse to participate	
Individual	Yes
Institution	Private
Mandate counseling includes	
Breast cancer	No
Fetal pain	No
Serious psychological effects	No
Abortion alternatives and support services	No
Waiting period (in hours) after counseling	No
Parental involvement required for minors	Consent of one parent required. Judicial bypass option available.

Index